Sociology, Education and Schools

An Introduction to the Sociology of Education

Robert G. Burgess

B. T. BATSFORD LTD
LONDON

First published 1986

Typeset by Deltatype, Ellesmere Port
and Printed in Great Britain by
Billings Ltd, Worcester

Published by B. T. Batsford Ltd
4 Fitzhardinge Street, London W1H 0AH

British Library Cataloguing in Publication Data

Burgess, Robert G.
Sociology, education and schools: an introduction to the sociology of education.——(Batsford studies in education)
1. Education——Social aspects
I. Title
370.19 LC191

ISBN 0 7134–1016–7
ISBN 0 7134–1017–5 Pbk

Contents

Preface

There are now numerous texts, readers and monographs on education and the sociology of education that report on specific issues and areas of study. As a consequence it becomes difficult to define the scale, scope and substance of the sociology of education. Some writers have approached this task by outlining the main themes and topics in the subject, while others have argued for a particular perspective or provided a catalogue of studies that they consider constitute this subject area. While bibliographic guides and summaries of research findings have a place within a discipline, they cannot communicate the richness of the field. The way in which researchers address key questions and controversies in a subject cannot be communicated through an encyclopaedic coverage of an area of study.

This text, therefore, provides a selective review of major topics in the sociology of education with special attention being given to key issues and questions that sociologists have examined when studying education and schools. This book does not, therefore, cover every topic in the sociology of education. It is an introduction, not a comprehensive guide to work that has been mainly conducted in Britain. The focus is upon empirical material and therefore considerable space is given over to an examination of statistical data and case studies to see what light they shed on the contribution that sociologists can make to the study of education. It is hoped that this approach will assist students of sociology and education, teachers and policy makers to appreciate how sociological studies can help to advance their understanding of education and schools.

In the course of writing this book I have been helped by many friends and colleagues. In particular, I am indebted to Stephen Ball, Janet Finch, Simon Frith and Ivor Goodson who provided helpful comments on earlier drafts of particular chapters. Meanwhile, Hilary Burgess was kind enough to read the complete manuscript and to provide me with detailed comments. I am also indebted to Olive Banks and to Tony

Seward who both initially encouraged me with this writing project. Finally, I would like to thank Hilary Bayliss, Frances Jones, Jeanne Summers and especially Fiona Stone for their first rate secretarial support. Needless to say, none of these people is responsible for any errors or omissions in this book which are, of course, my own.

Robert Burgess

University of Warwick
June 1985

1 Sociological perspectives and the study of education

Everyone who reads this book will have some experience of education and schools. Indeed, the process of education has played and continues to play an important role in people's lives. Many people have vivid memories of education and their school days, as shown by the following remarks:

> I remember the first morning, 'cos me Mum came in and said 'Come on you've got to go to school'. I said, 'Alright, I'll try it – do I have to go back if I don't like it?' And she said, 'You've got to go there for quite a long time'. I went up there and went into the classroom. I remember the other kids crying, but I don't remember myself crying. It was just a room with a whole load of desks in it. I thought, 'What the heck have I let myself in for?' (Andrew Pearce, aged 16, St Austell, Cornwall quoted by White with Brockington, 1983, p.9)

While this recollection of the first day at school from a sixteen year old may be familiar to some readers, others may identify more with the following observation made by the anthropologist Jules Henry in a school classroom where he recorded the following incident:

> Boris had trouble reducing $^{12}/_{16}$ to the lowest terms and could only get as far as $^{6}/_{8}$. The teacher asked him quietly if that was as far as he could reduce it. She suggested he 'think'. Much heaving up and down and waving of hands by the other children, all frantic to correct him. Boris pretty unhappy, probably mentally paralysed. The teacher quiet, patient, ignores the others and concentrates with look and voice on Boris. She says, 'Is there a bigger number than two that you can divide into the two parts of the fraction?' After a minute or two she becomes more urgent, but there is no response from Boris. She then turns to the class and says, 'Well, who can tell Boris what the number is?' A forest of hands appears, and the teacher calls Peggy, who says that four may be divided into the numerator and the denominator. (Henry, 1963, pp.295–6)

Both of these incidents are a part of the educational experience. The first situation will be familiar to many parents as well as to adults who can recall their first day at school. Similarly, the scene from a classroom, no doubt, reminds many of us about our experiences as pupils, while for teachers it also provides an illustration of a very familiar scene.

It is situations such as these that people talk about and write about when analysing their experiences of education and schools. However, they may examine such experiences from the point of view of a pupil, a teacher, a parent, a school governor or an educational administrator. In turn, these experiences are also examined by sociologists who not only describe those situations they have heard about or observed, but also at tempt to understand and explain what education and schooling is like. Sociological work is certainly not confined to 'factual' description but takes a critical stance where commonsense knowledge, fact and evidence are critically examined. It is this element of sociology that is well captured by Tom Burns when he writes:

> Sociology defines itself as a critical activity. The purpose of sociology is to achieve an understanding of social behaviour and social institutions which is different from that current among the people through whose conduct the institutions exist; an understanding that is not merely different but new and better. The practice of sociology is criticism. It exists to criticize claims about the value of achievement and to question assumptions about the meaning of conduct. It is the business of sociologists to conduct a critical debate with the public about its equipment of social institutions (Burns, 1967, pp.366–7)

As far as Burns is concerned sociology challenges many assumptions that people hold about social life. Indeed, he argues that it is the role of the sociologist of education

> to examine, to question, to raise doubts about, to criticize the assumptions on which current policy, current theory and current practice are based. (Burns, 1967, p. 358)

It is this kind of role that sociologists have been seen to play as they have examined different dimensions of education and schools. However, there has never been a unanimous view on the kinds of questions that are posed as different theoretical approaches have resulted in different kinds of social research. Accordingly, the sociological perspectives that are used by sociologists result in different questions being posed, different methods of study being used and different kinds of evidence being produced. It is this emphasis upon research problems and research evidence that is emphasized throughout this book. In particular, attention is drawn to the ways in which different sociological perspectives give rise to different questions and different sets of evidence on the same substantive topic. The different perspectives that are used assist sociologists in questioning basic assumptions. Furthermore, they also give rise to very different viewpoints among research reports. It is, however, the kind of questions that are posed from different sociological perspectives which distinguishes sociology from other disciplines (cf. Burgess, 1986; Lee and Newby, 1983).

In addition, sociologists can also use a range of theories and methods in their research activities in order to distinguish their work from that of other researchers. It is not the purpose here to outline the theories and methods in sociology, as these have been reviewed by others (see for example Lee and Newby, 1983, on theory and Bulmer, 1984, on methods). In turn, theories in the sociology of education have been examined by Demaine (1977) and the use of methods in the study of education have been discussed by Burgess (1984a, 1985a) and by Cohen and Manion (1980). However, it is important to illustrate the way in which sociological perspectives have been used to pose questions and provide explanations in the sociology of education and to outline some of the main issues in this area of study.

As Karabel and Halsey (1977a) have indicated, any classification of traditions in the sociology of education results in some simplification. Nevertheless, many commentators have drawn a distinction between 'old' or 'traditional' sociology of education, which is taken to include studies that were broadly concerned with social class and education, and the 'new' sociology of education, which is based on studies that focus on the curriculum as the main unit of study (for a detailed discussion of these divisions see Bernbaum, 1977). In addition, writers have also distinguished between macroscopic and microscopic analysis which is concerned with the scope of the research enquiry. The distinguishing features are well summarized by Woods and Hammersley, who comment:

> By a macro-focus we mean analysis at a relatively high level of abstraction, for instance concerned with whole societies, their structure and change. Micro-focus, on the other hand, designates a concern with specific settings at particular times, in other words with specific events. (Woods and Hammersley, 1977, p.15)

However, as they rightly indicate, macro- and micro-explanations are not research orientations that are used independently, but often complement each other in the sociological study of education. Nevertheless, the macro- micro-issue, together with the possible links between these approaches, has been the subject of speculation and debate among many sociologists (cf. Banks, 1978; A. Hargreaves, 1980a; Archer, 1981; Hammersley, 1984a, 1984b). It is, therefore, with these various distinctions in mind that we turn to a brief review of some of the main sociological perspectives that have influenced the research agenda in the sociology of education. In examining functionalism, interpretative sociology, neo-Marxism and feminism it is my intention to illustrate some of the ways in which these perspectives, along with many others, have shaped our understanding of schools and education.

Functionalism

A brief glance at sociology of education textbooks written some twenty years ago (Banks, 1968; Musgrave, 1965; Shipman, 1968) is sufficient to discover that functionalism was the dominant perspective which provided the main conceptual guide and influenced the research agenda. The focus of structural functionalism is upon consensus, equilibrium, and shared values. In an institution such as education it is assumed that all the parts are interdependent and work together to contribute to the functioning of society. Accordingly, the different parts of the educational system are considered in terms of their functions or purposes which are regarded as necessary for the survival of society.

In Britain, sociologists of education did not automatically embrace this tradition since they were involved in examining education as an aspect of the studies in social stratification and social mobility directed by David Glass (1954). Nevertheless, these interests were set within a functionalist perspective whereby education was seen in terms of its function to provide a literate and adaptable workforce for an advanced industrial society. In addition, functionalism was coupled with an interest in the wastage of working class ability. It was this style of research that Eggleston (1974) claims brought together structural functionalism, economic determinism and cultural discontinuity – a view he supports by quoting Halsey, Floud and Anderson's introduction to *Education, Economy and Society* (1961) when they state:

> modern industrial societies are distinguished in their structure and development from others of comparable complexity principally by the institutionalization of innovation – that is to say by the public and private organization, on an increasingly large scale, of scientific research in the service of economic and military growth. Their occupational structures are characteristically diversified, with relatively high educational qualifications for employment at all levels but the lowest. Education attains unprecedented economic importance as a source of technological innovation, and the educational system is bent increasingly to the service of the labour force, acting as a vast apparatus of occupational recruitment and training. (Halsey, Floud and Anderson, 1961, p.2)

The main concerns of those sociologists working from a functionalist perspective can also be seen from the contents of the first edition of Peter Musgrave's basic text entitled *The Sociology of Education* (1965). A central section of his volume examined the social functions of education by addressing four major questions which he states as follows:

> What part does education play in the balance between stability and change, in maintaining a democratic political system, in ensuring the full use of the talented people in our society and, finally, in supplying trained manpower to the economic system? (Musgrave, 1965, p.12)

Functionalism was applied to an analysis of relations between education and the economy, between education and the political system and to the selective mechanisms in the educational system as well as to an analysis of early childhood socialization. It was these concerns that dominated much early British and American work.

Within this tradition several major pieces of research can be identified, especially from American sociologists (Parsons, 1959; Clark, 1961; Turner, 1961). The most significant piece of work was Talcott Parsons's analysis of the school class as a social system and the relationship of its structure to its functions as an agency of socialization and allocation. Within his analysis Parsons is concerned with the following problem:

> how the school class functions to internalize in its pupils both the commitments and capacities for successful performance of their future adult roles, and second of how it functions to allocate these human resources within the role structure of the adult society. (Parsons, 1959, p.297)

Here Parsons is concerned with the ways in which these problems are interrelated. In particular, he takes socialization as a crucial function in integrating patterns of interaction in the school and in teaching pupils the value of achievement. In addition, he highlights the ways in which achievement differentiates pupils while performing an integrative function for the school system – a problem that was subsequently taken up by sociologists working from other perspectives such as interpretative sociology (cf. Hargreaves, 1967; Lacey, 1970; Ball, 1981).

Nevertheless, the functionalist perspective has helped sociologists to locate educational institutions in relation to wider elements of social structure. It was this advantage that Banks identified in her outline of the field when she wrote:

> In any consideration of either the socializing or the selective function of education regard must be had to the context in which the educational institutions operate and the influences at work upon them. Of these, the economy is obviously of paramount importance, determining as it does the complexity of the skills required according to the level of technology. At the same time its differentiating and selective functions bring education inevitably into close relationships with the demographic aspects of society and with the stratification system. The controlling and integrating functions of education and its role in the transmission of values also necessitate close ties with the value system of society, with religious institutions and with the State itself as an instrument of control. Moreover in so far as the educational process is a shared one, other socializing agencies of which the family is the most important, must be recognized for the part they play and their relationship with the more specialized educational agencies must be explored. (Banks, 1968, p.5)

As a consequence, Banks argues that sociologists of education working within this perspective focused their research activities on the relationship between education and other major institutions.

Although this approach has influenced the direction of much research in the 1950s and early 1960s, it has also attracted several criticisms. In particular, the emphasis upon shared values, integration and consensus is regarded by many, including Halsey and Floud (1958) to be a difficult notion to apply to the study of education in societies that are characterized by social change. Furthermore, such an approach overlooks conflict and the content of education (cf. Young, 1971b). In recent years, functionalism has also been criticized for its failure to question the gender order in society (Purvis, 1984). For example, June Purvis argues that, because functionalists accepted rather than questioned the allocation of sex roles, questions concerning the relationship between educational inequalities and the sexes were often overlooked. Furthermore, questions concerning the search for talent mainly consisted of a search for talented boys and men rather than individuals from both sexes. It is research questions such as these that have been taken up by feminist writers, while some of the other topics have been examined by writers working from other perspectives.

Interpretative sociology and the 'new' sociology of education

By the end of the 1960s many of these criticisms that were directed at functionalism were widely acknowledged by sociologists and attracted the attention of sociologists of education who were seeking alternative perspectives to examine their field of study. In particular, sociologists of education were concerned about broadening their subject area so as to include topics relating to the school, the classroom and the curriculum.

For sociologists of education 1970 was an important turning point in the development of their subject in Britain. In that year the annual conference of the British Sociological Association took as its central theme the sociology of education. The papers from that conference were subsequently published (Brown, 1973) and attempted to provide an assessment of current work *as well as* new problems. Among the papers given at the conference were contributions from Michael F. D. Young and Basil Bernstein, both of whom provided a critique of much current work. In particular, Young argued that sociologists had overlooked the content of education, methods of teaching and the way in which knowledge is organized in the school curriculum. However, he also addressed a broader set of problems by criticizing much of the current work on the sociology of education which he argued took educators' concepts and categories for granted and never explored the educators' meanings, assumptions and interpretations of issues such as 'the less able', 'school achievement', 'curriculum objectives' and 'the content of the curriculum'. In particular, Young pointed to the importance of focusing on classroom processes and the content of the curriculum, both of which have been examined in subsequent empirical studies (see Chapters 8 and 9 in this volume).

Although the impetus for research on the curriculum has been generally identified with the collection of papers edited by Young (1971a) which was entitled *Knowledge and Control*, it is much broader. The main perspective that was used brought together work based upon social phenomenology and symbolic interactionism in relation to the study of the curriculum and the analysis of school classrooms. For example the way in which these perspectives influenced the sociologist's research questions are well illustrated by Gorbutt (1972) when he states:

> If we take the notion that intelligence is not an intrinsic quality of the child but is imputed to him by others then we can ask questions like how does the teacher define an intelligent child? What is the implicit concept of intelligence being used by the teacher and where did he acquire it? Are the teacher's judgements about intelligence linked to his belief about social class? (Gorbutt, 1972, p.8)

Here the focus is upon the way in which teachers' perspectives are socially constructed, on the meanings teachers attribute to social situations and the ways in which educational activities are defined. Such an approach requires detailed observational work to be conducted in the classroom (for a discussion of this approach, see Hammersley and Atkinson, 1983; Burgess, 1984a).

It was the classroom and the curriculum that was the subject of the only empirically based paper in *Knowledge and Control*. This paper was written by Nell Keddie (1971) and focused attention on the content of the curriculum in the humanities department of a comprehensive school. The central task here was to examine education from the participants' point of view by focusing on their perceptions, interactions and assumptions. As well as a change in perspective there was also a change in method as questionnaires and interview schedules were replaced by observation and unstructured interviews. In turn, the problems investigated were also modified, and revealed a shift in emphasis. No longer was the major concern about which children fail or why they fail but with the state and status of classroom knowledge. Questions were now being posed about knowledge and the curriculum as well as about the achievement of working class and middle class pupils. A concern with issues such as these heralded a new direction in the sociology of education whereby researchers were interested in the kinds of assumptions held by teachers and pupils, the ways in which teachers formulated their ideas about success and failure, the way in which distinctions were made between different kinds of pupils and the contrast between what teachers say they do as opposed to what they actually do.

This approach focuses on the way in which individuals construct their own actions, attribute meanings to social situations, and define them. In turn, attention is directed towards perspectives, cultures, strategies and negotiations – especially between teachers and pupils in schools. As Woods (1983) has indicated, much of this research is conducted from an interactionist perspective and includes detailed ethnographic studies based on observation, participant observation and interviewing. The main questions that have been posed about schools from this perspective are summarized by Woods as follows:

> – How do teachers and pupils interpret school processes, personnel and organization, such as lessons, the curriculum, their peers, and each other?

> – What factors bear on these interpretations? What significant or generalized others have influenced them?
>
> – How do teachers and pupils experience school processes?
>
> – How do teachers and pupils organize their school activity? Having defined the situation (through perspectives in context) and experienced it (in relation to their identity concerns), what strategies do they adopt?
>
> – How do teachers and pupils perceive their careers in the school? What forms of commitment do they show and what are their identity concerns?
>
> Such questions place the centre of inquiry within individuals, as the constructors of their own action. But the locus of interaction is in neither, but between them. The most important root question, therefore, is: – What happens among teachers and pupils in school? (Woods, 1983, p.16)

The focus of this perspective is therefore upon the activities that occur within schools and classrooms and the content of the curriculum. In this respect, this kind of research focuses attention upon the analysis of small-scale situations. As a consequence, some of the proponents of this approach have suggested a sharp dividing line between themselves and those researchers who have been concerned with questions about the relationship between education, social structure and social change, all of which have been discussed by those working from a Marxist perspective.

Neo-Marxist approaches

Among those approaches that have made the most serious challenge to the 'new' sociology of education and to interpretative sociology have been various versions of Marxism. As a consequence there has been a shift back to macro-sociology and to an analysis of the importance of economic and political forces upon education. One version of Marxism that has been particularly influential in the sociology of education is concerned with theories of reproduction which are well represented in the work of Bowles and Gintis (1976). Reproduction theories are concerned with the way in which schooling assists in the reproduction of a capitalist society. In particular, Bowles and Gintis turn their attention to the American educational system and examine the extent to which the educational system reproduces the class structure. Central to their analysis is the view that there is a high degree of correspondence between school and work, as they argue that the educational system helps to integrate young people into the economic system. In particular, they maintain that schools socialize pupils into the discipline of work and to the main social habits that are demanded by the world of work. They continue by stating:

> Specifically the social relationships of education – the relationships between administrators and teachers, teachers and students, students and students, and students and their work – replicate the hierarchical division of labor. Hierarchical relations are reflected in the vertical authority lines from administrators to teachers to students. Alienated labor is reflected in the student's lack of control over his or her education, the alienation of the student

from the curriculum content, and the motivation of school work through a system of grades and other external rewards rather than the student's integration with either the process (learning) or the outcome (knowledge) of the educational 'production process'. Fragmentation in work is reflected in the institutionalized and often destructive competition among students through continual and ostensibly meritocratic ranking and evaluation. By attuning young people to a set of social relationships similar to those of the work place, schooling attempts to gear the development of personal needs to its requirements. (Bowles and Gintis, 1976, p.131)

Bowles and Gintis argue that, through its schools, the educational system produces the appropriate types of personality for positions in the hierarchy and fragments the subordinate class. In particular, they argue that schools are like work as they adhere to a hierarchy and service the economy by feeding pupils into different levels. They suggest that differences in social relationships within schools are reflected in the social backgrounds of students and their likely future economic positions, as they state:

blacks and other minorities are concentrated in schools whose repressive, arbitrary, generally chaotic internal order, coercive authority structures, and minimal possibilities for advancement mirror the characteristics of inferior job situations. Similarly, predominantly working class schools tend to emphasize behavioral control and rule following, while schools in well-to-do suburbs employ relatively open systems that favour greater student participation, less direct supervision, more student electives, and, in general, a value system stressing internalized standards of control. (Bowles and Gintis, 1976, p.132)

While Bowles and Gintis's argument is directed at American society it is also implicitly claimed that the features they have identified apply to capitalist societies in general (an issue that is examined in Chapter 2).

A small-scale study that also adopts a neo-Marxist perspective and attempts to examine the correspondence principle in operation has been conducted by Paul Willis (1977). The study consists of an observational account of the transition from school to work of boys in the English Midlands in which Willis examines youth subculture as an aspect of working class experience in a capitalist society. The key question for Willis is: 'Why do working class kids get working class jobs?' To address this issue Willis, in common with those sociologists working from an interactionist perspective, examines the way in which the 'lads' are involved in adherence to a set of values that result in school failure and which in turn prepare them for low grade manual jobs. It is on this basis that the school is considered to serve the 'needs' of a capitalist economy by locking the boys into a world of manual labour.

Such a study has some similarity with interactionist work as it focuses on the routines of schools and classrooms. However, the difference comes through the way in which classroom processes are situated in relation to capitalist society. In a similar way Sharp and Green (1975), in studying a progressive primary school, focus on teachers' perceptions not only in the classroom context but also in relation to the constraints that relate to the structure of capitalist society. As David Hargreaves (1978) argues, such an analysis needs to focus on the actual links between the constraints on the teachers and the demands of a capitalist economy if the relationship between these two levels is to be explained. At the secondary school level a similar analysis has been attempted by Bellaby (1979) but as Banks (1982a) has noted this kind of analysis omits to specify the link between the school and society. Nevertheless, this line of development takes us away from merely focusing on the school towards setting the activities of schools and classrooms in a broader context.

In addition, neo-Marxist work has also been introduced into the sociology of education through historical analyses of education in the nineteenth century (cf. Johnson, 1970; 1976; McCann, 1977). Here the emphasis is upon the way in which schools have prepared children for life in a capitalist society and the ways in which pupils were socialized in schools that ostensibly served the interests of the ruling class. The main research issue involves an analysis of the struggle between social class groups in the course of establishing and defining schools and schooling.

A neo-Marxist perspective has therefore helped to extend the research agenda that has been developed in the sociology of education. First, it has focused on macro- as well as microscopic analyses. Secondly, it has utilized historical as well as sociological evidence; and finally, it has broadened the subject matter of the sociology of education in terms of problems, theoretical perspectives and methods. In these ways it shares much in common with a feminist perspective that has been used in the sociology of education and to which we now turn.

A feminist perspective

Throughout the last ten years feminists and feminism have had a considerable impact upon sociology (cf. Stacey, 1981; 1982) and the sociology of education (cf. Deem, 1978; 1984a). The work that has been conducted from this perspective has not so much been united in terms of theory or method, but in terms of its critique of other sociologies of education that have neglected the study of girls and women together with questions about sexual inequality. The kinds of criticisms that can be made of many earlier studies are neatly summed up by Sandra Acker in her review of twenty years work in the sociology of education, when she invites readers to imagine the impression that a Martian would get of British society and the English educational system on the basis of reading sociological work on education. She writes:

> The Martian would conclude that numerous boys but few girls go to secondary modern schools; that there are no girls' public schools; that there are almost no adult women influentials of any sort; that most students in higher education study science and education; that women rarely make a ritual transition called 'from school to work' and never go into further education colleges. Although

> some women go to university, most probably enter directly into motherhood, where they are of some interest as transmitters of language codes to their children. And except for a small number of teachers, social workers and nurses, there are almost no adult women workers in the labour market. (Acker, 1981a, pp.81–2)

As a consequence of such neglect, feminists have developed much research that explores gender differences and education in general as well as research on the education of girls and women in particular. Accordingly, the kinds of questions that have been posed focus their attention on sexual divisions and the experiences of girls and women in the educational system. In a recent review of research in this area, Arnot (1983) focuses on four questions that have directed research attention to the education of girls. First, she asks: what factors are involved in explaining the differences between girls' responses to school life? Here, she highlights the importance of looking at the relationship between class *and* gender and how these variables have influenced girls' responses to socialization. Secondly, she asks: what are the effects of the development of state education on the education of girls? Such an approach focuses on differential patterns of educational achievement between men and women. In turn this leads her to analyse material on school achievement which suggests that there is still a pool of untapped female talent. Thirdly, she asks: what were the reasons for educating girls and how did they affect girls' schooling? Here, ideologies of educational provision are considered in terms of gender and social class. In particular, she demonstrates how such ideologies constructed girls' underachievement by directing their schooling towards limited goals and by directing them towards a domestic vocation rather than paid employment. Such an analysis highlights how those involved in educational planning have contributed to educational inequality and to the underachievement of girls and women. Finally, she asks: what sort of schooling do girls now receive and what implications has this for their future lives? Such a question focuses attention on the use of gender categories in the organization of schooling and the extent to which the concept of femininity limits the aspirations of girls and women.

The perspectives that have been reviewed are by no means exhaustive of sociological analysis in general or of work in these areas in particular. They have been used to illustrate some of the concepts that may be used in sociological analysis and the ways in which these influence the questions posed and the explanations that are provided. In particular, they draw attention to the fact that the material with which the sociologist of education works may be examined from a number of different perspectives. For example, familiar elements of schools and schooling may be examined from all the different perspectives that have been discussed in this chapter.

Perspectives on schooling

Schools are characterized by a number of familiar elements: bells, the marking of registers, morning assembly, dinner queues and lesson periods. Of all these aspects of schooling, morning assembly is probably most familiar to anyone who has been to school. Yet the researcher who is conducting an analysis of school situations has to choose what observations to record of an assembly. In the course of deciding what to record a number of questions might be posed: do the pupils stand or sit? Are they assembled into particular groups? Are boys and girls separated? Are all the pupils present? Are teachers present? What do pupils do? What do teachers do? What is said? What is not said? How do the activities in morning assembly relate to other activities in the school? While such a range of questions might be useful in orientating a researcher to an area of study, some questions can also highlight a particular perspective that is taken. For example, a researcher who is interested in 'improving' school assembly might ask: how effective is the process of communication between the headteacher and the pupils? What other approaches might be used? Meanwhile, a functionalist might ask: how does morning assembly function to maintain social order? A neo-Marxist might consider the extent to which school assembly is a part of the pupils' training and indoctrination in a capitalist society, while a feminist might examine the extent to which gender is used as a principle of organizing the assembly and the extent to which gender socialization occurs within an assembly. Finally, an interactionist might be more concerned with the way in which definitions are imposed on pupils and teachers by a headteacher. In short, the theoretical perspective that is taken by the researcher will result in different questions being posed and different explanations being advanced about the activities that occur within an educational setting. It is then for the reader to assess the relative merits and demerits of particular perspectives – that is, particular theories and methods and their relative usefulness in explaining what occurs in different settings. It is in this respect that the chapters that follow examine the kinds of research evidence that have been used by sociologists in the course of examining various aspects of education and educational activity.

In this brief review we have highlighted some of the main perspectives that have been used by sociologists in recent years in posing questions about education. In some commentaries it has become fashionable to suggest that the sociology of education is no more than an area of study in which structural functionalism has been replaced by symbolic interactionism and the survey method by ethnography. Yet such generalizations not only result in crude subdivisions of the sociology of education into 'old' and 'new' sociologies of education but also grossly oversimplify the diverse range of problems, theories and methods that are used in this field of study. Accordingly, it is the purpose of the chapters that follow to show how different kinds of research have been conducted on similar topic areas concerned with the role of education and schools in society.

The organization of the book

This book develops a topic-based approach to the sociology of education. At first glance it might seem that some of the early chapters deal with macroscopic analysis that has been identified with the 'old' sociology of education, while the later chapters consider microscopic issues which have become identified with the 'new' sociology of education. However, this is far too simple as many of these chapters bring together theoretical and empirical evidence, as well as statistical material and data from case studies in the course of reviewing research material.

We begin in *Chapter 2* by questioning the relationship between education and the economy, and the links between school and work and unemployment, before turning in *Chapter 3* to a review of the literature concerned with educational opportunity, and patterns of social mobility. *Chapter 4* begins to examine the basic patterns of social and educational inequality with special reference to social class, while *Chapter 5* explores the patterns of social and educational inequality in relation to gender and race. In both these chapters an attempt is also made to review some of the explanations that have been used to account for the patterns of inequality. However, this is only part of the subject matter of the sociology of education, as in recent years much attention has also been given to schools themselves.

In reviewing some of this literature we turn in *Chapter 6* to accounts of teachers and teaching and examine some of the social divisions that exist among this occupational group. In the next two chapters we focus upon the patterns of interaction among teachers and pupils. In *Chapter 7* we turn to an examination of different patterns of school organization and the implications this holds for teacher–pupil relationships – a theme that is also taken up in *Chapter 8* in connection with the activities that occur in classrooms. Meanwhile, *Chapter 9* turns our attention to the school curriculum which again picks up some of the themes that have been raised earlier in the volume regarding social class, gender and race and also teacher–pupil interaction. Finally, a brief concluding chapter highlights some areas that have yet to be fully developed, and discusses ways in which sociological research in education might be further explored.

The emphasis of this book is upon the research evidence that has been collected by sociologists of education. In particular, the different kinds of questions that have been used, the research evidence that has been provided and the explanations that sociologists have advanced are reviewed. Obviously, in a book of this scale it has not been possible to review all the material that is included in the sociology of education, but key areas have been examined with a view to illustrating some of the ways in which sociologists have attempted to deepen our understanding of education and schools.

Suggestions for further reading

This chapter has provided a brief introduction to some of the sociological perspectives that have been used to examine education. It does not provide a summary of trends and developments in the subdiscipline as these can be found in the following material:

Acker, S. (1981) 'No-woman's land: British sociology of education 1960–1979', *Sociological Review*, vol. 29, no. 1, pp.77–104. A review of the sub-discipline from a feminist perspective. Very useful in challenging assumptions and stereotypes. This article is also in Cosin and Hales (1983) pp.106–128.

Banks, O. (1982) 'Sociology of Education' in L. Cohen, J. Thomas and L. Manion (eds) *Educational Research and Development in Britain 1970–1980*, Windsor, NFER-Nelson, pp.43–54 contains a good synthesis of the major developments and debates. For a thirty year review see Banks (1982b).

Bernbaum, G. (1977) *Knowledge and Ideology in the Sociology of Education*, London, Macmillan. A short review of the field that is particularly good in distinguishing key features in the 'old' and 'new' sociologies of education. However, it is important to consider whether this subdivision can still be sustained.

Burgess, R. G. (1984) 'Exploring frontiers and settling territory: shaping the sociology of education', *British Journal of Sociology*, vol. 35, no. 1, pp.122–137 reviews a range of studies in the early 1980s drawing special attention to the way in which the field of study is defined.

Davies, B. (1983) 'The sociology of education', in P. H. Hirst (ed) *Educational Theory and its Foundation Disciplines*, London, Routledge and Kegan Paul, pp.100–145 provides a discussion of sociology alongside other essays that examine those disciplines which relate to educational theory.

Demaine, J. (1977) *Contemporary Theories in the Sociology of Education*, London, Macmillan. A useful introductory guide to theoretical issues and perspectives in the sociology of education.

Halsey, A. H. and Floud, J. (1958) 'The sociology of education: a trend report and bibliography', *Current Sociology*, vol. 7, pp.165–235 is a trend report on this field of study in the 1950s (especially in Britain and the U.S.A.).

Hartnett, A. (1982) (ed) *The Social Sciences in Educational Studies*, London, Heinemann is a series of bibliographic essays on different areas of education although many focus on issues in the sociology of education. It is well worth consulting to identify major themes and related reading.

Karabel, J. and Halsey, A. H. (1977) 'Educational Research: A Review and an Interpretation' in J. Karabel and A. H. Halsey (eds) *Power and Ideology in Education*, Oxford University Press, pp.1–85 reviews major theoretical and methodological issues in the sociology of education.

Woods, P. (1983) *Sociology of the School: An Interactionist Viewpoint*, London, Routledge and Kegan Paul. A useful synthesis of recent work on schools and classrooms from an interactionist perspective.

EMPIRICAL STUDIES

This chapter has provided a brief guide to functionalist, interpretative, neo-Marxist and feminist perspectives. The following four studies that focus on schools provide accounts that are written from each of these perspectives in turn. In particular, readers should examine the questions, concepts and explanations used in these studies.

Parsons, T. (1959) 'The school class as a social system', *Harvard Educational Review*, vol. 29, pp.297–318, is one of the classic papers in the sociology of education that provides a functionalist analysis of the elementary and secondary school class as an agency of socialization and allocation.

Woods, P. (1979) *The Divided School*, London, Routledge and Kegan Paul is an interactionist analysis of a secondary modern school with a theoretical focus.

Willis, P. (1977) *Learning to Labour*, Farnborough, Saxon House. An account of the transition from school to work. The first part focuses on data, while the second part is theoretical.

Stanworth, M. (1981) *Gender and Schooling: A Study of Sexual Division in the Classroom*, London, Women's Research and Resources Centre. A study that illustrates the kinds of questions and explanations that are provided in feminist analyses of schooling (a further edition was published by Hutchinson, 1983).

2 Education, the economy, work and unemployment

> We must not delay. Upon the speedy provision of elementary education depends our industrial prosperity. It is of no use trying to give technical teaching to our artisans without elementary education; uneducated labourers – and many of our labourers are utterly uneducated – are for the most part, unskilled labourers, and if we leave our workfolk any longer unskilled, notwithstanding their strong sinews and determined energy, they will become overmatched in the competition of the world. (Forster, 1870, quoted in Hansard 17th February 1870)

> It is vital to Britain's economic recovery and standard of living that the performance of manufacturing industry is improved and that the whole range of government policies, including education, contribute as much as possible to improving industrial performance and thereby increasing the national wealth. (DES, 1977a, p.6)

These two statements concerning education are separated by just over 100 years. The first set of remarks was made by Mr W. E. Forster when introducing to Parliament the 1870 Education Act which was designed to establish universal elementary education. The second statement appeared in a Green Paper which was produced, immediately following the 'Great Debate' on education that was inaugurated by the Prime Minister, James Callaghan, in the mid 1970s. Both accounts concern the relationship between education and the economy and testify to the way in which the link between education and economic circumstances has been part of a recurring debate throughout the period in which there has been a state educational system in England (cf. Reeder, 1979). Indeed, these remarks, together with numerous other commentaries, research reports and policy statements underline the extent to which it has been assumed that there should be a relationship between education and the economy. While this issue has been at the heart of much policy making it has also been a concern in academic discussion and debate about education, for economists, political scientists, sociologists and historians have been concerned to examine the different ideological positions associated with this topic. For example, David Reeder (1979) indicated how nineteenth-century debates in Britain and the USA resulted in conflict between those who considered that education should be concerned with transforming the social order and those concerned with educational change for social efficiency. In the twentieth century, Reeder identifies a continuing set of debates about vocational education, the purpose of schooling and the industrial order. In particular, these debates have been between groups who have different sets of objectives as far as state education is concerned. Raymond Williams (1961), for example, has identified three groups who are concerned with the development of state education. First, public educators who argue that individuals have a right to be educated. Secondly, old humanists who consider that education should be more than mere training; while a third group, the industrial trainers, ostensibly define education in terms of preparation and training for adult work – a situation that results in attempts being made to meet the 'needs' of industry and the economy (although the 'needs' are often unspecified). Groups such as these may enter into conflict over school effectiveness, curriculum content and the extent to which a suitably qualified labour force emerges from the school system. In addition, questions concerned with the relationship between school and work, employment and unemployment have in recent years come under active scrutiny. Indeed, sociologists have frequently engaged in these debates using statistical evidence in support of their arguments.

Among the sets of statistical data that have been widely used are those that focus on the relationship between socio-economic groups and the last school, college or university attended (see table 1). As can be seen from table 1, such evidence highlights the relationship between professional and non-manual grouping and further and higher education in contrast to those in manual occupations. Further data sets from the General Household Survey (OPCS, 1984) also suggest a relationship between educational qualifications and occupational categories (see table 2) although as we shall see later in this chapter this is the subject of some debate, especially where school leavers are concerned.

These statistical data indicate that higher qualifications have been obtained by those in the professional and the intermediate non-manual groups, while junior non-manual groups and skilled and semi-skilled manual groups are less likely to have higher academic qualifications, and in turn there is a tendency for those in the lower categories to have some but not many academic qualifications. Academic qualifications are also found to be of significance when earnings are considered, and evidence drawn from the *General Household Survey* (OPCS, 1984) again confirms that there is a correlation between education and earnings whereby those people who are regarded as the 'better educated' earn more per week than those individuals with less education as revealed by formal academic

TABLE 1: *Educational establishment last attended full-time by sex and socio-economic group*

Economically active persons aged 25–69 not in full-time education — Great Britain: 1981 & 1982 combined

Educational establishment last attended full-time	*Socio-economic group*						
	Professional	*Employers and managers*	*Intermediate non-manual*	*Junior non-manual*	*Skilled manual and own account non-professional*	*Semi-skilled and unskilled manual and personal service*	*Total*
	%	%	%	%	%	%	%
Males							
School	29	78	58	83	94	96	83
Polytechnic, college of further education, other college*	29	14	30	13	6	4	11
University	42	8	12	4	1	Ø	6
Base=100%	757	2358	1238	875	5246	2465	12939
Females							
School	[13]	67	41	82	90	95	79
Polytechnic, college of further education, other college*	[18]	27	51	17	9	5	19
University	[43]	6	8	1	1	Ø	3
Base=100%	74	570	1505	2783	710	3047	8689

NOTE: *Colleges of further education include colleges of education in Scotland, Northern Ireland, and outside the UK, as well as former colleges of education in England and Wales.

SOURCE: Office of Population, Censuses and Surveys (1984) table 7.10, p. 145.

TABLE 2: *Highest qualifications level attained by age, sex and socio-economic group*

Economically active persons aged 25–69 not in full-time education

Great Britain: 1981 & 1982 combined

*Age and highest qualification level attained**		*Socio-economic group*						
		Professional	*Employers and managers*	*Intermediate non-manual*	*Junior non-manual*	*Skilled manual and own account non-professional*	*Semi-skilled and unskilled manual and personal service*	*Total*
		%	%	%	%	%	%	%
Males								
All aged 25–69	Higher education	90	28	49	13	5	1	18
	Other qualifications	9	44	35	49	41	20	36
	No qualifications	1	28	17	38	55	78	46
Base=100%		722	2239	1205	847	4985	2354	12352
Females†								
All aged 25–69	Higher education	[64]	21	55	3	4	1	13
	Other qualifications	[8]	42	27	52	30	17	33
	No qualifications	[1]	37	18	45	66	82	54
Base=100%		73	563	1498	2772	702	3015	8623

NOTES : *'Higher education'=qualifications above GCE 'A' level standard; 'other qualifications'=qualifications at or below GCE 'A' level standard.
†The numbers of economically active women aged 60–69 were too small to show separately.

SOURCE: Office of Population Censuses and Surveys (1984) table 7.11, p. 147 adapted.

TABLE 3: *Usual gross weekly earnings, hours worked, and age by highest qualification level attained and sex*

Persons aged 20–69 in full-time employment — Great Britain: 1982

		Highest qualification attained						
		Degree or equivalent	*Below degree higher education*	*GCE 'A' level or equivalent*	*GCE 'O' level or equivalent/ CSE grade 1*	*CSE other grades/ commercial/ apprenticeship*	*No qualifications*	*Total***
Earnings								
Usual gross weekly earnings (index numbers, total=100)								
Males		156	122	106	102	93	89	100
Females		173	149	108	101	93	86	100
Median weekly earnings	(£)							
Males	(£)	204	160	139	133	122	116	131
Females	(£)	151	130	94	88	82	75	87
Earnings of females relative to those of males	%	74	81	68	66	67	65	67
Median hourly earnings	(£)							
Males	(£)	5.20	4.00	3.40	3.20	3.00	2.80	3.20
Females	(£)	4.20	3.40	2.50	2.30	2.10	1.90	2.30
Earnings of females relative to those of males	%	82	85	71	70	72	69	71
Hours: Mean hours worked per week								
Males		41.3	41.0	42.1	43.3	43.4	44.3	43.2
Females		37.6	37.5	37.8	38.8	37.9	39.2	38.6
Mean hours of females relative to those of males	%	91	91	90	90	87	88	89
Age: Mean age (years)								
Males		38.2	37.4	33.6	34.5	42.3	44.5	40.4
Females		34.0	37.8	28.8	30.5	35.2	43.8	37.3

NOTE: **Including foreign and 'other' qualifications.

SOURCE: Office of Population Censuses and Surveys (1984) table 7.15, p. 152

qualifications (see table 3). Indeed, this relationship has been identified in many studies apart from the work of Jencks *et al* (1972) which itself has been questioned by Psacharopoulos and Wiles (1980) for its dubious methodology. However, statistical data are only part of the story, as we need to ask questions about the patterns that are revealed. For example, Layard and Psacharopoulos (1974) argue that the question which is of interest is not whether education increases earnings but why this occurs.

Sociologists have also posed questions about the relationship between school and work and the process of certification. Among the major questions with which they have been concerned in recent years are:

Does education promote economic enhancement?
Do schools prepare pupils for the world of work?

However, as Richard Brown (1984a) perceptively remarks, the key question that confronts policy makers, politicians and sociologists is: education for what work? For as Brown indicates, the assumptions of the 1960s concerning the intrinsic worth of education no longer hold true and as a consequence we have witnessed a situation since the mid 1970s whereby there has been a return to an instrumental view of education as preparation for work and a general concern about the extent to which schools prepare pupils for employment. In addressing these questions, statistical evidence about the changing economic circumstances has been used but in turn this has been accompanied by a belief that the right relationship can be established between education and work through changes in education, school organization and the curriculum. However, as Brown remarks:

> What has given this long running debate a different twist in the last few years has been the growing realization that work is changing and that traditional patterns of employment and customary job opportunities for school leavers have disappeared and may never return. (Brown, 1984a, p.97)

It is in these circumstances that sociologists have needed to view the school to work phenomenon as a long term issue rather than a brief transition. Questions have been posed not merely about education and employment but also about education and unemployment (cf. Watts, 1983) and the form that education and training takes during a period of recession (cf. Gleeson, 1983; Bates *et al*, 1984; Raffe, 1984). The focus of this chapter will, therefore, be upon the kinds of theoretical and empirical evidence that sociologists have assembled, especially since the 1960s, when examining the relationship between education, the economy, work and unemployment.

Theoretical conceptions of education and the economy

Accounts that consider the relationship between education and the economy can be broadly subdivided into those that are pluralist and those that are Marxist. The pluralist account considers that society is composed of a number of interest groups who compete with each other for influence with the result that educational policy emerges out of consensus and compromise. From this perspective the entry of pupils into the labour market is seen to depend on individual circumstances and market forces. In turn, it is argued that work from a Marxist perspective is economically determinist. By contrast, Marxist accounts are critical of the pluralist perspective, as it is argued that such work ignores economic power, interest and class which it is believed underlie all policy formation. A key feature of Marxist accounts is a belief that the educational system is similar to the structure of the capitalist mode of production. In particular, it is argued that educational institutions stratify pupils and students according to the structure of the labour market, that they provide appropriate types of educated labour for the benefit of capital and that economic interests have played a significant role in the formation of educational policy and educational practice. Even a brief glance at these competing perspectives suggests that they cannot fully account for the ways in which educational institutions relate to the economy. It is, therefore, our intention to begin by evaluating two of the dominant theoretical approaches that have been used to conceptualize the relationship between education and the economy and the school to work relationship, that have been widely discussed by sociologists in the 1960s and 1970s: human capital theory and Bowles' and Gintis' correspondence principle.

HUMAN CAPITAL THEORY

This approach became popular in the 1960s in the context of debates about human resources. In particular, a Presidential Address delivered by Theodore Schultz to the American Economic Association in 1960 on 'investment in Human Capital' gave force to the industrial trainer model of education. At the centre of his address was the idea that education is not only a form of consumption but is also an individually and socially productive investment. On this basis, it is argued that investment in knowledge and skills has given labourers the possibility of owning valuable capacities. However, human capital theory merely explained the low earnings of minority groups as a reflection of inadequate investment in education, as Schultz (1961) argued:

> Laborers have become capitalists not from a diffusion of the ownership of corporation stocks, as folklore would have it, but from the acquisition of knowledge and skill that have economic value. This knowledge and skill are in great part the product of investment and, combined with other human investment, predominantly account for the productive superiority of the technically advanced countries. (Schultz, 1961, reprinted in Karabel and Halsey, 1977b, p.314)

Such an approach which carried with it numerous policy implications was taken up by many countries in the 1960s and served as a basis for rising educational expenditure. In turn, human capital theory held implications for the development of the school curriculum and the promotion of new approaches to teaching and learning.

However, as Esland and Cathcart (1981) have argued, the greatest impact that this approach had in England was upon higher education in the 1960s. This was the period when technological universities were developed, when polytechnics were established and when new universities were built (cf. Sanderson, 1972a). Indeed, by the end of that decade questions were being posed about the extent to which economic interests were influencing development strategies in higher education, – a situation that reached a high point at Warwick University in the late 1960s (cf. Thompson, 1970).

Significantly, by the end of the 1960s the human capital approach was under considerable criticism. In particular, the main assumption that differences in economic growth could be attributed to educational investment was subject to doubt. For example, Berg (1973) challenged the notion that education is related to productivity by arguing that the demand for educated labour had been overstated with the result that there has been an upgrading of qualifications required to enter particular occupations. Furthermore, as Bluestone (1977) indicates, the anti-poverty policies that could be derived from human capital theory had met with relatively little success as a consequence of educational investment. In turn, criticism has also come from a Marxist perspective, as Hussain (1976) has argued that within human capital theory there is too great a concentration on the idea that the possession of educational qualifications will guarantee a continual income, while Gintis (1971) and Bowles and Gintis (1975) have argued that, while the model of educational choices advanced by the human capital theorists was not wrong, severe doubt could be cast on the individual choice framework that was advanced. For as far as Bowles and Gintis were concerned, mass schooling had developed to ensure a suitably docile labour force who could work in bureaucratic and industrial hierarchies. It is, therefore, to their model that we now turn.

THE CORRESPONDENCE PRINCIPLE

The American economists Samuel Bowles and Herbert Gintis published a number of articles in the early 1970s that contributed to a Marxist analysis of schooling (cf. Gintis, 1971, 1972; Bowles and Gintis, 1975). From this perspective it was argued that through mass schooling inequalities were perpetuated, capitalist power sustained and a principle of correspondence has operated whereby the authority relations of capitalist production have been reinforced in schools. It was this perspective that was central to their book *Schooling in Capitalist America* (1976).

It is this notion of correspondence that lies at the heart of their analysis, for they argue that the educational system shapes future workers for the occupational structure. Indeed, as far as they are concerned, schools and industrial enterprises have the same basic structure:

> The educational system helps integrate youth into the economic system, we believe, through the structural correspondence between its social relations and those of production. The structure of social relations in education not only inures the student to the discipline of the workplace, but develops the type of demeanours, modes of self presentation, self image and social class identifications which are crucial ingredients of job adequacy. (Bowles and Gintis, 1976, pp.130–131)

Indeed, they go on to argue that schools and work places correspond as:

> Different levels of education feed workers into different levels within the occupational structure and, correspondingly, tend toward an internal organization comparable to levels in the hierarchical division of labour. (Bowles and Gintis, 1976, p.132)

Here it is argued that the internal organization of schools are compatible with the needs of industry which they outline in three ways. First, both schools and workplaces are hierarchical organizations. Secondly, schools are like workplaces as they exact alienated labour for extrinsic rewards, as the work on which pupils and workers are engaged is characterized by fragmentation. Furthermore, just as workers lack control of the production process so this is also paralleled by pupils and students who lack control over their education and who are alienated from the curriculum. The focus here is upon the social and authority relationships which schools develop. For it is argued that school organization is comparable to different levels in the hierarchical division of labour, as they demonstrate how, in America, black pupils are concentrated in schools where the internal organization coupled with few opportunities for advancement are a mirror image of low grade jobs. Furthermore, they argue that if schools in working class areas are compared with those in middle class areas, the former emphasize rule following, while the latter highlight less supervision and control. On this basis they argue that the internal organization of schools reflects the organization of the economy and fulfils its needs.

While Bowles and Gintis cite evidence from America to support their correspondence thesis, questions can be raised about its applicability to other societies. For example, Musgrove (1979) has argued that if industrial development and educational provision are examined historically in the nineteenth and early twentieth centuries, they show a lack of correspondence. In order to demonstrate that the Bowles and Gintis thesis is basically wrong, he draws on historical evidence from Tyack (1976) on the development of compulsory schooling in the USA, from a study by Lawrence Stone (1969) on the development of literacy and education in England from the early seventeenth century until the turn of the twentieth century and from a study by Sanderson (1972b) of literacy in nineteenth-century England. In particular, Musgrove argues that a rural-urban distinction in literacy rates explains nothing, but it does question the close connection that Marxists claim between urban-industrial capitalism and mass schooling. Indeed, he maintains that in nineteenth-century England the schools failed to involve lower working class children who were not in great demand by industry. On the basis of this material he maintains there is insufficient evidence to suggest a correspondence between schooling and industry or to suggest that mass schooling would provide a disciplined work force.

But what evidence do we have concerning Britain in the twentieth century? Questions can be asked about the mechanisms that exist to ensure a high degree of correspondence between education and employment in a decentralized educational system. However, as Finn, Grant and Johnson (1978) suggest, we are not witnessing a situation whereby education serves industry so well but one in which it serves it so badly, for as Frith (1978) argues, employers often complain about the attitudes that young people bring to the work situation. In addition, many writers have pointed to the way in which schools are not merely required to prepare pupils for work (cf. Finn, 1982). Yet despite these reservations about the wholesale applicability of Bowles and Gintis's theory to contemporary schooling there is some evidence to suggest that schools do influence the attitudes and aspirations that their pupils have concerning work (cf. Willis, 1977; Troyna and Smith, 1983) and future choices in the labour market. However, recent studies (Finn, 1984; Moore, 1984) suggest that young people do not merely acquire knowledge about the world of work from schools but also from their own experience of part-time employment. In particular, Finn (1984) argues that pupils acquire knowledge of the labour market through part-time jobs which in turn may provide them with knowledge, experience and access to informal job finding networks that will be important in their search for work – a situation that is confirmed by Richard Jenkins' study of working class youths in Belfast (cf. Jenkins, 1983). However, some sociologists have argued that it is not sufficient to focus on work experience and informal networks but that it is essential to examine the relationship between education and qualifications, a debate to which we now turn.

Educational qualifications and occupations: a tightening bond?

In recent years some commentators such as Freeman (1971) have argued that there is a tightening bond between educational qualifications, occupational attainment and starting salaries, as qualifications have been used to control entry to particular jobs (Dore, 1976; Banks, 1976; Tyler, 1976).

On the basis of studying 350 employing organizations, Maguire and Ashton (1981) have argued that it would be misleading to see educational qualifications being used in a uniform way in the selection process. They point to five strategies that are used by employers in selecting individuals for employment:

> *Strategy 1* is where the employer stipulates a minimum level of educational qualifications as a necessary condition for entry to the job, but in practice tends to select the candidates with the highest educational qualifications. Non-academic criteria can play a part, usually at the final interview, but they are normally subordinated to academic criteria.
>
> *Strategy 2* involves the use of educational qualifications as a means of pre-selection or screening. Minimum educational qualifications are stipulated, and candidates who fail to meet these conditions are automatically excluded from consideration. However, the final decision about which of the candidates with the minimum qualifications to employ is then made on the basis of non-academic criteria.
>
> *Strategy 3* is one in which the balance between academic and non-academic criteria shifts in favour of the non-academic. Educational qualifications perform a focusing function, directing the recruitment drive at students with a given level of ability. Employers stipulate a number of such qualifications as desirable, but if a candidate has other non-academic qualities which meet their requirements, they will not rigidly enforce the educational ones.
>
> *Strategy 4* places almost all the emphasis on non-academic criteria. In this strategy, educational qualifications are functionless. The qualities that educational qualifications measure are seen either as irrelevant or unnecessary for the effective performance of the jobs for which recruitment is taking place. Decisions about which of the applicants to employ are made on the basis of the personality or physical attributes which are perceived as being desirable for the job.
>
> *Strategy 5* is where the educational qualifications disqualify young people for consideration for a job. They are regarded by the employer as an indication of ability and ambition which could not be satisfied by the undemanding jobs for which this strategy is used. The decision about who to employ is made on the basis of non-academic criteria. (Maguire and Ashton, 1981, p.26)

As a consequence, they argue that rather than seeing the relationship between education and the labour market as a single tightening bond, it is better to see it as a series of disparate links. In particular, they maintain that the relationship between education and the labour market at lower levels is much looser. Indeed, in line with many other British studies (cf. Silverman and Jones, 1973; Reid, 1980) they argue that the stress is put on non-academic rather than academic criteria in the selection process. However, they do add that those with academic qualifications are often likely to hold the non-academic qualifications that are required (cf. Gray, McPherson and Raffe, 1983). Yet this explanation, like others, does not appear to take account of gender and race in considering the relationship between education and employment.

Education and employment: gender and race

Much of the theoretical work within the sociology of education and for that matter in sociology has until relatively recently taken little note of the importance of gender and race in explaining social situations (cf. Brittain and Maynard, 1984). While many of the explanations concerning relationships between education and the economy and school and work appear to take relatively little note of gender differences, Wolpe (1978) has argued that the relationship between education and employment is different for boys and girls. In particular, she highlights the importance of the sexual division of labour and the way in which divisions based on class and gender result in situations whereby working class school leavers end up in jobs that are of lower status than middle class school leavers (cf. Ashton and Field, 1976), while women end up in lower status jobs than men. Indeed, Wolpe sees that it is the sexual division of labour rather than education which determines women's job prospects. In particular, she argues that the jobs which women obtain are largely determined by opportunities in the labour market and by the sexual division of labour. Accordingly, jobs involving long periods of training rarely include women. In turn, she maintains that women's domestic labour commitments reduce women's employment in professional and skilled work (cf. Llewellyn, 1980) with the result that educational qualifications have relatively little impact on employment opportunities.

In reviewing evidence on race and the labour market Jenkins and Troyna (1983) point to the importance of examining the relative educational failure of black pupils in the course of providing explanations that account for their failure in the job market, for they argue that education and employment are two important dimensions of racial disadvantage. Indeed, the Rampton report (Rampton, 1981) focuses on the importance of educational qualifications when it states that the employability of a pupil is

> determined largely by the academic qualifications he or she has obtained at school and since West Indians . . . are underachieving at school, they will clearly be at a disadvantage in the job market. (Rampton, 1981, p.52)

Such evidence suggests that lack of educational qualifications and educational underachievement results in unemployment. This assumes that credentials offer some protection against unemployment and that school leavers will get jobs in relation to their ability. However, research evidence by Cross (1982) and by Roberts, Duggan and Noble (1981) indicate that black youths who were unemployed were better qualified than their white counterparts. Such evidence suggests that educational credentials do not have the same meaning for black youths as for whites. Accordingly, it would point to the importance of sociologists not arriving at generalizations about the relationships between education, employ-

TABLE 4: *Educational and economic activities of 16 year olds*[1] *in Great Britain*

Percentages & thousands

	1975/76			*1981/82*			*1982/83*		
	Boys	*Girls*	*Total*	*Boys*	*Girls*	*Total*	*Boys*	*Girls*	*Total*
Percentage of 16 year olds who were[2]:									
In full-time non-advanced education									
– in schools	28	28	28	29	33	31	30	34	32
– in further education establishments[3]	11	15	13	12	19	16	13	20	16
Mainly in employment outside Youth Opportunities Programme									
– with part-time day education	19	6	13	11	5	8	10	4	7
– other[4]	32	43	37	20	17	19	10	12	11
On Youth Opportunities Programme/New Training/Initiatives[5]	.	.	.	14	14	14	20	18	19
Registered/claimant unemployed[6]	10	8	9	14	12	13	16	13	15
Total 16 year olds (100%) (thousands)	428	406	834	478	453	931	467	443	910

NOTES: 1. The activities in January each year of those who had attained the statutory school-leaving age (16 years) by the previous 31 August.
2. In addition to the activities shown, some 10 per cent of 16 year olds attended evening classes.
3. Includes sandwich students and a small number in higher education.
4. Includes prior to 1982/83 the unregistered unemployed and those who were neither employed nor seeking work, and in 1982/83 those who were seeking work but not claiming benefit and those who were neither employed nor seeking work.
5. Includes those in further education establishments attending YOP or NTI courses.
6. The registered unemployed (prior to 1982/83) are Department of Education and Science estimates.

SOURCE: Central Statistical Office (1985) p. 49

ment and unemployment without taking race as well as gender seriously. In the course of reviewing some of the empirical studies that have been conducted by sociologists on the transition from school, 'youth' is not treated as a homogeneous group as account is taken of differences based on gender and race.

Sociological studies of the transition from school to . . .

In the 1950s and 1960s it was common to talk of the transition between school and work as being a short period in which young unqualified school leavers searched for work and shifted jobs prior to settling down in their early twenties. However, by the mid 1970s this pattern had shown a marked change with the search for work and the transition between school and work being punctuated by short term jobs, periods on government sponsored schemes and periods of unemployment. The main trends in the educational and economic activities of sixteen year olds in Great Britain since the mid 1970s are shown in table 4. One trend that is of particular significance is the number of young people who now leave school and go on to a training scheme. Between 1978/79 and 1982/83 young people went on to the Youth Opportunities Programme, after which it was replaced by the Youth Training Scheme.

While table 4 outlines the main trends in Great Britain, Rees and Gregory (1981) have indicated that they did not occur uniformly. They emphasize how the transition from school to work, to a scheme or to unemployment often varies according to the regional location of individuals, and is also dependent on gender and ethnic origin. Nevertheless, they argue that three broad categories can be identified in the transition between school and work:

> First of all, there is what we may term a 'traditional' approach to the school-to-work transition with a clearly demarcated interface at age 16, in so far as the majority of secondary schools are concerned. Second, we identify a more 'progressive' approach which recognises the inadequacies of the present relationship between the institutions of secondary education and those of work. An effort to improve the linkages between the two, focused on the immediate pre-school leaving years, would be a feature of this approach. Lastly, there is a 'radical' view which would not accept the traditional breakpoint at 16, but rather would see school-to-work as a continuum stretching from 13–20 along which schools present themselves as a resource. A key feature here would be the interchange of resources and time between schools and the world of work, together with the possibility of secondary-school students spending blocks of time in properly supervised work experience well before their final school year. (Rees and Gregory, 1981, p.21)

In turn, they demonstrate the ways in which these approaches may be viewed, as seen in figure 1.

Figure 1: Educational pathways from school to work

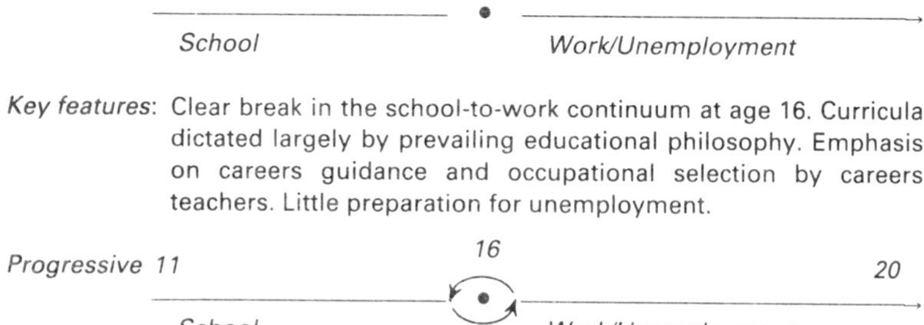

Key features: Clear break in the school-to-work continuum at age 16. Curricula dictated largely by prevailing educational philosophy. Emphasis on careers guidance and occupational selection by careers teachers. Little preparation for unemployment.

Key features: Clear break in the school-to-work continuum but with efforts to locate the final year at school in a more realistic setting via school/industry projects, forums, conferences etc. Some attempts to 'tailor' final-year curricula for some pupils to fit perceived needs of local industry.

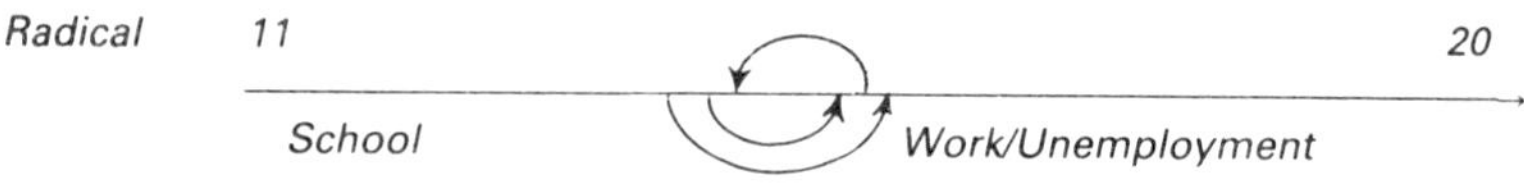

Key features: No clear-cut break in the school-to-work continuum. Emphasis on two-way interchange between school and industry via programmed work experience for students from the age of 13 onwards. Equally on teachers spending time in local industry and representatives from industry spending time in school.

(SOURCE: Rees and Gregory, 1981, p. 22)

As Rees and Gregory indicate, the two predominant patterns of transition that are found in Britain are those that they describe as the 'traditional' and the 'progressive' approaches. Nevertheless, a small number of local authorities, especially those who are pioneering community education, would argue that the arrangements that they are making in secondary education come close to the 'progressive' and 'radical' approaches where work experience is a part of the curriculum for all pupils (cf. Coventry Education Committee, 1983, and see the essays in Eggleston, 1982). On this basis it would seem appropriate to consider sociological evidence on the traditional school-to-work relationship, and the school to government scheme or unemployment relationship.

From school to work

The classic British ethnographic study that has been conducted on the transition between school and work concerns white working class boys in the Midlands in the early 1970s. Here, Paul Willis (1977) examines the way in which careers teaching and careers lessons transmit the notion that there is a degree of fit between ability, behaviour and work. As a consequence many of the teachers in Willis's study argued that non-conformist attitudes and behaviour would not fit the 'needs' of industry (a term that they do not clarify). Willis illustrates how teachers often used some form of blackmail which suggested that if pupils did not co-operate, they would not get a good report which in turn would result in little chance of a job. For example, Willis reports a careers teacher talking to fifth year pupils in the following terms:

> I've just heard of a case, a lad at Easter, he got sacked after three weeks. He resented authority and wouldn't obey the rules. His attitude was wrong, the manager just sacked him, he said, OUT, he wasn't going to put up with it, why should he. I've told you before bad habits at school take a lot of throwing over, if you're resentful of authority here, and have a bad attitude towards discipline, it will carry on at work, it will show there and they won't have time for it. Now's the time to start making an effort, show you are up to it now. (Willis, 1977, p.92)

However, as far as the lads in Willis's study were concerned there was no need to take any notice for they found that it was possible to meet with success without formal qualifications and without doing school work. For them it was possible to meet with success by obtaining jobs through local networks, and proving evidence of ability 'on the job' (cf. Jenkins, 1983; Finn, 1984). However, we might consider the extent to which the lads' rejection of the school is based on a particular view of masculinity which helps them to identify with male manual workers. But what, we might ask, is the experience of working class girls?

In a study of 760, 16-year olds in the Bradford Metropolitan District in 1980 Helen Roberts (1986) has focused on the period of transition from school to work for girls. In her study she asks:

> Did equal opportunities' legislation mean that girls were now being offered – and taking up – the same opportunities as boys?
> Were they employed or unemployed in similar numbers? Were they going on to Youth Opportunities Programme schemes and were the schemes they went on different from the schemes offered to or chosen by the boys?

Already it becomes apparent that in the three year period since Willis's study had appeared it had become essential for sociologists to modify the kinds of questions that could be addressed in relation to the opportunities that were available. Indeed, Roberts summarises the main opportunities for 16-year old pupils in 1980 as: remaining in school, further education, work, unemployment, a youth opportunities scheme and, for the girls, full-time domestic labour – an opportunity that reflects the sexual division of labour.

In order to focus on the experiences of girls leaving school without qualifications Helen Roberts examines the case of a girl she calls Patsy. For Patsy school was seen as a prelude to work and in the twelve months since leaving school she had held four jobs and experienced five months of unemployment. In common with many working class boys, she had obtained her jobs through family connections and through her personal social network (cf. Lee and Wrench, 1981; Finn, 1984). However, in common with many girls, but unlike the boys in Roberts' study, she was not in a job that involved further training. She was willing to take jobs that 'came her way' and for which few skills were required and no training. Indeed, as Roberts remarks:

> The notion of a career is probably not an appropriate one for most girls going into employment at sixteen. The name of the game is getting a job, getting a wage, keeping off the dole. (Roberts, 1986)

Among the key findings in Roberts' study is the differences between the aspirations and experiences of boys and girls in the job market. But we might ask: how does race modify the dominant patterns?

In a review of young blacks and Asians in the labour market, Dennis Brooks (1983) indicates that until relatively recently most working class young people have found the transition from school to work relatively non-problematic as they have been adequately prepared for their future roles. However, he makes three qualifications to this model. First, the aspirations-opportunities match has broken down. Secondly, the breakdown has occurred on the supply side, and finally, for black and Asian young people aspirations do not match those of their white contemporaries.

As far as job aspirations are concerned it is essential to distinguish between blacks and Asians and between boys and girls. As far as black boys are concerned there is a tendency to want similar jobs to members of the 'respectable' white working class, while black girls also want respectable occupations, which again lays stress on the similarity between blacks and the indigenous white population (cf. Lee and Wrench, 1983; Rex and Tomlinson, 1979). However, among young Asians it has been found that aspirations are much higher than among white youths – a situation that is also shared by Asian girls (cf. Taylor, 1976). But what of the search for jobs? As far as the transition from school to work is concerned for blacks and Asians, Brooks (1983) argues that they are more dependent on the careers service, have to make more job applications and take longer to secure jobs than their white peers. In these circumstances, we might ask what is the relationship between job aspirations and job attainment? Drawing on evidence from statistical surveys where data could be compared for boys and for girls in different ethnic groups, Brooks (1983) is able to offer the summary shown in table 5.

TABLE 5: *The relationship of job attainments to job aspirations of school leavers*

Researcher/s Date	*Brooks 1975*			*Singh 1975*		*CRE 1977*				*Lee & Wrench 1979*		
Racial or ethnic group	W	W	A	W	A	W	B	W	B	W	WI	A
Gender	M–F	M–F	M–F	M–F	M–F	M	M	F	F	M	M	M
Attained type of job aspired to	54%	68%	28%	50%	25%	61%	39%	55%	49%	49%	15%	15%
Did not attain type of job aspired to	37%	30%	72%	50%	75%	24%	48%	33%	41%	44%	57%	45%
Other/no answer	9%	3%	—	—	—	15%	13%	12%	10%	7%	28%	40%
Number	35	37	18	87	127	112	109	115	66	57	46	67

KEY: W = White
A = Asian
B = Black
WI = West Indian
M = Male
F = Female

NOTE: the first two columns of the Brooks data represent two separate samples. For details see Brooks in Brooks and Singh (1979) pp. 76–78

SOURCE: Brooks (1983) p. 89

A dominant trend that emerges from these comparative data is that whites were much more likely than either blacks or Asians to realize their job aspirations – a situation that Brooks concludes is the result of discrimination rather than unrealistic job aspirations. However, it has been found that there is a lower level of job satisfaction among Asians and blacks – a situation that is consistent with their lower levels of job attainment and with the wider gap between aspirations and attainments compared with whites. Nevertheless, these data do not take into account the situation of rising unemployment and the transition from school to government schemes to which we now turn.

From school to schemes and unemployment

One of the main characteristics of the 1970s was the rise in unemployment. In 1975 there were just over a million unemployed, a figure which rose to just over two million in 1980 and to three million in 1983. However, these figures underestimate the true level of unemployment, as they exclude those who do not or cannot claim benefit, those involved in short term work, those on job creation schemes and school leavers, of whom 112,200 were unemployed in March 1983 (Department of Employment, 1983). Indeed, between 1972 and 1977 school leaver unemployment rose by 120 per cent compared to 45 per cent among the working population as a whole (Rees and Gregory, 1981). It is, therefore, in these circumstances that the Manpower Services Commission has been able to establish its position (cf. Education Group, 1981) whilst examining the main patterns and processes associated with the transition from school and developing courses for school leavers. In particular, the Holland Report on *Young People and Work* (1977) considered the distribution of youth unemployment to be a significant part of the problem when it stated:

> The impact of unemployment is most severe on those young people who have few or no qualifications. In comparison with the better qualified they suffer longer duration of unemployment, are more frequently unemployed and when employed they tend to work in lower status jobs with poorer prospects of promotion and fewer opportunities for training. Moreover, when there is a high level of unemployment, people with poor qualifications encounter increased competition for jobs from those of higher ability and with better qualifications. (Holland Report, 1977, p.17)

In turn, the report also indicated that among those most adversely affected were individuals from households whose members were unemployed, girls and first or second generation Commonwealth immigrants. The report also suggested that it was essential to devise a government scheme that would cater for these groups so as to change the distribution as well as the level of unemployment.

It is in these circumstances that the Holland Report (1977) advocated that the special programmes that had been established to provide work experience or training for unemployed young people should be replaced by the Youth Opportunities Programme (YOP) which would offer courses or work experience schemes from two weeks to one year in length for unemployed young people aged 16 to 18. Indeed, the government promised to find a YOP place for every young person who had not found a job (initially by Easter but later by Christmas) after leaving school. As a consequence the scale of YOP was substantial. To begin with about 160,000 young people entered YOP in 1978–79 and 216,000 in the year 1979–80. During 1979–80 the average number of filled places was 77,000 and an estimated 24,000 entered the programme each month. Indeed, YOP was expanded to cater for 250,000 young people in 1980–81 and was expected to receive almost double that number of young people in 1981–82. As a consequence YOP has become the experience of young people entering the labour market from school (see table 4). But we might ask: how has YOP influenced the school to work relationship?

David Raffe (1983) has argued that YOP has acted as a filter which influences the criteria for selection for employment by increasing the information that is available to future employers about their recruits. In particular, Raffe demonstrates how YOP schemes have tended to provide work experience with ordinary employers. In turn, it is this experience that has been treated by many employers as equivalent to an educational qualification and which has been used as a means of screening future recruits. On this basis YOP has become more important, for as Raffe comments:

> Not only has YOP itself substituted for a number of permanent jobs; entry to many of the ordinary jobs which remain has been effectively restricted to young people who have been through a YOP scheme. By the logic of its situation, the MSC has been disposed to favour this trend. To maintain the credibility of the programme and the motivation of those on it, the MSC has needed to maintain high rates of post-scheme employment; it is therefore in its interest that the remaining jobs available for young people should be rationed in favour of those who have passed through YOP. (Raffe, 1983, p.302)

As a consequence, the criteria for occupational selection have changed, so much that Raffe (1981) found that, among unqualified school leavers in Scotland, it was those on YOP who were more likely to find work than those who had not been on YOP. It would, therefore, appear that YOP has had a significant influence on the school to work transition; but we might ask: what has been the experience of girls and ethnic minorities whom the Holland Report (1977) had shown were particularly disadvantaged?

Rees and Gregory (1981) have indicated that about half the places on YOP schemes are given to women. However, the significant feature is the distribution of the two genders on the YOP schemes. In particular, sex stereotyping persists as the majority of women trainees are on Work Experience on Employers Premises compared with 22 per cent on Project Based Work Experience and 27 per cent in Training Workshops. These trends are also echoed in data that Rees (1983) has collected on YOP schemes in Northern Ireland as shown in table 6. As Rees (1983) indicates, these data on Northern Ireland are not exceptional, as places and work have been distributed along traditional sex stereotypical lines throughout Britain as the YOP scheme is geared towards the reproduction of labour in predominantly male spheres of employment.

Among ethnic minorities participation in the Youth Opportunities Programme has been relatively high. For example, Bedeman and Harvey (1981) found, in a sample survey of YOP entrants in London between September 1978 and June 1979, that 54 per cent of trainees were from ethnic minorities and of these the largest group (41 per cent) were black. In turn, a report by Stares, Imberg and McRobbie (1982) compared ethnic minority representation on YOP with the total registered youth unemployed in Southall, Handsworth and Moss Side as shown in table 7. As Brooks indicates, apart from Southall, ethnic minorities are over-represented on YOP schemes compared with the registered un-

TABLE 6: *Trainees entering YOP by scheme and gender, April 1981–March 198*

	Male	*Female*	*Total*	%	*Females*
Apprentice Training					
in Government Training Centres (GTCs)	1038	3	1041	6.1	0.2
in Employers' Premises	1891	323	2214	13.0	14.6
Attachment Training Scheme	871	1966	2837	16.6	69.2
Work Experience					
Work Preparation Units	1943	890	2833	16.6	31.4
Work Experience Programme	955	1147	2102	12.3	54.6
Courses					
Young Persons courses at GTCs	1725	162	1887	11.0	8.6
Youthways / Work Preparation Course	496	455	951	5.6	47.8
Job Creation					
Young Help	91	367	458	2.7	80.1
Enterprise Ulster	900	2	902	5.3	0.2
National Trust	105	6	111	0.6	5.4
Other					
ESF Pilot Projects/ERU	53	28	81	0.4	52.8
TOTAL	10901	6192	17093	100.0	36.2

NOTE: Calculated from information supplied by the Department of Manpower Services.
SOURCE: Rees (1983) p. 176

employed. In turn, evidence on the post-YOP experience of blacks compared with Asians and whites has been found by Bedeman and Harvey (1981) to be such that blacks do not experience the advantage of having been YOP trainees.

Such experiences of YOP have resulted in a number of critical questions being raised which have been well summarized by Raffe (1983, p.304).

> Are enough trainees receiving an educational input?
> Is the quality of the work experience itself adequate?
> Is the balance between general work skills and specific vocational skills right?
> Is social and life skills training any more than an agency of social control and a regressive departure from the liberal tradition of social education?
> Is the whole of YOP any more than a clumsy ideological manoeuvre to blame the victims of youth unemployment for their own predicament?

Such questions raise the whole issue of the shape and substance of

TABLE 7: *Ethnic minority representation within YOP compared to representation on the unemployment register by locality*

Area		*Male*	*Female*
Southall	YOP	86%	100%
	Unemployment	93%	59%
Handsworth	YOP	89%	94%
	Unemployment	46%	51%
Moss Side	YOP	22%	15%
	Unemployment	20%	12%

Based on Stares, Imberg and McRobbie (1982)
SOURCE: Brooks (1983)

education and training. Here the significance of the content of the courses becomes important. Indeed, schemes such as YOP contribute to our understanding of the relationship between education and training and have helped to fuel the debate about the extent to which schools should become directly involved in preparing young people for work. Eggleston (1982) suggests that work experience may be provided in a number of ways:

1. by infusion into the whole curriculum whereby subjects are taught giving explicit attention to the relevance of industry, commerce and the professions;
2. by work experience courses through placements with local employers;
3. by work creation schemes whereby schools organize the provision of services for themselves and the local community;
4. by link courses for school pupils in the local colleges of further education;
5. by work simulation schemes whereby a school based enterprise is established to give individuals the range of experiences associated with the activities required to produce and sell goods.

It is schemes such as these that bring us back to the question of the relationship between education and the economic structure and school and work. Furthermore, these schemes also pose problems about the meaning of the 'needs of industry' and the content of work 'experience'.

Conclusion

This chapter has focused on the relationship between education and the economy and in turn the relationship between school, work and unemployment. Throughout this long running debate is a tendency to blame the educational system and in turn the schools for failing to provide school leavers who are fully equipped for the world of work. Alternatively, there is a tendency to blame young people for lacking the skills, habits of mind and work experience that is thought to be required by employers. Yet such accounts overlook analyses of the labour market and fail to understand the distinction between education and training. At the present time we have a number of new schemes both within schools and beyond them: the technical and vocational education initiative (TVEI), the certificate of pre-vocational education (CPVE) and the Youth Training Scheme (YTS) which it is planned to extend to a two year programme. Clearly, all these initiatives call for critical scrutiny by their participants and also by sociologists. For if sociologists place these issues firmly on the research agenda we shall be able to question some of the assumptions associated with these schemes alongside furthering our understanding of the relationships between education and industry. In this sense, further research evidence can contribute to what is a recurring debate among sociologists.

Suggestions for further reading

Bowles, S. and Gintis, H. (1976) *Schooling in Capitalist America*, London, Routledge and Kegan Paul is the key text that discusses the 'correspondence principle' between school and work. All the illustrative material relates to the USA. This book has been widely quoted and attracted considerable debate and criticism – see for example Musgrove (1979) and Cole (1983).

Dale, R., Esland, G., Fergusson, R. and MacDonald, M. (1981) (eds) *Education and the State, Volume 1 Schooling and the National Interest*, Lewes, Falmer Press contains a collection of papers in section 2 on education, the economy and the labour process, see especially papers by Hussain, Braverman and Sanderson. The key paper by David Reeder (1979) on the education-industry debate is also reprinted.

Esland, G. and Cathcart, H. (1981) 'Education and the corporate economy' in Open University, *The State and the Politics of Education* (Course E353, Block 1, part 1, Unit 2) Milton Keynes, Open University Press, pp.57–100 provides a guide to pluralist and Marxist approaches to this field of study together with illustrative material on higher education (cf. Sanderson, 1972a)

Finn, D. and Frith, S. (1981) 'Education and the labour market' in Open University, *The State and the Politics of Education*, (Course E353, Block 1, Part 2, Unit 4) Milton Keynes, Open University Press, pp.41–85 complements the material by Esland and Cathcart by examining the education and industry question in Britain in the 1960s and 1970s.

Gleeson, D. (1983) (ed) *Youth Training and the Search for Work*, London, Routledge and Kegan Paul contains papers on the sociology of further education. It contains sections devoted to further education and the labour market, further education and training and further education and unemployment.

Halsey, A. H., Floud, J. and Anderson, C.A. (1961) (eds) *Education, Economy and Society*, New York, Free Press is a classic collection of papers that examines education and the economy from a functionalist perspective. See especially parts one and two.

Karabel, J. and Halsey, A. H. (1977) (eds) *Power and Ideology in Education*,

Oxford, Oxford University Press provides a review of educational research which locates the ways in which theories on education and the economy have been developed and used. There is also a complete section (pp.307–365) devoted to education, 'human capital' and the labour market.

Watts, A. (1981) (ed) *Schools, Youth and Work*, special issue of *Educational Analysis*, vol. 3, no. 2, pp.1–106. A collection of papers on employment, unemployment and the school to work relationship. The papers by Rees and Gregory (1981) and by Maguire and Ashton (1981) are well worth consulting.

Watts, A. (1983) *Education, Unemployment and the Future of Work*, Milton Keynes, Open University Press provides a useful review of the relationships between education and unemployment. The author summarizes basic positions that have been adopted.

White, R. with Brockington, D. (1983) *Tales out of School*, London, Routledge and Kegan Paul. The first part of the book contains statements by seventy young people about their schooling and preparation for work, see especially chapters five, six and seven that deal with school and work and the Youth Opportunities Programme.

EMPIRICAL STUDIES

There are now numerous studies on the school to work transition, many of which monitor new schemes for school leavers. The following studies give insights into such work as well as material that articulates with key issues identified by sociologists.

Bates, I. *et al* (1984) *Schooling for the Dole? The New Vocationalism*, London, Macmillan is a set of essays that critically examine work experience programmes and youth training schemes. See especially the essays by Finn (1984) and by Moore (1984).

Fiddy, R. (1983) (ed) *In Place of Work: Policy & Provision for the Young Unemployed*, Lewes, Falmer Press. A collection of papers that provide reflections on policy and practice prior to the start of the Youth Training Scheme.

Griffin, C. (1985) *Typical Girls? The Transition from School to Un/Employment for Young Working Class Women*, London, Routledge and Kegan Paul is an ethnographic study that focuses on the transition from school to the labour market for young working class women. The study was designed to complement the earlier work of Paul Willis (1977). For the background to the study see Griffin (1985a).

Raffe, D. (1984) 'The transition from school to work and the recession: evidence from the Scottish school leavers surveys, 1977–1983', *British Journal of Sociology of Education*, vol. 5, no. 3, pp.247–265. A paper that focuses on survey data obtained from longitudinal studies of school leavers in Scotland and links up with key debates about school and work.

Rees, T. and Atkinson, P. (1982) (eds) *Youth Unemployment and State Intervention*, London, Routledge and Kegan Paul. A set of papers that examines state response to youth unemployment. See especially Finn (1982) on schooling and the 'needs' of industry and Williamson (1982) on clients' views of the Youth Opportunities Programme.

Willis, P. (1977) *Learning to Labour*, Farnborough, Saxon House is the classic ethnographic study of the school to work transition for working class boys in the 1970s.

3 Educational opportunity and patterns of social mobility

In concluding her classic study of English secondary education, Olive Banks (1955) maintains that the secondary school has been considerably influenced by its role in selection for social mobility – a case that she sustains by detailed reference to the development of the secondary grammar school. While education has been a possible avenue of social ascent, this has not always been the case, as Halsey (1977a) indicates: in the nineteenth century and even in the first half of the twentieth century education, and especially higher education

> was much more the stamp put on the social character of individuals whose jobs and life-styles were predetermined by social origin than an institutional ladder for the talented of humble birth. (Halsey, 1977a, p.176)

While there was some mobility between different generations, the most important developments were in terms of capital accumulation and on the job promotion rather than education. It is against this background that sociologists and educationalists have considered how equality of opportunity, especially in education, could provide the way forward to an egalitarian society. Much of this work and writing has been concerned with two linked concepts: *meritocracy* and *equality of opportunity*.

In a meritocracy individuals are rewarded on the basis of merit, as it is argued that the educational system allocates them to positions on the basis of ability. Such a situation is well summarized by Evetts (1973) when she states:

> In a meritocracy, economic, social and political rewards are distributed according to performance in intellectual accomplishments. Those who do best in the education system are allotted the most powerful, prestigious and best paid positions in the occupational structure. (Evetts, 1973, p.113)

As Evetts (1973) indicates, selection takes place through the educational system which provides an avenue of social and economic mobility. Here, individuals are selected for positions in the economic and social hierarchies according to educational criteria. On this basis, social origins do not determine educational success, so that those born into a wealthy family are not automatically destined for high status. Equality of educational opportunity would, therefore, break the chain of links between family background and social placement in adult life.

However, the concept of a 'meritocracy' is not without problems. First, it tends to assume that social inequality is inevitable. Secondly, as it focuses on placement in the occupational structure it overlooks the significance of elites and the role of the propertied upper class (for a review of this area see Philip Stanworth, 1984). Thirdly, a meritocracy is a society with structured social inequality in which individuals have an equal opportunity to obtain unequal power and reward. On this basis, privilege and disadvantage is not eradicated as the educational system provides a different set of criteria to allocate people to social positions. In particular, social positions are allocated according to talent which, according to Floud and Halsey (1961), finds its own level providing that there is a high rate of social mobility and the minimization or 'elimination of social factors in educational selection and occupational recruitment' (p.4). However, the emphasis on social mobility is open to doubt as Young (1958) and Herrnstein (1973) maintain that a meritocracy has low rates of social mobility. Furthermore, if a society is to become a meritocracy, social status would be *achieved* through education which itself would be determined by merit. Accordingly, this demands equality of educational opportunity.

The term equality of educational opportunity is surrounded by considerable confusion, although several writers have attempted to come to terms with this issue. In particular, Coleman (1968) indicates that in connection with his large scale project on *Equality of Educational Opportunity* (Coleman *et al*, 1966) five different definitions of equality of educational opportunity were considered. Broadly speaking, there were those definitions that were concerned with inputs into schools and those that focused on the effects of schooling. Those definitions concerned with inputs were defined as follows:

> (a) Differences in global input characteristics such as per pupil expenditure, physical facilities, and library resources.
>
> (b) The social and radical student composition of the school.
>
> (c) Intangible characteristics of the school such as teachers' expectations of students, teacher morale, and the level of interest of the student body in learning.
>
> (Marjoribanks, 1975, p.25)

While those definitions concerned with the effects of schooling were defined in terms of:

> (d) Equality of results given the *same* individual input.
>
> (e) Equality of results given *different* individual inputs.
>
> (Marjoribanks, 1975, p.25 emphasis in original)

As far as the study was concerned, Coleman (1968) indicates that the focus was upon the fourth definition which resulted in an assessment being made of the effects of various inputs upon student characteristics. In particular, he highlights the way in which this concept implied effective equality of opportunity – that is equality among elements effective for learning.

As Coleman (1975) indicates, a key problem concerns whether equality implies equality of input or equality of output. However, he suggests that neither inputs nor outputs are viable and so concludes that equality of educational opportunity is not a meaningful term. If it is examined on the basis of results, it is unachievable, and if looked at as the input of resources it is a weak term. Such an analysis focuses on the use of the concept in the USA so we need to consider the extent to which it is applicable to Britain.

As Evetts (1973) indicates, the term 'equal educational opportunity' is also problematic in Britain. In particular, she highlights two problems. The first concerns the way in which educational opportunities are achieved, while the second concerns what is meant by 'equal educational opportunity'. As Harold Silver (1973) has remarked in relation to British work on this subject:

> for most of this century, the discussion of education in relation to such concepts as 'equality', 'equality of opportunity', 'democracy' or 'social justice' has focused on the *structure* of the educational system and *access* by children from different social groups to its different component parts. (Silver, 1973, p.xi, emphasis in original)

However, as Halsey (1972) has shown, a great deal of sociological research and writing in Britain has been concerned with different aspects of equality of educational opportunity, some of which had direct implications for social and educational policy. In particular, Halsey identifies three trends in this work. First, a period in which research was concerned with access. Secondly, when research was concerned with achievement, and finally, a phase in which the functions of education were reappraised.

The first phase of this debate about equality of educational opportunity is identified by Halsey as lasting from the turn of the century until the end of the 1950s when discussion was in terms of equality of *access* for all children to the more advanced stages of education regardless of their sex, social class, religion, ethnic group or region of origin. On this basis, equality of opportunity was developed in such ways as establishing the scholarship ladder, abolishing grammar school fees, establishing secondary education for all and providing a route into higher education (for further discussion see Banks, 1955). However, 'parity of prestige' was never achieved, with the result that equality of access to education came to mean equality of opportunity in gaining access to a grammar school place. Nevertheless, large numbers of children did not gain access to grammar school places, so in these circumstances the notion of equality of opportunity was unreal.

The second phase charted by Halsey occurred throughout the 1960s when the meaning of equality of opportunity changed to become equality of achievement. On this basis, equality of educational opportunity comes about if the proportion of people from different social, economic or ethnic categories at all levels of education is more or less the same as the proportion of these people in the population. If this did not occur then injustice could be said to have taken place. During the late 1950s and early 1960s sociological research indicated that particular groups were at a disadvantage in terms of educational achievement. As a consequence, positive discrimination in the form of compensatory education was suggested. The main aim of compensatory education was to reduce educational disadvantage and to narrow the gap in educational achievement. This problem was tackled in the USA through the Project Headstart programme (Adam, 1969; Smith and Bissell, 1970) which was established to break the cycle of poverty by assisting pre-school children. In a similar way, in Britain the Plowden Committee (Central Advisory Council for Education, 1967) recommended the establishment of Educational Priority Areas (EPAs) where schools would be given greater resources and where attempts would be made to initiate change. Such programmes attracted considerable attention concerning the effects of these initiatives on the children involved. However, there was also much debate about the concept of compensatory education which Bernstein (1970a) argued carried with it the implication that something was lacking in the family and the child.

The key areas of debate over equality of educational opportunity therefore concerned equality of access and equality of outcomes. Halsey (1972) has argued that it is essentially a discussion 'about education for whom and to do what' (p.11). Finally, he indicates that the debate can be taken beyond equality of educational opportunity to a reappraisal of the function of education in contemporary society.

In the USA equality of educational opportunity has also been of central importance but it has taken a different turn (cf. Coleman, 1969). Firstly, it has meant the provision of free education up to entry into the labour market. Secondly, it has concerned the provision of a common curriculum for all children regardless of their social background. Thirdly, it has referred to the provision of education for children from diverse social backgrounds in the same school. Finally, it has meant providing for equality within a locality. On this basis, equality of opportunity in education would demand that all pupils need to be exposed to the same curriculum in similar schools through equal inputs. The evidence in the Coleman report (Coleman *et al*, 1966) showed that there was relative equality of educational inputs but inequality of results.

Accordingly, it is argued, if equality of opportunity is to be realized in the USA it is not sufficient to remove legal disabilities on blacks, women and other disadvantaged groups, but instead provision has to be made to give them the same effective chance as white male members of the population. Jencks *et al* (1972) has also used this evidence to highlight the inequalities that exist within groups as well as the differences that occur between them.

The directions that research has taken in Britain and the USA have been somewhat different. For the sake of clarity, it is therefore important to identify the way in which this debate has been pursued in Britain. The kinds of questions that have been central to recent British discussions are well identified by Halsey, Heath and Ridge in relation to the main concerns of their study *Origins and Destinations* (1980) where they asked:

1 What have been the class differences in access to education?

2 How far has the British educational system achieved its professed goal of meritocracy?

3 What are the handicaps which prevent individuals attaining educational success?

4 What are the likely consequences of comprehensive reform for the achievement of goals such as equality of opportunity and equality of results?

5 Is the structure of the educational system more important?

These questions were asked of a cohort of men aged between 20 and 64 in the summer of 1972. During the period covered by this study the number of selective secondary school places had increased, but did not keep pace with population growth. As a consequence, the relative class chances of gaining a selective school place remained the same. This situation has been well summarized by Robinson (1981b) when he states:

> Equality of opportunity is rather like an escalator. As the whole shifts, the relative position remains the same. (Robinson, 1981b, p.43)

It is this question of equality of opportunity that has been a major focus for sociologists of education who have been concerned with issues such as:

Does the process of equal opportunity favour those who are initially privileged in terms of family of origin?

Does education help to provide a society that is open to talent?

Does education provide a channel of upward social mobility?

Does education accentuate existing inequalities in terms of class, gender and race?

Questions concerning the extent to which Britain is an 'open society' and whether equality of opportunity exists are related to social mobility, for, as various commentators have indicated, an 'open society' with 'equality of opportunity' implies a certain amount of social mobility. Accordingly, if we are to examine the extent to which equality of opportunity is achieved in Britain it is to studies of social mobility that we must turn.

Studies of social mobility

There have been several studies in Britain that have contributed to our understanding of trends in social mobility during this century (for a review of some of this material up to the 1960s see Macdonald and Ridge, 1972). Among the studies that they include in their review are the longitudinal investigations by Douglas (1964) who has focused on all children born in Great Britain during the first week of March 1946, and a study sponsored by the Scottish Council for Research in Education that has followed a sample of Scottish children born in 1936 (cf. Maxwell, 1969). While these studies have their advantages as they follow individuals from birth to maturity, they also have disadvantages when attempts are made to examine trends in mobility. Accordingly, much of the main evidence that is available comes from special surveys of social mobility which have been based on national samples. The first major study was conducted in 1949 by David Glass and his colleagues at the London School of Economics (Glass, 1954). Secondly, there was a major study which was conducted as part of an investigation on voting by Butler and Stokes (1971). Thirdly, there was the Oxford Mobility Study conducted in 1972 by Goldthorpe *et al* (1980), and finally a study also conducted in 1972 by Psacharopoulos (1977). Of all these studies, the two that have attracted most interest are the Glass study of 1949 and the Oxford Mobility Study of 1972, although as we shall see these studies are not strictly comparable.

Before turning our attention to the studies themselves we need to examine briefly some of the terminology that is used in relation to social mobility. The concept 'social mobility' is used to refer to movement up or down the social class hierarchy and can refer to any movement, long-range (from social class VII to social class I or vice versa) or the more common phenomenon of short range mobility. Sociologists have generally made distinctions between the social status of individuals. First, there is *ascribed* status which is fixed, rigid and transmitted across generations; it is acquired at birth on the basis of the social standing of an individual's parents. Secondly, there is *achieved* status which may be higher or lower than the position that is acquired at birth and which is obtained on the basis of individual achievement. Here the key questions concern the way in which achieved status is obtained and the degree of movement that takes place across generations. It is in these circumstances that social mobility becomes important, as sociologists examine the way in which individuals compete for unequal positions. In studying social mobility the sociologist compares the actual amount of social mobility with the ideal of free movement through equal opportunity. As a consequence, the social position that an individual achieves may bear no relationship to the position he acquired at birth. Movement up or down the social scale is based on merit. In these circumstances attention is focused on two aspects of social mobility:

1. *Intergenerational mobility* that refers to mobility between generations and is measured by comparing the occupational status of sons with that of their fathers.
2. *Intragenerational mobility* that refers to mobility within a generation, to a situation where an individual acquires a different status from that which was previously held. It is measured by comparing an individual's occupational status at two or more points in time.

It is on these two patterns of social mobility that sociologists have focused, together with a study of cross-class mobility – that is movement across the manual/non-manual line. It is, therefore, these elements that will be examined in the two major British studies. Much recent discussion concerning education and social mobility has focused on the study conducted from Oxford in 1972 by John Goldthorpe and his colleagues. However, it is important to recall that this study was considerably influenced by the work of David Glass in 1949 and it is therefore important to trace some of the issues that are held in common by both studies.

In a discussion of both these investigations, Halsey (1977a) outlines some of the basic issues and assumptions involved in the Glass study when he writes that it was:

> strongly influenced politically by a radical stance towards the powers, privileges and dubious efficiency of the elite professions, and expressed both a condemnation of waste and frustration through the neglect of ability among working class children and a hope that expanded educational opportunity would produce a more efficient and socially sensitive elite. Its assumptions about stratification implied a greater interest in status than in class and conceived of the social structure in terms of a hierarchy of layers in which occupation was closely associated with distinct styles of life. (Halsey, 1977a, pp.174–5)

The Glass team looked at a sample of 10,000 men who were 18 and over who lived in England, Scotland or Wales in 1949. Among the data collected were: the respondents' age, marital status, schools attended, qualifications obtained and details of their own and their fathers' occupations. Such data were used to address two major questions. First, how 'open' was British society? Second, was there equality of opportunity for those of equal talents? In addressing these questions, Glass looked at intergenerational mobility by comparing the occupational status of fathers and sons to examine the extent to which sons follow the occupations of their fathers.

TABLE 1: *Intergenerational mobility among men in Great Britain, 1949 sample*

	Father's occupational group (ranked as in original classification)	*Per cent of sons who –*									*All sons (aged 18+)*
		*Stayed in father's group**	*Moved, but stayed on same side of non-man./manual line*				*Moved, and crossed the non-man./manual line*				
			To adjacent groups	*To non-adjacent groups*		*Sub total*	*To adjacent groups*	*To non-adjacent groups*		*Sub total*	
				Up	*Down*			*Up*	*Down*		
I	Professional, high admin.	39 (3)	15	—	31	46	—	—	15	15	100
II	Managerial, executive	27 (5)	33	—	19	52	—	—	21	21	100
III	Inspect., supervis., etc. (higher)	19 (9)	29	4	10	43	—	—	38	38	100
IV	Inspect., supervis., etc. (lower)	21 (13)	19	6	—	25	—	—	54	54	100
VA	Routine non-manual	16 (7)	15	14	—	29	29	—	26	55	100
VB	Skilled manual	41 (34)	17	—	13	30	7	22	—	29	100
VI	Semi-skilled manual	31 (17)	50	—	—	50	—	19	—	19	100
VII	Unskilled manual	27 (12)	24	32	—	56	—	17	—	17	100
All sons (aged 18+)		31 (19)	24	6	8	38	4	13	14	31	100

NOTE: Based on data calculated from Miller (1960). The data are those of the national sample survey the results of which where analysed in detail in Glass (1954) (especially Chapter VIII). But the figures reproduced in Miller's paper are used here, because – unlike the original published figures – they distinguish between occupational categories VA and VB above.

* The figures in brackets in the first column show the percentage of sons from each group of origin who *would* have stayed in the same group (i.e. their father's group) if there had been 'perfect mobility' – that is, if a son's destination in life were in no way influenced by his parental origin. (These figures are equivalent to the percentage distribution of all sons among the different job levels, in terms of their own jobs. Thus, 12 per cent of all sons had unskilled manual jobs; and if parental origin did not affect chances in life, 12 per cent of the sons of each particular origin – including the sons of unskilled workers – would have gone into unskilled jobs. In fact, 27 per cent of the sons of the unskilled workers did so – over twice as many as would have done so if there were 'perfect mobility'.) SOURCE: Westergaard and Resler (1975) p.298

On the basis of this study Glass (1954) found that there was a high degree of self-recruitment at the two ends of the social scale. Secondly, that most mobility was short range as individuals moved mainly between lower white collar and skilled manual positions in both directions. Finally, that the middle of the occupational hierarchy was a 'buffer zone' so that movement between manual and non-manual occupations was short range.

The evidence concerning intergenerational mobility is summarized in table 1. Here, Glass found that fewer than a third of the men were in the same job as their fathers. Westergaard and Resler (1975) illustrate how Glass's data show that inequality is not fixed at birth and that there is a fair degree of fluidity of circulation. However, as they point out, Glass's evidence does demonstrate that although children from high status origins may be downwardly mobile compared with their fathers, they may still have a better chance than their working class peers of getting to higher level jobs. Accordingly, three major conclusions have been drawn from this work. First, that most mobility in Britain is short-range, and long-range mobility is very rare. Secondly, that there is a barrier to movement across the manual/non-manual line, and finally, that there is a high degree of self-recruitment at the top of the social scale.

The evidence that is available in the Glass study together with the arguments that have been deduced from it have come in for considerable criticism from Ridge (1974), from Payne, Ford and Robertson (1977) and from Frank Musgrove (1979). The bulk of the criticism concerns the methodology of this study. In particular, Payne, Ford and Robertson cast doubt on the validity of Glass's sample, as a comparison of the number of sons born in the first four status categories with the number in those categories in 1949 suggests a contraction of white collar occupations. Yet as they indicate, there was a 16 per cent expansion in white collar jobs prior to 1949. Such material suggests that Glass and his colleagues underestimated the rate of social mobility and the degree of long-range mobility. Even more stringent criticism comes from Musgrove when he writes that the study provides:

> a (highly statistical) picture of Britain in the first half of the twentieth century, not as a land of increasing but actually diminishing opportunity in spite of its expanding educational provision . . . it is a serious distortion of the past. The picture of opportunity in Britain which it offers is not only empirically implausible, it is a logical absurdity and an arithmetical impossibility. (Musgrove, 1979, p.123)

This argument is extended by Musgrove who maintains that the national sample of men had experienced more downward than upward social mobility even though evidence from the census suggests that the number of higher level occupations and opportunities had increased in number. It is on this basis that he concludes that Glass made a major sociological blunder. Nevertheless, the study by Glass did highlight the importance of a grammar school education for those who were of working class or lower middle class origin, as he maintained that they were more likely to be socially mobile than those who attended elementary schools. Attendance at grammar school also resulted in a high relationship between father's and son's occupation in the middle class. Meanwhile, for the working class it greatly increased occupational ascent. It is these data that Anderson (1961) used in relation to data sets obtained from the USA and from Sweden. On the basis of this evidence he argued that there was more mobility than could be expected if education was the only criterion to be used. But we might ask: to what extent does Anderson's sceptical note on the relationship between education and social mobility apply to the contemporary picture of patterns of social mobility in Britain? To address this issue we turn to a consideration of the Oxford Mobility Study to see if the situation that Glass presented holds true.

The Oxford study was conducted by Goldthorpe and his associates (Goldthorpe with Llewellyn and Payne, 1980) and consisted of a sample of 10,000 adult men aged 20 to 64 who were resident in England and Wales in 1972. Here the respondents were required to provide data on their own occupational and educational biographies as well as those of their fathers, mothers, wives, brothers and friends. As Halsey (1977a) indicates, this study involved an examination of the impact of post war reform and economic change on the degree of openness in British society. Furthermore, the team also wished to examine the influence of post war educational policy and the degree of movement between generations of individuals from the same family. The focus was, therefore, once again upon patterns of intergenerational mobility. However, it was not possible to make a direct comparison with Glass's work. The Glass team had used a status classification based on occupational prestige to categorize respondents, while the Oxford team used a sevenfold classification based on social class (see the notes in table 2). These seven classes were grouped into three broader categories as follows:

1. Classes I and II of professionals, administrators and managers are a *Service* class.
2. Classes III, IV and V of clerical, self employed artisans and supervisors are an *Intermediate* class.
3. Classes VI and VII of manual workers are a *Working* class.

Nevertheless, data from the Oxford study can be examined in the light of the conclusions reached by Glass's work concerning short-range and long-range movement, movement across the manual/non-manual line and the degree of self-recruitment at the top of the social scale.

SHORT-RANGE AND LONG-RANGE MOBILITY

The basic data are presented in table 2 which shows the 'outflow'; that is the destinations of men from different social origins.

TABLE 2: *Intergenerational mobility in England and Wales 1972: outflow*

Father's class	*Respondent's class (% by row)* I	II	III	IV	V	VI	VII	Total	N
I	48.4	18.9	9.3	8.2	4.5	4.5	6.2	100.0	582
II	31.9	22.6	10.7	8.0	9.2	9.6	8.0	100.0	477
III	19.2	15.7	10.8	8.6	13.0	15.0	17.8	100.1	594
IV	12.8	11.1	7.8	24.9	8.7	14.7	19.9	99.9	1223
V	15.4	13.2	9.4	8.0	16.6	20.1	17.2	99.9	939
VI	8.4	8.9	8.4	7.1	12.2	29.6	25.4	100.0	2312
VII	6.9	7.8	7.9	6.8	12.5	23.5	34.8	100.2	2216
%	14.3	11.4	8.6	9.9	11.6	20.8	23.3	99.9	(8343)

Based on: Oxford Social Mobility Group.
Sample: men aged 25–64 in 1972.
NOTE: The classes are defined as follows:

I Higher-grade professionals; administrators; managers in large establishments; large proprietors
II Lower-grade professionals; higher-grade technicians; lower-grade administrators; managers in small establishments; supervisors of non-manual employees
III Routine non-manual (clerical) employees; sales personnel; other rank and file service workers
IV Small proprietors; self-employed artisans; non-professional 'own account' workers
V Lower-grade technicians; supervisors over manual workers
VI Skilled manual wage-workers
VII Semi- and un-skilled manual wage-workers

SOURCE: Heath (1981), p.54

The evidence indicates that there has been considerable intergenerational mobility and dispels the view that an individual's class position is fixed at birth. The figures on the diagonal (top left to bottom right) give the percentage of men in the same class as their fathers. Only 28 per cent of the sample has been intergenerationally stable. There has also been an increase in upward mobility which is in line with the trend towards an expansion of professional and managerial jobs. In addition, the evidence in table 2 indicates that while there is little long-range mobility from Class I to Class VII and from Class VII to Class I there is evidence of more short-range mobility between, for example, Classes II and VI.

THE MANUAL/NON-MANUAL BARRIER

The notion that a barrier exists between the middle and the working class now needs to be examined. Taking Classes I, II and III as above the barrier, it is apparent from table 2 that about a quarter of the men from working class origins crossed this barrier. In addition, they were as likely to end up in Class I as in Class III. In turn, fewer men from Class I crossed this barrier into the working class, a pattern that has also been found in studies in the USA (cf. Blau and Duncan, 1967).

PATTERNS OF ELITE SELF-RECRUITMENT

As in the evidence available from Glass's study, the picture that emerges is one of self-recruitment especially in Classes I and VII. As a consequence those in Class I are most likely to follow in their father's footsteps for, as table 2 illustrates, those born into Class I had a good chance of staying there. However, table 3 shows that the majority of men in Class I were newcomers. This trend can be accounted for by the expansion of Class I and the pattern of upward mobility.

The data that are available in table 3 show that Class I is heterogeneous in composition – that is three-quarters of Class I are upwardly mobile – while Class VII is homogeneous, as three-quarters are 'second generation' members of the working class. A similar pattern has also been repeated in data available for Scotland in the work of Payne, Ford and Robertson (1976) (see table 4).

TABLE 3: *Intergenerational mobility in England and Wales 1972: inflow*

Father's class	*Respondent's class (% by column)* I	*II*	*III*	*IV*	*V*	*VI*	*VII*	%
I	23.6	11.6	7.5	5.8	2.7	1.5	1.9	7.0
II	12.7	11.4	7.1	4.6	4.5	2.7	2.0	5.7
III	9.5	9.8	8.9	6.1	7.9	5.1	5.5	7.1
IV	13.1	14.3	13.3	36.7	10.9	10.4	12.5	14.7
V	12.1	13.1	12.2	9.0	16.1	10.9	8.3	11.3
VI	16.3	21.6	26.9	19.6	29.2	39.4	30.2	27.7
VII	12.7	18.1	24.1	18.1	28.6	30.0	39.7	26.6
Total	100.0	99.9	100.0	99.9	99.9	100.0	100.1	100.1
N	1197	948	721	830	969	1734	1944	(8343)

NOTE: For a definition of the classes see table 2.
SOURCE: Heath (1981) p. 63

TABLE 4: *Social mobility, Scotland, 1975*

		Mobility Table for 1975 Respondent's Current Occupation and 'Father's' Occupation when Respondent was 14 years old							*Inflow*
		1	2	3	4	5	6	7	Total
Father's	1	23.3	10.3	2.8	10.9	1.5	1.6	1.8	6.2
occupational	2	19.6	28.0	9.6	16.9	5.6	8.0	5.3	12.2
category	3	13.8	13.8	18.8	9.7	9.7	12.2	11.4	12.8
when R	4	7.5	5.1	2.5	5.6	2.2	1.6	1.7	3.3
was 14	5	16.5	18.6	26.7	23.6	42.6	29.5	32.9	28.7
	6	9.3	13.4	20.3	17.6	20.6	28.6	23.0	19.9
	7	10.0	10.9	19.3	15.7	17.7	18.6	23.9	16.9
		100.0	100.0	100.0	100.0	100.0	100.0	100.0	
Total		11.8	14.8	13.9	5.7	20.2	19.3	14.2	100.0

NOTES: In Scotland the socio-economic categories are defined as follows:

1 Professionals, proprietors and managers of large organizations, and senior supervisory staff
2 Semi-professionals, higher technicians, proprietors and managers of small organizations (including farmers)
3 Supervisors of manual workers, self-employed artisans, and lower technicians
4 Routine non-manual workers
5 Skilled manual workers
6 Semi-skilled manual workers
7 Unskilled manual workers

SOURCE: Payne, Ford and Robertson (1976) p. 70

The main trends that can be derived from this evidence concern patterns of social mobility among men. First, there has been a considerable pattern of self-recruitment. Secondly, there has been considerable upward mobility as the upper socio-economic groups have recruited individuals from those of manual origins. Such a pattern of upward mobility has been the consequence of a growth in professional, administrative and managerial occupations as shown by the census data from 1951 onwards. However, the fact that these positions have been filled by the sons of manual and non-manual workers undermines the idea that there is a 'buffer zone' or that there is any closure of the upper status groups.

At this point it is important to emphasize that these trends only apply to men, as women have been excluded from studies of social mobility and no comparable studies to those that have been reviewed have been conducted among women. Questions concerning the absence of women from such studies has been criticized by several writers (cf. Blackstone,

1980; MacDonald, 1981). In particular, they point out that the absence of women from these studies is a consequence of the way in which social class is defined in terms of male occupational status. The result is that women are classified according to the status of men, regardless of their own work experience. Such an approach, which is claimed to be the 'conventional view' of class analysis (Goldthorpe, 1983, 1984), has been used in the Oxford Mobility Study. Here Goldthorpe and his colleagues (1980) attempt to justify the exclusion of women on the grounds that if women had been included in the sample it would have been at the expense of men. Furthermore, they argue that

> it is difficult to envisage any factors which, over the period in question, would be likely to result in any *sizeable* number of women occupying *markedly* different class positions from those of the male 'heads' of their families, or possessing attributes or engaging in activities which would in themselves materially influence the class position of the family unit. (Goldthorpe *et al*, 1980, p.288)

In response, MacDonald (1981) claims that this is a circular argument as the class position of the family is defined in terms of the male 'head of household', but she also argues that there is a complete neglect of the contribution that women make to the material conditions of the family –a point she supports with data derived from Goldthorpe's work (cf. Goldthorpe *et al*, 1980, pp.60–1). Similar criticisms have also been levelled at this view by Britten and Heath (1983), and by Michelle Stanworth (1984), but Goldthorpe has still argued that it is essential to maintain the conventional view.

As far as mobility patterns are concerned, Heath (1981) has used those data that are available to consider women's occupational and marital mobility – a pattern that he defines by comparing the woman's father's status with her husband's status. His findings indicate that women have inferior opportunities for occupational mobility compared to men. Yet he found that single women who had pursued a career had better chances of upward mobility than men and access to lower level professional and managerial work. In addition, women from manual workers' homes have a better chance than men of obtaining non-manual jobs, while few women from non-manual backgrounds are downwardly mobile into manual occupations.

In all studies of social mobility it is widely assumed that the educational system has been the main mechanism of upward mobility. But we need to consider what part education plays in this process and the relative importance of social origins – that is home and family background – as well as schooling in terms of an individual's occupational attainment.

In an attempt to address issues such as these, Otis Dudley Duncan has established a processual model to examine the determinants of an

Figure 1: The Basic Model of the Attainment Process

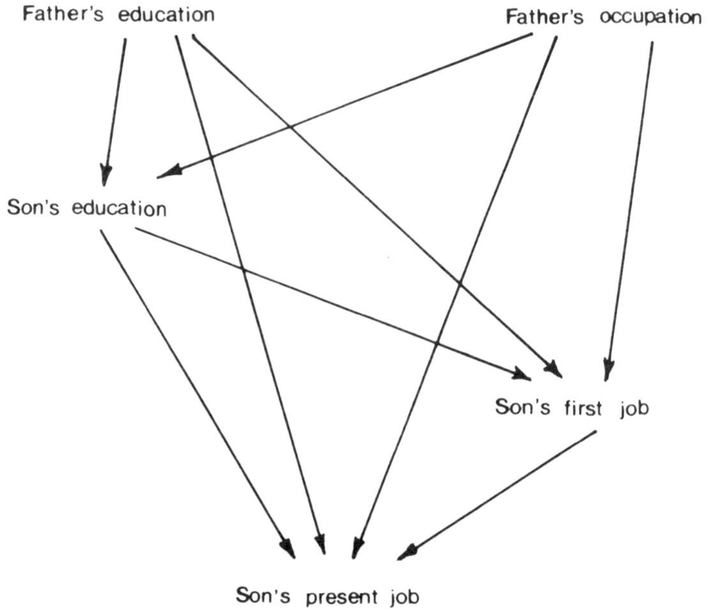

SOURCE: Heath (1981) p.139

individual's attainment at different stages of the life cycle. Duncan claims that an individual's social origins and family background, which can be measured in terms of father's occupation and educational level, may influence educational achievement. Together educational achievement and social origins may influence the individual's first job in the labour market. In turn, the subsequent career that is followed is the result of social origins, educational achievement and first job. It is this pattern that is set out in figure 1.

However, such a pattern leads to questions about the relationship between social origins and educational attainment: how far do social origins influence educational attainment? How far does educational attainment influence occupational placement? Is there a tight bond between schooling and life chances? On the basis of data available for men aged 25–59 in 1972, Halsey (1977a) has constructed a path diagram (as shown in figure 2) which allows sociologists to interpret 'the direct effect which one variable has on another, *controlling for other variables already included in the model*' (Heath, 1981, p.141, emphasis in original).

Figure 2: The Attainment Process in England and Wales

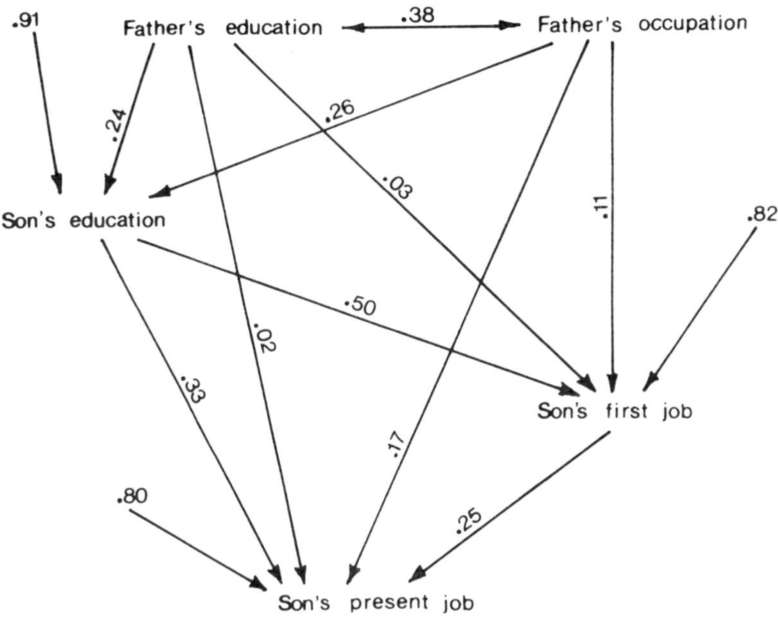

Based on Halsey (1977a)
SAMPLE: men aged 25–59 in 1972 and resident in England and Wales at age 14.

VARIABLES:
(1) Father's education: school examinations, professional/academic qualifications
(2) Father's occupation at respondent's age 14
(3) Respondent's education as in (1)
(4) Respondent's first job as in (2)
(5) Respondent's 1972 job as in (2)
NOTE: The numbers represent the size of the direct effect one variable has upon another.
SOURCE: Heath (1981) p.142 adapted.

On the basis of this evidence, it appears that there is a powerful effect between education and the first job that is obtained in the labour market. In turn, education not only helps the individual to get a first job but also has an indirect effect on subsequent jobs (cf. Bourdieu and Passeron, 1977). Indeed, Halsey (1977a) has noted that education plays an important part in occupational status and income. He also argues that family background indicators and educational qualifications – that is ascriptive and achievement factors – are at work in the transmission of occupational status between generations. In addition, he argues that there has been a shift in the occupational structure with more opportunities at the top and net upward mobility. However, he maintains that over the past generations:

> What has happened is the weighting of the dice of social opportunity according to class, and 'the game' is increasingly played through strategies of child rearing refereed by schools through their certifying arrangements. (Halsey, 1977a, p.184)

On the basis of all this evidence it can be concluded that social origin does not fix subsequent status, as an individual's position in the social hierarchy is not fixed at birth. However, it is not possible to conclude that education directly influences social mobility as it is mediated by both class and status (and we need to add by gender and race), all of which will be discussed in subsequent chapters. Meanwhile, we turn to examine another aspect of mobility, namely an ideological dimension based on different sets of values which relate to different modes of mobility.

Modes of social mobility

The ways in which individuals are recruited through particular modes of mobility have been suggested by Turner (1961), who outlines two different patterns of social mobility based on conflicting sets of values. In this instance, Turner is concerned with the predominant modes of mobility that he sees as a means of organizing the educational system. For this purpose, Turner examines the educational systems of England and the USA. Both educational systems, he argues, have open class systems and provide mass education, but he maintains that it is possible to provide a contrast between England with a system of sponsored mobility and the USA with a system of contest mobility. Here, the system of contest mobility is described by Turner in the following terms:

> a system in which elite status is the prize in an open contest and is taken by the aspirants' own efforts. While the 'contest' is governed by some rules of fair play, the contestants have wide latitude in the strategies they may employ. Since the 'prize' of successful upward mobility is not in the hands of the established ethic to give out, the latter are not in a position to determine who shall attain it and who shall not. (Turner, 1961, p.122)

In these circumstances, there would be open access to all institutions that are of equivalent status. In particular, Turner quotes the example of the USA where there is no sharp separation between students taking particular courses and where there is relatively open access to institutions of higher education. In these circumstances, control over selection relies upon assessment, examination and testing procedures. In contrast, he defines sponsored mobility in terms of an educational system where:

> elite recruits are chosen by the established elite or their agents, and elite status is *given* on the basis of some criterion of supposed merit and cannot be *taken* by any amount of effort or strategy. Upward mobility is like entry into a private club, where each candidate must be 'sponsored' by one or more of the members. Ultimately, the members grant or deny upward mobility on the

> basis of whether they judge the candidate to have the qualities that they wish to see in fellow members. (Turner, 1961, p.122, emphasis in original)

In this instance, Turner draws on examples taken from the English educational system, where, he argues, segregation takes place at an early age and where training and credentials are of importance and are judged by experts. However, it is important to remember that both these modes of mobility are based on ideal types using examples drawn from America and Britain almost thirty years ago. On this basis, it is important to consider the way in which these ideal types might now be modified in the light of changes that have occurred within the educational systems. Nevertheless, there are a number of key issues that they still raise.

Each of these modes of social mobility involves not only the question of who shall have elite credentials but also the patterns of socialization involved. Turner argues that the most conspicuous control problem is ensuring loyalty in the disadvantaged to a system in which they get less and less. Under a contest system each individual is encouraged to think that they may compete for a position and absolute points of selection for mobility and immobility are awarded. Meanwhile, under sponsorship, control is maintained by training 'the masses' to regard themselves as incompetent to manage, by restricting access to the skills of the elite and by cultivating the idea of the superior competence of those who are selected.

Many commentators have been quick to point out that Turner has made a sharp distinction between the two systems (Noel, 1962), but as Davies (1976) indicates, Turner is clear that mobility occurs in terms of *both* modes in *all* societies. Yet, it is still maintained that had Turner witnessed the demise of grammar school selection, the rise of the comprehensive school and the expansion of higher education he might have argued that England was undergoing a shift from sponsored towards contest mobility. Nevertheless, it can be argued that even changes such as comprehensive schooling include a range of specialist training based on ability grouping that results in a strong link through to higher education. However, Turner's model still needs to be empirically tested as, apart from his own work (Turner, 1964), little empirical evidence has been collected using his conceptual scheme.

Yet it has been argued that these two ideal types that have been identified by Turner are far too basic. For example, Hopper (1971a) has maintained that in Turner's model, people are seen as mobile or non-mobile and that the mode of mobility occurs along one route. Furthermore, it is argued that Turner's model does not take into account the different stratification systems, and the different educational systems in Britain and the USA which result in a variety of educational experiences.

As a consequence, Hopper attempts to extend Turner's typology by focusing on the classification of the selection process in educational systems using the following terms:

1 *how it occurs:* that is the mode of implementation;

2 *when it occurs:* that is in terms of timing and the degree of educational specialization;

3 *to whom it occurs*;

4 *why it occurs*.

However, Hopper eventually substitutes the two categories devised by Turner with two categories of his own. In particular, he identifies ideologies of implementation and ideologies of legitimization whereby the former concerns the how and when questions, while the latter refers to questions concerning whom and why. It is on this basis that Hopper attempts to establish a typology that justifies selection, but he has been criticized for not taking sufficient account of the structure of educational systems which have to respond to different ideologies that exist alongside each other in a society. Nevertheless, as far as Hopper (1971b) is concerned, this model of school selection involves training, recruitment and allocation and also the regulation of ambition. Such an approach, which examines the attributes of upward social mobility, demands an analysis of the school experience of *all* recruits so as to identify the processing of the majority as well as the educational elite. As a consequence the process involves examining every route in the selection process including the 'warming up' of students who receive further specialized training and those who are 'cooled-out' and sent into the labour market.

A further criticism of this work has been made by Ioan Davies (1971) who argues that Hopper has been so concerned with selection that he has neglected the way in which education is involved with the transmission of culture and the management of knowledge. In turn, Smith (1976) has included the transmission process in a model of how the educational system is involved in the distribution process. In particular, he highlights the ways in which the selection of students and the transmission of knowledge occur. Here, there is concern with *who* is selected, *what* they are taught and *how* it is transmitted. As a consequence, Smith's analysis uses Turner's work, which he links to Bernstein's studies of the curriculum (Bernstein, 1971a). The result is that the analysis of structural processes and knowledge properties are brought together.

A further model that has attracted some attention has been outlined by Boudon (1974, 1977) who looks at the relationship between intelligence, scholastic attainment, social background and aspirations. On the basis of his analysis he proposes a two tier theory of attainment based on 'primary effects' of social background, which are similar to intelligence and school achievement, and 'secondary effects', which apply when children of equal intelligence and achievement have to choose between different kinds of curricula. Boudon goes on to suggest that upper class children choose courses that lead to the same social status as their parents. Indeed, he maintains that a large amount of mobility will take place despite the bias of the educational system in favour of the middle class and the fact that the hiring process gives the advantage to those who are more qualified. However, given the competition that exists for places in the educational system and the occupational system there is no guarantee that the children from more privileged groups will be favoured. Indeed, he shows how high status children are demoted and low status children promoted. As a consequence, Tyler (1977) considers that Boudon helps to explain why there is a degree of randomness in occupational attainment, why education does not seem to affect mobility and why patterns of social ascent appear to remain stable across generations. However, on the basis of evidence from the study *Origins and Destinations*, Halsey, Heath and Ridge (1980) suggest that Boudon's views demand modification, as those who survive in the school system are assimilated to the pattern of survival and performance of service class pupils (cf. Halsey, Heath and Ridge, 1980, pp.126–147).

Some implications

Having reviewed patterns, processes, models and explanations of social mobility we now turn to examining questions relating to these issues. For example, what are the consequences of different modes of mobility? To what extent have selection strategies resulted in equality of educational opportunity? In examining questions such as these, we turn to evidence drawn from Britain by writers who have examined educational opportunity and social mobility within a dynamic framework (cf. Little and Westergaard, 1964; Westergaard and Resler, 1975).

During the twentieth century there has been an increase in educational opportunities, but how have children from different social backgrounds fared? The evidence that is most frequently used concerns access to selective secondary education and access to university education. Drawing on evidence for selective secondary education (see table 5) Westergaard and Resler (1975) argue that while only 1 in 3 children from professional and managerial families went to grammar or independent secondary schools up to 1910, over 3 in 5 went in the 1930s. Furthermore, children lower in the social hierarchy also increased their chances of selective secondary education, but by the late 1930s 90 per cent of their number were still outside the selective schools. On this basis it is concluded that 'educational deprivation' has been reduced far more at the top than at the bottom of the social hierarchy (cf. Halsey, Heath and Ridge, 1980). In turn, Westergaard and Resler (1975) indicate that class differences in the period referred to in table 5 were reduced. The chances of a child from a professional or managerial background getting a selective school place, as against a child from a semi or unskilled background, were reduced from 37:1 to 6:1. However, they suggest that a shift to comprehensive schooling may mean more pupils receive an academically orientated education but that it is impossible at this stage to assess accurately who gets what kind of education within the comprehensive system (cf. Halsey, Heath and Ridge, 1980). In turn, evidence on access to a university education indicates a number of trends that are shown in table 6. In particular, Westergaard and Resler (1975) indicate how the pattern of inequality widened up until the 1950s, but narrowed very slightly in recent years. Nevertheless, they conclude that even in the 1970s children from skilled and semi-skilled manual workers' homes were nine times less likely to gain a university education than those from a professional and technical background.

TABLE 5: *The trend of class inequalities of opportunity for entry to selective secondary education, England and Wales*

Social origin – i.e. father's occupation	*Per cent of children, of different social origins, who obtained education in grammar and independent schools: among these born –*				
	Before 1910	*1910–1919*	*1920–1929*	*Late 1930s*	*Approx. 1957/60*
Professional and managerial	37	47	52	62	47
Other non-manual and skilled manual	7	13	16	20	22
Semi-skilled and unskilled	1	4	7	10	10
All children	12	16	18	23	25

Based on the following data: For children born before 1910 and up to the late 1930s – Westergaard and Little (1967). (Estimates from data in earlier studies by others.) For children born 1957/60 – calculated from *The General Household Survey (1971), Introductory Report* (OPCS, 1973) p. 234, for children 11–14 in secondary schools.

NOTES:

(i) The occupational categories used are roughly, but not perfectly, comparable over the years.

(ii) The figures for the last generation shown, those born approx. 1957/60, cannot be directly compared with the earlier figures, because nearly 28 per cent of all children born 1957/60 obtained secondary education in 'comprehensive' (mixed ability) schools, whereas very few in the previous generations did so.

(iii) Differences between boys and girls in respect of entry to selective secondary education were very slight.

SOURCE: Westergaard and Resler, (1975) p. 320

A further theme that Halsey, Heath and Ridge (1980) maintain needs to be examined in the context of educational expansion and the social distribution of educational chances is what has been described as the

TABLE 6: *The trend of class inequalities of opportunity for entry to university education*

Social origin – i.e. father's occupation	*Per cent of different social origins, who obtained a university education:*		
	Those born –		
	Before 1910	*1910–1929*	*Late 1930s*
Profess., manag. and 'intermediate'	3	6	14½
Remaining non-manual and skilled manual	½	1	2½
Semi-skilled and unskilled	—	½	½
All children	1½	2½	4

Social origin – i.e. father's occupation	*Per cent of children, of different social origins who obtained a university education:*		
	Those born –		
	Late 1930s	*Approx. 1953/54*	
Profess. and technical	10 (Profess. and technical, Admin. and managerial, Other non-manual combined)	18 (Profess. and technical, Admin. and managerial, Other non-manual combined)	35
Admin. and managerial			21
Other non-manual			10½
Manual, all levels	1½	4	
All children	4	9	

Based on the following data: For the first series (generations born before 1910 and up to the late 1930s) – Westergaard and Little (1967). For the second series – as above in respect of those born in the late 1930s; with calculations from Universities Central Council on Admissions (1973) for the estimate in respect of the latest generation shown.

NOTES:

(i) Comparison of the figures for different generations, even within each of the two series, can be made only in rough terms, because the occupational classifications used for the generations born up to 1929, in the late 1930s and around 1953/54 do not fully coincide; and because the figures for the 1953/54 generation relate to the UK, earlier figures to England and Wales.

(ii) There were and are very sharp differences between the sexes in chances of university entry. More than twice as many boys as girls entered university education throughout the period covered (with a slight increase in the share of girls in recent years), and these disparities between the sexes widened down the class scale.

SOURCE: Westergaard and Resler (1975) p. 322

'alternative route' and the provision of part-time further education. Indeed, it was the objective of the Crowther Committee (Ministry of Education, 1959) to develop further education as an alternative route for the working class. As Raffe (1979) has shown, part-time further education has recruited from those with the lowest level of school success. However, the *greatest use* of part-time further education is by those from the intermediate class and by poorly qualified boys from the service class. Using these data, Halsey, Heath and Ridge (1980) illustrate the trends in class access to part-time further and post secondary education as shown in tables 7a and 7b. On the basis of this evidence, Halsey, Heath and Ridge conclude that in earlier decades part-time further education could hardly be described as an alternative route for the working class. However, for the last cohort they conclude that the 'alternative route' is a reasonable description. Indeed, in the context of post school educational opportunity it has brought a diminution of class inequality. However, as Halsey, Heath and Ridge point out, the service class is not slow in using this alternative route. Nevertheless, apart from class VII they found class chances of access to further education were equal.

TABLE 7a: *Percentage attending part-time further education by social class and birth cohort*

Father's social class	*1913–22*	*1923–32*	*1933–42*	*1943–52*
I, II	50.0	46.2	59.3	45.1
III, IV, V	40.3	41.7	55.1	57.2
VI, VII, VIII	29.9	36.9	46.4	50.8

TABLE 7b: *Percentage attending any form of post-school education by social class and birth cohort*

Father's social class	*1913–22*	*1923–32*	*1933–42*	*1943–52*
I, II	60.6	64.4	77.1	73.9
III, IV, V	43.5	48.0	60.4	67.4
VI, VII, VIII	31.5	38.9	49.9	54.6

NOTE: For a definition of the classes see table 2.
SOURCE: Halsey, Heath and Ridge (1980) p. 192

Conclusion

But, we might ask, what are the consequences of this evidence? How do people react to their class situations and to the experience of social mobility? Schools, colleges and universities are geared to the procedure of social selection – a procedure that may well raise aspirations. But can these aspirations be realized? Certainly, and if we turn to the evidence of Halsey, Heath and Ridge (1980) we find that they strike a pessimistic note as they echo the comments of Antony Crosland writing in 1956 when he remarked:

> . . . we shall still not have equality of opportunity so long as we maintain a system of superior private schools, open to the wealthier classes, but out of reach of poorer children however talented and deserving. This is much the most flagrant inequality of opportunity, as it is cause of class inequality generally, in our educational system; and I have never been able to understand why socialists have been so obsessed with the question of the grammar schools, and so indifferent to the much more glaring injustice of the independent schools. (Crosland, 1956, pp.260–1)

Certainly, since Crosland was writing there have been changes in state school provision and in higher education. But as we have seen, educational expansion alone is not sufficient to change the relative chances of the 'disadvantaged' in obtaining high status positions. Nor for that matter will the development of the comprehensive secondary system *alongside* the independent sector diminish inequality and promote equality of opportunity (cf. Stenhouse, 1983a). Accordingly, we need to explore further the patterns of inequality in education that have been identified by sociologists of education and the explanations that have been advanced.

Suggestions for further reading

This chapter has concentrated predominantly on British material. The suggestions for further reading, therefore, focus on some of the source material and provide some guidance on comparative material from the USA.

Blackstone, T. (1980) 'Falling short of meritocracy', *The Times Higher Education Supplement* 18th January provides a useful critique of the Oxford studies. For an extract see Burgess (1985b) pp.55–58.

Halsey, A. H. (1977) *Change in British Society*, Oxford, Oxford University Press consists of a series of essays that were originally delivered as Reith lectures in which Halsey drew upon material on social mobility from the Oxford Mobility Study.

Halsey, A. H., Floud, J. and Anderson, C. A. (1961) (eds) *Education, Economy and Society*, New York, Free Press is the classic collection of papers in the sociology of education in the 1960s. It includes Turner (1961) on modes of social mobility and Anderson's (1961) sceptical note on social mobility.

Heath, A. (1981) *Social Mobility*, London, Fontana provides an excellent introduction to the study of social mobility drawing on major British and American material.

Karabel, J. and Halsey, A. H. (1977) (eds) *Power and Ideology in Education*, Oxford, Oxford University Press. The second section on selection includes a number of relevant papers including Halsey (1977a), and Boudon (1977). There is also a paper by Hopper (1977).

Payne, G., Ford, G. and Robertson, C. (1977) 'A reappraisal of social mobility in Britain' *Sociology* vol. 11. pp.289–310 contains a critique of Glass's data.

Musgrove, F. (1979) *School and the Social Order*, Chichester, Wiley includes a critical review of the literature on educational opportunity and social mobility in Chapter 6.

Silver, H. (1973) (ed) *Equal Opportunities in Education*, London, Methuen consists of an excellent collection of British material concerned with equal opportunity together with a very good review essay.

Tyler, W. (1977) *The Sociology of Educational Inequality*, London, Methuen provides a critical review of British and American research on the sociology of educational opportunity.

Westergaard, J. and Resler, H. (1975) *Class in a Capitalist Society*, Harmondsworth, Penguin provides a review of the Glass (1954) mobility study together with an analysis of some of its implications for education.

EMPIRICAL STUDIES

Blau, P. M. and Duncan, O. D. (1967) *The American Occupational Structure*, New York, Wiley provides data that can be compared with some of the data from the Oxford Mobility Study.

Coleman, J. *et al* (1966) *Equality of Educational Opportunity*, Cambridge, Mass., Harvard University Press is the classic American study on this topic.

Glass, D. (1954) (ed) *Social Mobility in Britain*, London, Routledge and Kegan Paul is the classic 1950s social mobility study that had implications for the study of education from a sociological perspective.

Goldthorpe, J. (with Llewellyn, C. and Payne, C.) (1980) *Social Mobility and Class Structure in Modern Britain*, Oxford, Clarendon Press provides the major findings of the Oxford Mobility Study. It includes many of the early papers such as Goldthorpe and Llewellyn (1977a, 1977b).

Halsey, A. H., Heath, A. and Ridge, J. M. (1980) *Origins and Destinations*, Oxford, Clarendon Press is a study of equal opportunity and meritocracy in education based on the male sample used in the Oxford Mobility Study.

Hope, K. (1984) *As Others See Us: Schooling and Social Mobility in Scotland and the United States*, Cambridge, Cambridge University Press. A study that examines longitudinal data from Scotland between 1947 and 1964. In addition, the author compares boys' performances in Scotland and the USA.

4 Patterns of inequality 1: social class and education

A persistent theme that is documented in much of the literature on the sociology of education is the relationship between social class and educational inequality. Such a topic covers a range of issues and includes a consideration of social class background and its influence on the family, patterns of child rearing, language and socialization and in turn education in the school system and beyond it. It is themes such as these that have been central to sociological research on education in Britain since the pre-second World War study of Gray and Moshinsky (1938) on ability and opportunity in the English school system. It was this study, which focused on individual ability and the wastage of talent, that marked the early stages of a tradition of research in the sociology of education known as political arithmetic (cf. Szreter, 1984).

Central to work on political arithmetic was a concern with who succeeded and who failed in the school system. The way in which researchers approached this topic was by collecting statistical evidence on such issues as wastage and educational injustice among working class children. As a consequence, the tradition had a political edge as many of the researchers were committed to the political left and chose research topics that were influenced by a left wing perspective committed to social reform (cf. Heath, 1980; Halsey, 1982). The work within this tradition therefore reflects a merger of survey based methods of investigation with value laden topics that were used to investigate aspects of inequality. Indeed, Bernstein (1974) has argued that this approach was very much in keeping with applied sociology in Britain, being atheoretical, pragmatic, descriptive and policy focused. When examining studies in this area it is as well to keep this comment in mind as there is a tendency for some commentators to suggest that all the work within this tradition is cumulative and can be linked together. While this is broadly the case it is essential to examine how social class and education have been defined in different studies over the years (cf. Reid, 1981; Marsh, 1986; Burgess, 1986b), for different researchers have defined social class and education in so many ways that comparability among projects becomes a central problem (cf. Stacey, 1969; Gittus, 1972; Burgess, 1986c).

Much of the data on social class and education relies not only on individual research projects but also on official statistics produced by the Department of Education and Science and large-scale projects such as the General Household Survey which has been conducted since 1971 (for a complete guide to major surveys concerned with education see Hakim, 1982). However, a major problem concerns the availability of these data. Invariably, we do not have continuous data sets available, with the result that much statistical evidence on education may appear dated or may not provide a portrait of education over time. In the case of work on social class and education, sociologists have had to rely on government surveys that have been conducted intermittently and longitudinal studies that were conducted in the 1950s and 1960s. Accordingly, a range of different data is drawn on in this chapter. However, there are further problems as many of these data were collected with little concern for theoretical questions. Indeed, Williamson (1981) has argued that in much of the work on the sociology of education, the concept of class has been used as a category rather than a relationship, as it is used to refer to:

> groups of people with certain socio-economic characteristics which they share and in terms of which they are distinguished from other groups. It matters not at all here whether the people themselves conceive of themselves as part of a group, for this concept of class makes no reference to questions of identity, or consciousness, or feelings of solidarity. (Williamson, 1981, pp.18–19)

While Williamson argues that this results in a disadvantage in attempting to provide sociological explanations, it does have the advantage of allowing the concept to be operationalized within empirical projects. We begin, therefore, by examining the ways in which social class has been used to raise questions about education, before turning to some explanations.

Patterns of social class and education

One writer who has persistently pointed to the importance of social class in understanding educational opportunity, educational attainment and patterns of inequality has been A. H. Halsey, who has argued that liberal policy makers

> failed to notice that the major determinants of educational attainment were not schoolmasters but social situations, not curriculum but motivation, not formal access to the school but support in the family and the community. (Halsey, 1972, p.81)

Here, Halsey points to a lack of understanding about social and economic circumstances, for, as he argues elsewhere (Halsey, 1975), the concept of class has been trivialized by many writers and researchers because:

> A theory which explains educational achievement as the outcome of a set of individual attributes has lost the meaning of those structural forces which we know as class. An adequate theory must also attend to those structural inequalities of resource allocation which are integral to a class society. (Halsey, 1975, p.17)

In reviewing patterns of social class and education in relation to different age groups, account will be taken of structural inequalities when drawing on data from research studies and official sources.

PRE-SCHOOL PROVISION

One of the ways in which it has been argued that it is possible to promote equality of educational opportunity is through the provision of nursery education. Indeed, the Plowden Committee (Central Advisory Council for Education, 1967) argued that the provision of nursery schools would help promote education, health and welfare among the under fives – a view that was subsequently reinforced in the 1970s by the White Paper entitled *Education: A Framework for Expansion* (HMSO, 1972). It was in the light of such recommendations that some developments took place in pre-school provision through playgroups, day nurseries and nursery schools. Indeed, according to data from the DES, attendance at nursery schools in England rose from 14 per cent in 1971 to 27 per cent in 1979 (OPCS, 1981). Furthermore, the proportion of children attending nursery or primary schools, playgroups or day nurseries rose to 40 per cent by 1979. Such provision of pre-school education has been seen as a possible means of promoting equality of educational opportunity (cf. Blackstone, 1970; Halsey, 1972; Lodge and Blackstone, 1982). In particular, it has been argued that nursery provision might help expose all children to similar cultural settings and help compensate for deficiencies in home background. However, drawing on data from the *General Household Survey, 1979* (OPCS, 1981) we can begin to assess the success of pre-school provision by examining the social class background of children receiving day care (see table 1). These data strike a rather pessimistic note when reviewed in relation to the degree to which equality of opportunity has been achieved through pre-school provision. In particular, it is noticeable that 57 per cent of children from a professional, managerial and employer background received some kind of day care or education and were more likely to attend playgroups or day nurseries than the children of semi-skilled and unskilled manual workers. Indeed, Finch (1983) has argued that playgroups are predominantly middle class because other social class groups are reluctant to use them (cf. Shinman, 1981) and they seldom cater for the child care needs of working women. Such evidence gives overwhelming support to the view that pre-school provision in general tends to favour the middle classes although Finch (1984) has provided some evidence on the facilities available in working class playgroups. While the experience of

TABLE 1: *Day care of children under five by type of facility used and socio-economic group of father*

Children under five[1] Great Britain: 1979

Type of facility used	*Socio-economic group of father*[2]									
	Professional, employers and managers		*Intermediate and junior non-manual*		*Skilled manual and own account non-professional*		*Semi-skilled and unskilled manual and personal service*		*Total*	
	%		%		%		%		%	
Nursery or primary school		12		13		14		12		13
Playgroup, day nursery		40		28		27		24		30
Individual other than parent:										
other member of household	1		1		1		1		1	
relative outside household	4		5		9		8		7	
neighbour, friend	1	9	2	8	2	12	4	13	2	11
childminder	1				1		1		1	
other	3		nil				nil		1	
Total receiving day care		57		43		47		45		48
Not receiving day care		43		57		53		55		52
Base=100%		453		332		689		363		1837

NOTES:

1. Children in households containing more than one family with children under five have been excluded.
2. The socio-economic group of the head of household has been used where the father was not a member of the household.

SOURCE: OPCS (1981) p. 108

pre-school playgroups has not been found to confer academic advantage (cf. Douglas and Ross, 1964; Blackstone, 1970), it does help to socialize children for mixing with teachers and pupils when they join infant schools.

THE PRIMARY SCHOOL

Much of the evidence on social class and educational attainment in the primary school relates to the traditional transition period from infant to junior school at the age of seven and to the transition from junior to secondary school at the age of eleven. Here, the data sets that are available come from two longitudinal studies. The first is by J. W. B. Douglas and consists of an analysis of data from a cohort of 5,386 children born in the first week of March 1946 (Douglas, 1964; Douglas *et al*, 1968), while the second study (the National Child Development Study) is based on a cohort of 16,000 children born in the first week of March 1958 (Fogelman, 1983). Both groups have been followed throughout their primary and secondary school careers when data have been collected through educational tests, questionnaires, medical examinations and interviews with parents (for methodological discussions see Douglas, 1976 and Fogelman, 1983, pp.1–7).

TABLE 2: *Reading and Arithmetic attainment test scores of seven year old children by father's social class (percentages) in Great Britain*

	REGISTRAR GENERAL'S SOCIAL CLASS						
	I	*II*	*III(N)*	*III(M)*	*IV*	*V*	*ALL*
Grouped Southgate Reading test scores							
0–20	8	15	14	30	37	48	29
21–28	37	39	43	41	38	34	39
29–30	54	47	43	29	25	17	32
Grouped problem Arithmetic test scores							
0–3	12	19	19	30	34	41	29
4–6	38	39	43	42	42	37	41
7–10	50	42	38	28	24	22	31
N=15,496							

NOTES: Whole sample included those without father or social class information.
Based on data derived from Tables A165 and A168 in Davie, Butler and Goldstein (1972).
SOURCE: Reid (1981) p. 215

The investigation by Davie, Butler and Goldstein (1972) which was conducted within the National Child Development Study found that at the age of seven, social class was the variable that was most strongly associated with attainment in reading and arithmetic, although at the age of seven it was found that girls were significantly ahead of boys in their reading test scores. The data that are available on class differences in reading and arithmetic are reported in table 2 and show the relationship between parental social class (as defined by the Registrar General's classification) and test scores. In particular, these data point to the differences in reading ability between children in social class I and those in social class V. In this study, it was found that a child in social class V was six times as likely to be a poor reader as a child from social class I. Furthermore, the lowest percentage of poor readers was in social class I, while the highest percentage of pupils with poor reading scores was in social class V.

Further data on differences in attainment in the primary school can be derived from the test scores of children in Douglas's study (1964). Here pupils were given tests of intelligence, reading, vocabulary and sentence completion at the age of eight and a similar range of tests including arithmetic at the age of eleven. The trends shown in table 3 indicate that at each age there is a gradient in test scores, especially between the middle and the manual working classes. Furthermore, there is a greater increase in test scores for the middle as opposed to the manual working class at the age of eleven.

Similar trends have also been found among children in the National Child Development Study, as Fogelman and Goldstein (1976) found that at the age of eleven children whose fathers were in non-manual occupations were about one year ahead of those in social class III manual and IV who were 0.4 years ahead of social class V. These differences were in addition to the differences at the age of seven, with the consequence that the overall differences at the age of eleven were 1.9 years for the non-manual children and 1.1 years for the manual children in terms of reading ability. Similarly, in arithmetic it was found that among the non-manual children there was a difference of 1.1 years from children in social class III manual and IV and 6.6 years between the latter and social class V. This research has also considered the extent to which sex is a significant variable in school performance during the primary school phase – a topic that is discussed in the following chapter.

SECONDARY SCHOOLING

Much of the data that are available on secondary schooling relate to the period of selective schooling. Nevertheless, these data reinforce the trends that have been found in the primary years. For example, Douglas, Ross and Simpson (1968) report on the progress of their sample of pupils in the secondary schools where the relationship between social class and

TABLE 3: *Average test scores of children in each social class at the ages of eight and eleven years*

	Social Class			
	Upper Middle	*Lower Middle*	*Upper Manual Working Class*	*Lower Manual Working Class*
Eight year tests:				
Picture intelligence	56.13	52.73	50.17	48.82
Reading	56.74	53.45	49.86	47.80
Vocabulary	58.33	53.88	50.19	47.63
Sentence completion	57.30	53.79	49.83	48.02
Eleven year tests:				
Non-verbal ability	57.03	54.31	50.25	47.99
Verbal activity	57.43	54.32	50.12	47.78
Reading	57.54	54.01	49.89	47.52
Vocabulary	59.18	54.81	50.33	47.36
Arithmetic	57.18	54.43	49.86	47.30

NOTE: Douglas's definitions of social class categories are as follows:
Upper Middle Class: The father is a non-manual worker, and
(a) both parents went to secondary school and were brought up in middle class families, or
(b) both parents went to secondary school and one parent was brought up in a middle class family, or
(c) both parents were brought up in middle class families and one parent went to secondary school.
Lower Middle Class: The rest of the non-manual workers' families.
Upper Manual Working Class: The father is a manual worker and either the father or mother or both of them had a secondary school education, and/or one or both of them were brought up in a middle class family.
Lower Manual Working Class: The father is a manual worker, and both the father and the mother had elementary schooling only, and both the father and the mother were brought up in manual working class families.

SOURCE: Douglas (1964) p. 185

education is maintained. In particular, they show how there is a relationship between social class and pupils obtaining 'good' 'O' level certificates, which they define as four passes including three from English language, mathematics, science and a foreign language, and those obtaining general certificates, defined as at least one 'O' level pass and any number and combination of passes in subjects other than those

TABLE 4: *Proportions of children staying at school and gaining certificates related to ability and social class (some data from the 1960s)*

Social class:		*Percentage Table* 60 and over	55–59	*Ability at 15 years* 50–54	45–49	44 and less
Middle	Upper	97	93	86	69	40
	Lower	94	79	59	36	17
Manual	Upper	90	67	35	22	6
	Lower	80	46	27	12	3
		% Starting Session 1962–63				
Middle	Upper	90	82	71	42	20
	Lower	78	52	37	20	8
Manual	Upper	67	43	20	10	3
	Lower	50	20	12	4	2
		% Gaining Good Certificates				
Middle	Upper	77	33	11	4	—
	Lower	60	18	6	—	—
Manual	Upper	53	15	2	1	—
	Lower	37	9	3	—	—
		% Gaining General Certificates				
Middle	Upper	94	79	54	27	20
	Lower	87	59	38	13	1
Manual	Upper	86	45	17	5	—
	Lower	69	31	12	2	—

NOTE: For the way in which Douglas defines social class categories see table 3.
SOURCE: Douglas, Ross and Simpson (1968) p. 216

TABLE 5: *Social class and school examinations*

Father's social class	*Percentage staying on until 16 or later*	*Percentage obtaining school certificate or 1 or more 'O' levels*	*Column 2 as a proportion of column 1 ('O' level success rate)*	*Percentage staying on until 18 or later*	*Percentage obtaining higher school certificate or 1 or more 'A' levels*	*Column 5 as a proportion of column 4 ('A' level success rate)*
I, II N=1,072)	70.0	58.1	0.83	28.2	26.9	0.93
III, IV, V (N=2,475)	32.6	24.2	0.74	7.7	6.9	0.90
VI, VII, VIII (N=4,482)	26.8	11.8	0.71	3.0	2.8	0.93

NOTE: The classes are defined as follows:

I Higher grade professionals, administrators, managers and proprietors.
II Lower grade professionals, administrators and managers. Supervisors and higher grade technicians } The Service Class

III Clerical, sales and rank-and-file service workers.
IV Small proprietors and self-employed artisans. The 'petty bourgeoisie'.
V Lower grade technicians and foremen. The aristocracy of labour. } The Intermediate Class

VI Semi-skilled manual workers in industry.
VII Semi- and unskilled manual workers in industry.
VIII Agricultural workers and smallholders. } The Working Class

SOURCE: Halsey, Heath and Ridge (1980) based on table 8.12, p. 142

that are said to constitute a 'good' certificate. The main trends are shown in table 4 which highlights how those social inequalities that were present in the primary school were reinforced in the secondary school. In particular, it is shown that pupils from manual backgrounds were particularly handicapped with poor examination results. Furthermore, it is only a relatively small proportion of manual working class pupils who obtain 'good' certificates.

Subsequent evidence from the all male sample of Halsey, Heath and Ridge (1980) suggests that it is not just social class origins and success in public examinations that have to be considered, but the relationship between social class and the proportion of pupils (by which they mean boys [cf. Acker, 1981b]) staying on at school, as shown in table 5. Here, the most striking feature is the number of working class boys who dropped out at the minimum school leaving age. Nevertheless, for those who survive there is a great similarity in the success rates of different social classes in public examinations. It is on this basis that Halsey and his colleagues are able to conclude that at 'O' and 'A' level, working class pupils (boys) *who survive* in school, compete on equal terms with pupils (boys) who are from other social classes. However, by this stage the class differentials are very wide as the boy from the working class family is more likely to drop out of school at the minimum school leaving age, is less likely to go into the sixth form and less likely to proceed into higher education.

However, we should note that much of this research relates to boys, to the period before comprehensivization and to the period before the raising of the school leaving age to sixteen. Together these features suggest that there might be some change in the relationship between social class and patterns of school achievement in the secondary school. On this basis, we need further data from sociologists about the ways in which changes in the pattern of secondary schooling have influenced the performance of boys *and* girls from different social classes since the mid 1970s. As a consequence, sociologists need to conduct further surveys on recent patterns of secondary school performance. However, they also need to consider whether the patterns of performance that occur in the school system are also repeated in the post school years.

POST SCHOOL EDUCATION

The most comprehensive survey that has been attempted on patterns of higher education comes from the Robbins committee (Robbins, 1963a) who conducted a survey of one in every 200 people born in 1940–1. The basic data that were collected are summarized in table 6. Here, it is apparent that the percentage of each social class attaining some form of higher education declines from the higher professional class to the semi and unskilled manual class. On the basis of the evidence it is possible to conclude that a person in the professional class was thirty-three times

TABLE 6: *Highest course of education by father's occupation for children born in Great Britain 1940–41*

	Percentages					
	Higher Education			*'A' level or SLC*	*Other post school or 'O' level*	*No post school or 'O' level/SLC*
	Full-time		*Part-time*			
Father's occupation	*Degree*	*Other*				
Higher professional	33	12	7	16	25	7
Management/other professional	11	8	6	7	48	20
Clerical	6	4	3	7	51	29
Skilled manual	2	2	3	2	42	49
Semi/Unskilled manual	1	1	2	1	30	65
All children	4	3	4	3	40	47

NOTES: 1. SLC is the Scottish School Leaving Certificate.
2. All children includes those whose father's occupation were not known/whose fathers were unoccupied or dead.

SOURCE: Robbins (1963b) derived from table 2, p. 40

TABLE 7: *Distribution of children (1971) and students in higher education (1956–1979) by social class of father*

<table>
<tr><td></td><td colspan="7">(Percentages)
Class</td></tr>
<tr><td></td><td>I</td><td>II</td><td>IIIN</td><td>IIIM</td><td>IV</td><td>V</td><td>N/C</td></tr>
<tr><td>1) Children aged 10–14 in 1971, GB</td><td>5.0</td><td>18.2</td><td>9.0</td><td>37.3</td><td>16.5</td><td>6.8</td><td>7.3</td></tr>
<tr><td>2) 'A' level pupils aged 18 in school & FE, FT, 1974, Eng.</td><td>20</td><td>40</td><td>12</td><td>18</td><td colspan="2">8</td><td>2</td></tr>
<tr><td>3) Univ. entrants, FT, 1956, GB</td><td></td><td></td><td></td><td></td><td></td><td></td><td></td></tr>
<tr><td>Male</td><td>21</td><td>41</td><td>11</td><td>22</td><td>4</td><td>1</td><td>—</td></tr>
<tr><td>Female</td><td>26</td><td>45</td><td>9</td><td>16</td><td>2</td><td>1</td><td>—</td></tr>
<tr><td>All</td><td>22</td><td>42</td><td>11</td><td>20</td><td>4</td><td>1</td><td>—</td></tr>
<tr><td>4) Univ. student, FT, 1961/2, GB</td><td></td><td></td><td></td><td></td><td></td><td></td><td></td></tr>
<tr><td>Male</td><td>17</td><td>40</td><td>12</td><td>19</td><td>6</td><td>1</td><td>5</td></tr>
<tr><td>Female</td><td>20</td><td>43</td><td>11</td><td>16</td><td>6</td><td>1</td><td>3</td></tr>
<tr><td>All</td><td>18</td><td>41</td><td>12</td><td>18</td><td>6</td><td>1</td><td>4</td></tr>
<tr><td>5) Univ. students by age,</td><td></td><td></td><td></td><td></td><td></td><td></td><td></td></tr>
<tr><td>19 and under</td><td colspan="2">64</td><td>11</td><td>21</td><td colspan="2">4</td><td>—</td></tr>
<tr><td>Mid-1960s 20–22</td><td colspan="2">71</td><td>8</td><td>17</td><td colspan="2">4</td><td>—</td></tr>
<tr><td>23 and over</td><td colspan="2">59</td><td>10</td><td>26</td><td colspan="2">5</td><td>—</td></tr>
<tr><td>6) Univ. entrants, FT, 1979, UK</td><td>19.8</td><td>38.0</td><td>21.1</td><td>14.7</td><td>4.5</td><td>0.9</td><td>9.8</td></tr>
<tr><td>7) Teacher training students FT, 1961/62, GB</td><td></td><td></td><td></td><td></td><td></td><td></td><td></td></tr>
<tr><td>Male</td><td>5</td><td>27</td><td>16</td><td>32</td><td>13</td><td>2</td><td>5</td></tr>
<tr><td>Female</td><td>8</td><td>35</td><td>14</td><td>28</td><td>8</td><td>2</td><td>6</td></tr>
<tr><td>All</td><td>7</td><td>33</td><td>14</td><td>29</td><td>9</td><td>2</td><td>6</td></tr>
<tr><td>8) AFE students, FT, 1961/62, GB</td><td>12</td><td>32</td><td>14</td><td>28</td><td>8</td><td>2</td><td>4</td></tr>
<tr><td>PT day</td><td>6</td><td>20</td><td>16</td><td>39</td><td>12</td><td>4</td><td>3</td></tr>
<tr><td>PT evening</td><td>5</td><td>22</td><td>14</td><td>39</td><td>12</td><td>3</td><td>4</td></tr>
<tr><td>9) Poly. degree students, FT & PT, 1972/73, Eng.</td><td></td><td></td><td></td><td></td><td></td><td></td><td></td></tr>
<tr><td>Male</td><td colspan="2">46</td><td>19</td><td colspan="3">26</td><td>10</td></tr>
<tr><td>Female</td><td colspan="2">51</td><td>17</td><td colspan="3">24</td><td>9</td></tr>
<tr><td>All</td><td>12</td><td>34</td><td>18</td><td>8</td><td>2</td><td>16</td><td>10</td></tr>
<tr><td>10) Poly. non-degree students, FT & PT, 1972/73</td><td>11</td><td>29</td><td>17</td><td>10</td><td>3</td><td>18</td><td>14</td></tr>
<tr><td>11) Poly. PT students, 1972/73, Eng.</td><td>9</td><td>23</td><td>19</td><td>12</td><td>4</td><td>18</td><td>15</td></tr>
<tr><td>The same, own occupation</td><td>9</td><td>38</td><td>29</td><td>2</td><td>0</td><td>15</td><td>7</td></tr>
<tr><td>12) Open Univ. PT entrants, 1971, UK</td><td>8</td><td>26</td><td>13</td><td>34</td><td>13</td><td>5</td><td>—</td></tr>
<tr><td>The same, own occupation</td><td>20</td><td>62</td><td>11</td><td>5</td><td>1</td><td>0</td><td>—</td></tr>
</table>

Based on (1) OPCS (1971) Household Composition Table 26; (2) Williams and Gordon (1975); (3) Kelsall (1957); (4), (7), (8) Robbins (1963c) pp. 4, 92, 128; (5) Hopper and Osborn (1975) table 4.8; (6) UCCA (1979) Table E5; (9), (10), (11) Whitburn, Mealing and Cox (1976) Tables 4.12, 4.A, 4B, 6.7 and personal communication with Farrant (students in (11) are also counted in (9) or (10)); (12) McIntosh, Calder and Swift (1976).

SOURCE: Farrant (1981) p. 85

more likely to end up in higher education than one from a semi or unskilled manual background. Indeed, at the other extreme only 7 per cent of the professional class failed to gain any educational qualifications compared with 65 per cent of those from the semi and unskilled manual class. Further evidence on the social class composition of university students is available from a survey of graduates conducted by Kelsall, Poole and Kuhn (1972). On the basis of data from graduates who obtained degrees in 1960 it is apparent that the children of middle class origin have a greater chance of becoming graduates than those from the working class. However, this evidence was gathered before the expansion of higher education and the implementation of the Robbins principle that opportunities in higher education should be provided for all young people who are qualified in terms of ability and attainment. Recent evidence (see table 7) suggests that it is still predominantly those from a non-manual rather than a manual background who have the opportunity of entering higher education. However, it might be considered that some changes in this pattern might have occurred with the developments that have taken place in terms of the provision of degree courses in polytechnics and colleges of higher education. As far as the non-university sector is concerned Whitburn, Mealing and Cox (1976) have shown that there is a trend for students from higher socio-economic groups to be enrolled in full-time degree courses. Indeed, as Williamson (1981) has noted, if there has been an improvement in the chances of working class students to obtain higher education it has been in those institutions that might be regarded by some members of the general public to be less prestigious than universities.

Nevertheless, it might be expected that the Open University with its different style of recruitment and different pattern of teaching would recruit students from a broader range of social class backgrounds. The evidence available in table 8 shows the pattern of recruitment in just over a decade. Once again the dominant trend is for individuals from non-manual rather than manual backgrounds to be represented. A significant increase has occurred among those who said they were not in employment. While this group may include those who had retired, and who had independent means, as well as students, prisoners and hospital residents, it also includes a significant number of unemployed people (Central Statistical Office, 1985). Further trends that are worthy of our attention include the proportion of teachers and lecturers and housewives who became Open University students. While the proportion of Open University students who were teachers and lecturers decreased by two thirds, the proportion of housewives increased by over two thirds between 1971 and 1983. However, as the Central Statistical Office (1985) points out, as teachers and lecturers only represent 2 per cent of the population aged 21 or over, they remain proportionately the best represented group among Open University students who are in employment.

TABLE 8: *Open University occupation of new undergraduate students*
United Kingdom *Percentages*

Occupation	*1971*	*1976*	*1981*	*1983*
Teachers & lecturers	40	27	20	14
Housewives	10	15	18	17
Technical personnel	12	11	12	12
Clerical & office staff	6	10	11	11
The professions and the arts	8	11	10	11
Shopkeepers, sales & services	3	4	5	5
Administrators & managers	5	5	3	4
Armed forces	2	3	3	3
Qualified scientists & engineers	6	4	3	3
In other employment	3	7	9	9
Not in employment	2	4	5	11
No information	2	—	—	—
Total new students (=100%)	19.6	12.2	14.5	18.2

NOTE: These data relate to finally registered new students at the commencement of their studies.
SOURCE: Data from tables in Central Statistical Office (1982, 1985).

Such trends as those that are shown in tables 7 and 8 reflect patterns of recruitment to higher education during a period of expansion in the 1960s and early 1970s. Here, the data that are available appear to bear out the case that has been advanced by Embling (1974) who states that:

> inequality, far from diminishing with the expansion of higher education and higher educational expenditure, has . . . increased for it is the non-manual classes that have exploited the extra opportunities. (Embling, 1974, p.37)

Having identified such patterns, sociologists have posed a number of questions about class inequality in education and have set about attempting to provide explanations of the phenomena that they have identified.

The main question that sociologists have addressed in their studies is: *To what extent is the social class distribution of the population reflected in the distribution of pupils and students in various sectors of the educational system?* This leads on to an analysis of the relative chances of individuals from different social classes obtaining particular opportunities in education. In addition, researchers have considered the source of educational inequality which has resulted in attempts to provide explanations for the patterns that we have so far reviewed.

One of the basic issues that social scientists have examined is the way in which individual differences in educability emerge. Some writers have argued that human abilities are inherited and that differences in attainment are accounted for by cognitive ability. Within this area of investigation, psychologists such as Herrnstein (1973) have been heavily involved. It was Herrnstein who argued that there are a number of psychological traits that constitute intelligence (IQ), that individual and group differences have a genetic component, that IQ is important if an individual is to attain high status and that differences in IQ account for differences in social status and life chances. However, Husén (1979) maintains that the way in which intelligence is defined within a meritocratic framework together with the methodology used will give the results expected. This debate has also turned towards a consideration of heredity and environment where psychologists have considered the relative importance of genetic and environmental factors (cf. Taylor, 1980). However, when sociologists and other educational researchers focus on these issues there is a tendency towards psychological reductionism as achievement is explained in terms of socialization and by reference to the nature/nurture debate (for further critical discussion see Bernstein and Davies, 1969; Archer, 1970). Many researchers have therefore utilised the concept of class in an attempt to provide explanations of patterns of child rearing (Newson and Newson, 1965, 1970, 1976), of the influence of home and family background on school achievement (cf. Douglas, 1964; Douglas *et al*, 1968; Davie, Butler and Goldstein, 1972), in studies of language (Bernstein, 1971b, 1975) and in ecological studies (Eggleston, 1977a). The remaining part of this chapter will, therefore, provide a review of some of this evidence.

Social class, the family and education

The evidence that is available on the family has traditionally been discussed in terms of material disadvantage and cultural disadvantage which we shall examine in turn. However, along with many other commentators it is important to stress that researchers have found difficulty in being able to isolate a particular variable in accounting for educational attainment. Indeed, there has been a tendency to suggest a complex interaction between a number of variables in relation to educational achievement.

MATERIAL DISADVANTAGE

It was in the classic longitudinal study by Douglas (1964) that reference was made to the importance of the material conditions of the homes from which children came. In particular, Douglas drew attention to the importance of housing, which included the size and number of rooms, the degree of overcrowding, the sharing of beds and other household amenities which, it was argued, was associated with lower ability and attainment. Such findings were also confirmed by data from the National Child Development Study (Davie *et al*, 1972; Fogelman, 1975) and by a range of other studies (cf. Rutter *et al*, 1970; Murray, 1974). The main trend throughout these studies is to point to the relationship between 'unsatisfactory' housing conditions and lower test scores. In particular, Douglas highlights the lowering of test scores among children from 'unsatisfactory' manual working class homes between the ages of eight and eleven, although this position is reversed for middle class children from 'unsatisfactory' homes beyond the age of eight. These trends were also confirmed by data from the National Child Development Study where it was argued that there was a social class trend with only 1 per cent of children from social class I living in overcrowded conditions and with less good amenities, while 37 per cent of children from social class V were in such situations. Accordingly, it is argued that these conditions were important in relation to school attainment. Such trends have also been used in the National Child Development Study to account for attainment at the age of 16 and to explain patterns of progress in the secondary school (cf. Fogelman, 1976 and Essen, Fogelman and Head, 1978).

A second major finding in Douglas's study concerned material conditions related to family size. Generally, it was argued that the impact of family size on attainment was such that there was a decline in measured ability with each increase in family size. Indeed, it was found that this was related more to manual working class homes than to middle class homes. Among middle class children it was boys from a family of four or more who could be said to be disadvantaged. This account links up with Townsend's (1979) study which indicates that the proportion of people in poverty increases with family size.

These are just two of the material disadvantages that are discussed in Douglas's work and which have been confirmed in subsequent studies where attempts have been made to account for the differences in measured educational attainment. However, as Mortimore and Blackstone (1981) indicate, there are many other material factors such as health, conditions of work and unemployment that researchers claim have some impact on educational attainment. As Deem (1984b) remarks, such accounts need to be treated carefully as unemployment may affect any family regardless of their class position. As a consequence there is an urgent need for researchers to investigate the effects of parents' unemployment on children's education in a set of changing social and economic circumstances. Nevertheless, previous studies on the family-education link indicate that it is not merely material conditions that influence educational attainment but also cultural conditions, to which we now turn.

CULTURAL DISADVANTAGE

A concept introduced into the literature in the 1960s was that of cultural deprivation which was used to explain the school failure of pupils (cf. Riesman, 1962). Children who were culturally deprived, it was argued, came from homes where there were not only material disadvantages but also cultural disadvantages in terms of the attitudes and values that were transmitted to them. In particular, sociological evidence drew attention to accounts of child socialization and to patterns of child rearing.

Turning to the classic study by Douglas (1964), we note how he found that parental encouragement was the most important single factor that accounted for the improvement of children's test scores between the ages of eight and eleven. In turn, this was confirmed by the Plowden Committee (Central Advisory Council for Education, 1967) when, on the basis of their survey, they found associations between social class and the initiative, interest, support and encouragement given by parents to children's school work. In addition, they confirmed that a more favourable attitude was likely to be associated with higher social class. Such trends were also confirmed by Douglas, Ross and Simpson (1968) in relation to high attainment, good 'O' level results and patterns of pupils staying on at school. Indeed, Douglas *et al* (1968) considered that parental interest could be shown through visits to school – a trend that teachers perceive as an indicator of parental interest. However, caution needs to be exercised here for, as Johnson and Ransom (1983) have argued, parents who do not come to school are not necessarily apathetic, as many forms of parental support and interest are invisible to teachers.

Data that are available in the Newsons' studies of child rearing also focus on the concept of class, as John and Elizabeth Newson remark:

> In our discussions of child rearing, from minutiae to the total schemata, we have given the class factor the attention which, without prejudging the issue, it seemed to deserve; and it is only in response to the inescapable salience of the social class patterns into which our data has fallen that we have presented class as the major isolable influence in the way people feel and act in bringing up their children. (Newson and Newson, 1976, p.30)

Indeed, the Newsons found that social class was the most important variable in understanding the way in which mothers behaved towards their babies (Newson and Newson, 1965). In subsequent studies the Newsons followed children from the pre-school years into the primary school (cf. Newson and Newson, 1970, 1977) where they found that parental interest could be examined through home-school links and through the general cultural interests of the parents. In particular, a class trend was revealed between the professional groups and the semi-skilled and the unskilled manual workers. Children in the lower social class groups were less likely to be helped with reading, and were less likely to have their knowledge extended. In turn, Newson and Newson (1977) also discuss the role of cultural interests such as visits to the cinema, the theatre and to museums as well as the importance of parents using books and newspapers with their children. Indeed, the Newsons move to a discussion of socialization processes as they argue that

> By taking him [by which they mean the child] on visits to places of interest, making sure that he has access to the written media, answering his questions and searching for answers elsewhere when her own knowledge is inadequate, the mother repeatedly characterizes cultural interest as relevant to herself, and by identification, to the child as well. (Newson and Newson, 1977, p.85)

It is here that such an explanation has some links with the work of Bourdieu (1973), Bourdieu and Passeron (1977) and Bernstein (1971a) who have examined the way in which culture is transmitted between parents and children in different social class groups. On the basis of research concerning cinema, theatre and museum attendances and the use of books, Bourdieu discusses the processes of cultural reproduction. He argues that education demands a linguistic and cultural competence that is not automatically provided by schools. Accordingly, the advantage is to those whose families are able to transmit elements of culture, as the 'high' culture which may be transmitted through family upbringing is also transmitted by schools. For Bourdieu, those families who control economic capital also have control over cultural capital, which insures that their children will obtain the necessary qualifications through school (cf. Bourdieu and Boltanski, 1978).

There are also links here with Bernstein's discussion of family role systems and the process of social reproduction. Bernstein (1971c) has discussed two types of family role structure: the positional family and the person-centred family. In the former there is a clear separation of roles and a 'closed' system of communication, while in the latter the importance of the child in relation to other members of the family is perceived and there is an 'open' system of communication. Clearly, in the person-oriented family there is importance attached to communication and language which has also been used to explain the relative advantage of different social class groups in education, to which we now turn.

Language studies

Sociological work on language, social class and education is synonymous with Basil Bernstein who, since the 1950s, has been concerned with studies that make links between social structure and educational attainment through analyses of language. It is important to recall that Bernstein's work is empirical as well as theoretical, although the theoretical discussions rest on a very thin empirical base consisting of a study of 61 post office messenger boys compared with 45 boys from a major public school. It is from this very small study in which the former group are said to constitute the 'working class' and the latter group the 'middle class' that Bernstein builds his theory which is of most significance to us here.

In his early writing Bernstein distinguishes between two forms of language. First, a *public language* and secondly a *formal language* which, in his later writing, is developed considerably so that it becomes the *restricted code* and the *elaborated code* respectively. It is these codes which regulate communication and generate speech. The restricted code, it is claimed, usually involves short simple sentences where the speech is descriptive and narrative rather than analytic and abstract, focuses upon concrete items and contains implicit meanings. In contrast, the elaborated code consists of much more explicit meanings, is difficult to predict, and is analytic and abstract.

As far as Bernstein is concerned, these two linguistic codes are linked to patterns of socialization between the social classes whereby the normative system of the middle class child gives rise to the use of elaborated code speech variants, while the working class child is socialized into using restricted code speech variants. However Bernstein adds that:

> children socialized within middle class and associated strata can be expected to possess both an elaborated and a restricted code while children socialized within some sections of the working class strata, particularly the lower working class, can be expected to be limited to a restricted code. As a child progresses through a school it becomes critical for him to possess, or at least to be oriented toward, an elaborated code if he is to succeed. (Bernstein, 1970b, p.183)

In these circumstances, Bernstein is suggesting links between educational opportunity and social class as a consequence of language use. However, Bernstein does not leave his analysis here, as he subsequently argues (along with many of his critics (cf. Rosen, 1972)) that the relationship between language and social class is too imprecise. As a consequence Bernstein adds to his theory by distinguishing between two ideal types of family role systems: positional and person-oriented families (see the previous section). Broadly, he argues that there is a relationship between the working class, positional family and the restricted code and the middle class person-oriented family and the elaborated code. However, he also adds that some working class families are more person-oriented – a situation that has consequences for his theory.

While Bernstein claims that access to the codes is broadly related to social class and that the middle class has access to both codes, he also argues that within the working class positional family we should expect the restricted code. In addition, he also claims that both family types are found in each social class – a situation that holds implications for his theory which Stubbs (1983) has attempted to summarize in a diagrammatic way (see figure 1).

As Stubbs indicates, the arrows represent links between levels where there is an expected link between working class, positional families and restricted code use. However, Stubbs argues that when the codes are set out in this way no real predictions are made. In turn, Gordon (1981) has

Figure 1: Bernstein's Theory (as summarized by Stubbs)

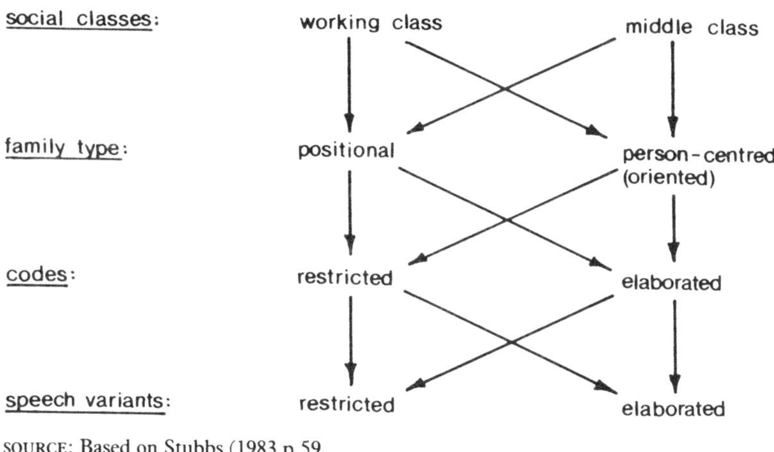

SOURCE: Based on Stubbs (1983 p.59

also attempted to summarize what Bernstein claims in the following way:

> social class ⟶ family structure ⟶ roles ⟶ modes of early socialization ⟶ roles . . . modes of perception . . . access to codes ⟶ codes ⟶ speech ⟶ educational attainment

Here the arrows represent causal links while the dots refer to obscure links in Bernstein's work. Overall, he argues that there is obscurity throughout the chain and that both 'social class' and 'educational attainment' are taken for granted.

As can be seen, Bernstein's work, whilst attempting to provide an explanation of the link between social structure and educational attainment through language, is controversial (cf. A. D. Edwards, 1976; Rosen, 1972; Stubbs, 1983; Fletcher, 1984; Atkinson, 1985). In particular, there has been considerable controversy over the extent to which Bernstein's restricted code user has a distinct educational disadvantage. In a widely quoted paper, Labov (1972) has challenged this view, arguing that the restricted code user's speech can contain complex sets of ideas; the result is that what Labov calls non-standard Negro English is different rather than deficient (a subject that will be discussed further in the following chapter). Meanwhile, there is space for further investigation to see the extent to which teachers use the elaborated code and the implications that this holds for the educational achievement of the restricted code user. However, Halliday (1973) has argued that, while educational failure cannot be restricted to linguistic failure, there is, nevertheless, a relationship between language use and success and failure in school. In these terms, language is one of the variables that can help explain educational attainment, but we need to turn to other accounts.

Education and social class: alternative explanations

The explanations that have so far been examined rest upon the child as the unit of analysis and carry with them the notion that educational provision is similar in all sections of society. Yet a brief glance at the annual figures produced by the Chartered Institute of Public Finance and Accountancy (see the figures that are produced annually by the Chartered Institute) highlight differences in provision across local education authorities, between primary and secondary schools and in terms of teacher–pupil ratios. Furthermore, evidence in government reports by the Newson Committee (Ministry of Education, 1963) and the Plowden Committee (Central Advisory Council for Education, 1967) and in research reports (cf. Taylor and Ayres, 1969) highlight differences between local authorities and local education authority resources. It is on the basis of such evidence that Eggleston (1977a) has argued the case for sociologists to conduct ecological studies of education. He maintains that the distribution of resources and the response to them may help to account for differences in educational achievement. Among the questions that he considers important are:

> Can the distribution and response to educational resources offer an alternative source of explanation for differences in opportunity and achievement? Can the ecology of schooling lead to an enhanced understanding of the ecology of attainment? (Eggleston, 1977a, p.23)

It is issues such as these that Eggleston (1967) and Byrne, Williamson and Fletcher (1975) have examined at the level of the school and the local authority respectively.

Of all sociological writing, the data provided by Byrne and Williamson (1972) and Byrne, Williamson and Fletcher (1975) have been used to develop a socio-spatial model of educational attainment which rests on Weber's concept of class. Here they develop three propositions. First, that social class refers to a relationship between groups that are differently placed in society to obtain the rewards of that society. Secondly, that relationships between social classes are based on control and domination, and finally, that rewards that social classes have are spatially distributed. These rewards include provision of a range of services and benefits. It is on the basis of these propositions that Byrne, Williamson and Fletcher (1975) ask whether there is a significant degree of socio-spatial inequality in the educational system of England and Wales. In addition, they also ask: can such inequality be assessed in terms of differential outcomes for groups placed differently in relation to the system of inequality? In their analysis of eleven local education authorities in north-east England they related measures of the socio-spatial system. These measures included: social class background, local environmental factors, local authority policy, local authority resources and local authority provision in relation to educational attainment (based on pupils staying on at school after the age of 16). On the basis of the evidence they argue that there is a relationship between measures of educational provision, measures of environmental condition and educational attainment. Indeed, they argue that school system inputs are of importance in explaining differences in attainment. Furthermore, there is a relationship between the class background of an area and the educational resources that are available as there is a general tendency for there to be better provision in areas where the social class composition is high. Accordingly, their model stresses a relationship between social class, educational resources, local authority policy and educational outcomes at school level.

While examining the relationship between social class and higher education, Williamson (1981) similarly rejects the class-culture paradigm as it ignores the structural position of different groups in society with respect to the control and funding of education and the structure of the social division of labour. For, as Williamson argues, such a model focuses more on socialization rather than upon children's different relationships to the wider structure of opportunity in society. Accordingly, Williamson uses a relational concept of class in order to examine patterns of social class bias in higher education. He argues that the social inequalities that are found in the decisions taken by school pupils have their roots in higher education and in the relationship of higher education to society. On this basis he maintains that the relative life chances of different groups in higher education cannot be discussed as separate from the form, control and social significance of higher education. Williamson identifies three principles:

1. The social determinants of differential educational attainments in secondary schools and processes of decision making which results in some children leaving school and others aiming for higher education;
2. the form and content of higher education together with the principles regulating access to it;
3. the influence of patterns of change in universities and higher education and which groups shape the direction of change.

In each of these contexts, class is operative, as shown in figure 2 which illustrates those factors that influence educational decision-making among different class groups. Williamson argues that he can overcome mechanistic accounts of some simple correspondence between education and the needs of the economy (Bowles and Gintis, 1976), as his model develops a relational concept of class which can provide a way of discussing the social mechanisms in education that result in class inequality in society. In particular, this model suggests firstly, that differences in aptitude, attitude and opportunity of those who are capable of higher education, from those who are not, are rooted in

Figure 2: Class and Higher Education: A model of processes

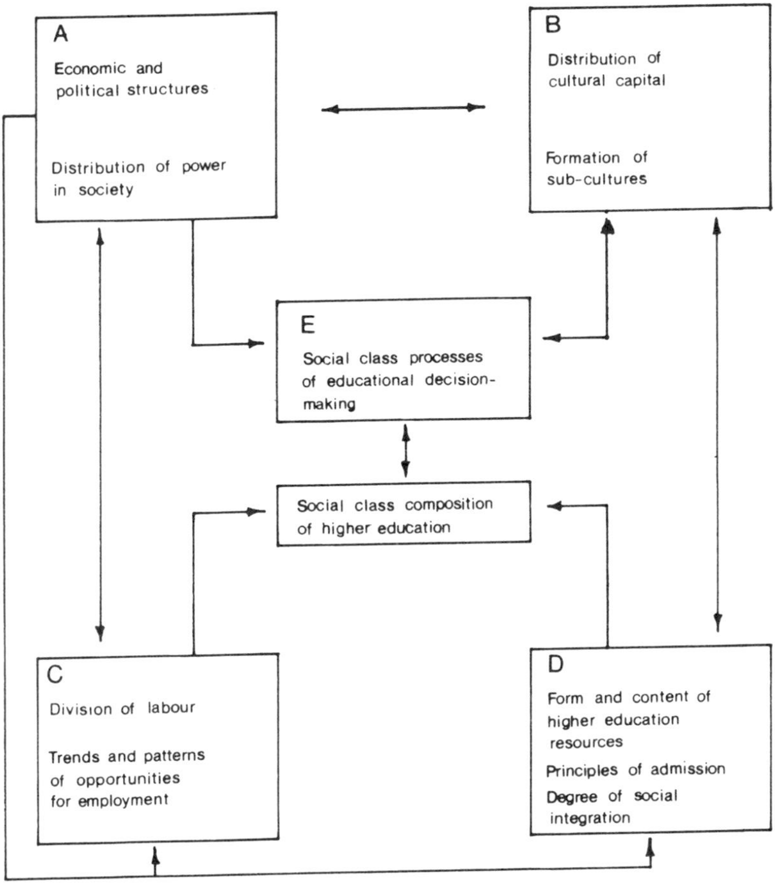

SOURCE: Williamson (1981) p.31

economic and political structures; secondly, that the structure of the labour market sets the value of educational qualifications and the demand for them; thirdly, that the form, content and admissions policies of higher education reflect the 'ideal of cultivation' of the dominant group; fourthly, that there is constant pressure for change in higher education in relation to changes in class structure; fifthly, that social class processes of decision-making cannot be separated from the opportunities available, the secondary school experiences of different groups and their perception of the value and accessibility of higher education; finally, that variations in the class profiles of higher education among societies of the same structural type reflect variations in industrialization and social class formation. Overall, this model points to the importance of having a broad analysis of the concept of educability and in turn directs our attention to the importance of unravelling the ways in which social class influences patterns of higher education.

Conclusion

This chapter has focused on one of the most pervasive divisions in education. Here, two tasks have been attempted. First, the basic patterns of class inequality in English education have been charted using data that are mainly drawn from sociological research projects conducted in the 1950s and 1960s together with available evidence from the 1960s and subsequent years that is included in official reports. Secondly, an attempt has been made to review some of the explanations that have been advanced by sociologists to account for class inequalities in education. Yet this is only part of the story. Social divisions based on sex and race also have a direct bearing on educational achievement and it is these issues that will be examined in the following chapter. Nevertheless, it is important for sociologists to bear in mind that the *relationship* between class, gender and race needs to be explored when providing accounts of patterns of inequality in education.

Suggestions for further reading

There is a vast range of material on class inequality relating to all phases of education. This list of suggested reading should therefore be supplemented by additional material listed in the bibliographies.

Bernstein, B. (1971) *Class, Codes and Control, Volume 1*, London, Routledge and Kegan Paul (2nd Edn. 1973) and Bernstein, B. (1975) *Class, Codes and Control, Volume 3*, London, Routledge and Kegan Paul are a pair of volumes in which Bernstein reprints the major papers that he has produced on language codes and social class and their relationship to educational attainment. The preface to each volume is especially useful as Bernstein traces various developments in his enquiries and makes some of the links much more explicit. For commentary see Atkinson (1985)

Burgess, R. G. (1984) 'Patterns and processes of education in the United Kingdom' in P. Abrams and R. K. Brown (eds) *U.K. Society: Work Urbanism and Inequality*, London, Weidenfeld and Nicolson provides a discussion of social inequalities in education. It traces patterns of inequality relating not only to social class but also to gender and race. The essays by Wainwright (1984) and by Stanworth (1984) are also important in this context.

Edwards, A. D. (1976) *Language in Culture and Class*, London, Heinemann provides a sociological analysis of topics on language and linguistics. There is a useful chapter on Bernstein's work.

Lodge, P. and Blackstone, T. (1982) *Educational Policy and Educational Inequality*, London, Martin Robertson contains a useful chapter on nursery education.

Mortimore, J. and Blackstone, T. (1981) *Disadvantage and Education*, London, Heinemann consists of a critical review of literature on the social factors influencing educational attainment.

Purvis, J. and Hales, M. (1983) (eds) *Achievement and Inequality in Education*, London, Routledge and Kegan Paul provides a range of papers on educational inequality; see especially part four.

Robinson, P. (1981) 'Whatever happened to educability?' in B. Davies (ed) *The State of Schooling*, special issue of *Educational Analysis*, vol. 3, no. 1, pp.37–46 reviews the trends in the political arithmetic tradition in research and writing.

Stubbs, M. (1983) *Language in Schools and Classrooms*, (2nd Edn.) London, Methuen contains a review and critique of recent literature including the work of Bernstein and Labov.

Williamson, B. (1981) 'Class bias', in D. Warren-Piper (ed) *Is Higher Education Fair?* Guildford, Society for Research in Higher Education is a review of statistical evidence on social class and higher education together with an explanation of the patterns.

EMPIRICAL STUDIES

Byrne, D. S., Williamson, B. and Fletcher, B. G. (1975) *The Poverty of Education: A Study in the Politics of Opportunity*, London, Martin Robertson provides a socio-spatial model of inequality that complements individualistic analyses.

Douglas, J. W. B. (1964) *The Home and the School*, London, Panther is the classic longitudinal study on home-school relationships and the influence of family background on primary education.

Douglas, J. W. B., Ross, J. M. and Simpson, H. R. (1968) *All Our Future*, London, Panther continues the longitudinal account in Douglas (1964) but in relation to secondary education.

Fogelman, K. (1983) *Growing Up in Great Britain*, London, Macmillan provides a set of papers from the National Child Development Study. It is a basic resource on this longitudinal study of children born in 1958.

Halsey, A. H., Heath, A. and Ridge, J. M. (1980) *Origins and Destinations: Family, Class and Education in Modern Britain*, Oxford, Clarendon Press contains data concerning the educational achievement of an all male sample in England and Wales.

Kelsall, R. K., Poole, A. and Kuhn, A. (1972) *Graduates: The Sociology of an Elite*, London, Routledge and Kegan Paul is an empirical study of graduate students in Britain.

5 Patterns of inequality 2: gender, race and education

Although the central issue in sociology has been social inequality (cf. Béteille, 1969; Walby, 1986) much of the discussion has focused on social class as this phenomenon has been seen as the basic dimension of social stratification. However, in recent years, sociologists have begun to recognize the ways in which gender and race contribute to patterns of inequality. Indeed, O'Brien (1981) has argued that the study of social stratification was not only 'mainstream' but also 'male stream' in sociological thought (cf. Stacey, 1981, 1982) with the result that women were excluded from study. As a consequence analyses of gender inequality have found a place on the research agenda of many sociologists along with studies of racial inequality. In turn, questions have also been raised about the interrelationship between class, gender and race in the course of attempting to understand patterns of social inequality.

Many commentaries on the sociology of education have indicated how researchers have shown a tendency to follow developments in the parent discipline (cf. Banks, 1976; Robinson, 1981a) and in this respect studies of social inequality in education are no exception. Indeed, many sociologists of education have pointed to the importance of extending our studies of social inequality so that they include a discussion of patterns of social differentiation and social division based on gender and race (Deem, 1984a). Much of the work that has taken place in these areas share common themes, as sociologists have documented the existence of these divisions, their implications, possible explanations for their persistence and possible 'solutions' to some of the problems that they have identified. Indeed, Brittain and Maynard (1984) have commented that much of the literature on gender and race in education

> focuses, in various ways, on underachievement or the underrepresentation of particular groups in critical areas of the school curriculum. This is demonstrated in the concern over women's poor science and mathematical qualifications, and Blacks' position in the lower and remedial classes in schools. Of course, these are extremely important matters for consideration. However, the

> descriptive rather than the analytic approach, often goes on to imply that 'solutions' may be found via the implementation of various ameliorative policies. Thus, for instance, the provision of special classes and compensatory techniques can lure young women away from the delights of English literature and office skills, to physics and computer science and can coax young Blacks out of the lower streams to compete equally with Whites for educational qualifications. (Brittain and Maynard, 1984, pp.153–154)

They go on to point out that it is not just disadvantage but also discrimination and repression that needs to be understood in education and schools. However, this is much easier said than done. For example, June Purvis (1984) has indicated how the range of literature that is available on women and education is limited, as it is only in recent years that women as well as men have been the topic of systematic investigation by sociologists, and as a consequence there are considerable gaps in our knowledge. Similar points have also been made with respect to studies of race and underachievement (cf. Tomlinson, 1983). Indeed, when the Rampton Committee and later the Swann Committee (Rampton, 1981; Swann, 1985a) wished to obtain evidence on West Indian achievement and underachievement in Britain, special studies had to be commissioned in order for the evidence to be readily available.

The kinds of questions that sociologists have directed their attention to when conducting studies in these areas have been well summarized by Deem (1984a) as follows:

> Is class a more dominant influence on schooling patterns and practices than gender?
> Is race a minor or a major determinant?
> Do gender, race and class have a cumulative effect upon individuals, trebly disadvantaging some, or is there a more complicated relationship between these three divisions? (Deem, 1984a, p.iv)

However, she also makes the point that work on gender and race is at an early stage of development both theoretically and empirically so that some of the formulations that can be made are somewhat speculative – a comment that is especially applicable to discussions that attempt to make links between class, gender and race (cf. Fuller, 1984a; MacDonald, 1981). Accordingly, this chapter will be devoted to a discussion of some of the patterns of differentiation by gender and race in the English school system, together with some of the possible explanations that have been advanced to account for the relative underachievement of a particular group. In addition, some of the possible 'solutions' that these explanations imply will be briefly reviewed.

Patterns and processes of gender differentiation in education

Within the scope of this section we will be predominantly concerned with contemporary patterns of gender differentiation in the English school system, although there is also a historical literature on developments in the late nineteenth and early twentieth centuries which has been well documented by Dyhouse (1981) and by Purvis (1984). Central to both historical and contemporary debates in this field of study is terminology, as Delamont (1980), Deem (1984a) and Morgan (1986) have all indicated the importance of making a distinction between two concepts: sex and gender. Among the different commentators Oakley (1981) has summarized the distinction in the following way:

> 'Sex' refers to the biological division into female and male; 'gender' to the parallel and socially unequal division into femininity and masculinity. (Oakley, 1981, p.41)

As such this points to a basic distinction being made between the biological and the social/cultural, the latter being of central significance to a sociological understanding of patterns of inequality in education (cf. Delamont, 1980). We begin by documenting patterns of gender inequality in education by examining the different phases of education which include the pre-school phase, the primary and secondary school period and the post-school years.

In terms of studies conducted in nursery schools (Walkerdine, 1981) and infant schools (King, 1978) we find sociologists arguing that pupils are socialized into a gender differentiated world through the school curriculum – a process that is reinforced in the junior school (cf. H. Burgess, 1983; 1986; Pollard, 1985) (see also Chapter 9 of this volume on the school curriculum). Indeed, the organizational procedures such as the sub-division of classes into single sex work groups and the division of names according to lists of boys and girls reinforces social divisions based on sex. In turn, the number of male and female teachers, their distribution and their positions also implicitly reinforce gender differentiation in primary and secondary schools (see Chapter 6 in this volume).

As far as large-scale surveys of academic performance among primary school pupils are concerned, much of the evidence comes from data that were collected when the eleven plus examination was used for secondary school selection. One of the features that was often the subject of some comment was the difference in scores between boys and girls at the age of eleven. The traditional pattern that was established was one where girls' scores were higher than those for boys in English, mathematics and intelligence tests. However the girls' superior performance was often explained away by those who constructed tests, as shown in the following statement:

> If the pass marks are made equivalent for the two sexes the number of girls admitted to grammar schools will in most areas substantially exceed the number of boys. In view of the fact that these differences exist at the age of eleven and that there is considerable uncertainty as to when and to what extent they eventually disappear the most satisfactory course . . . to adopt would

seem to be to treat boys and girls separately for the purpose of allocation to secondary school. (Yates and Pidgeon, 1957, pp.168–9)

Accordingly, discrimination frequently occurred as girls often had to achieve higher scores than boys if they were to obtain grammar school places.

Large-scale national surveys by Douglas (1964) and within the National Child Development Study (Davie *et al*, 1972) have provided consistent evidence to illustrate how girls obtained superior academic results in all areas of the primary school curriculum apart from mathematics. In terms of ratings for good behaviour it has also been found that girls have been ranked as superior to boys. However, the only tests that Douglas considered were valid for comparing changes in the achievement of boys and girls in the primary school were those for reading and vocabulary. Here, girls had higher scores than boys at the ages of eight and eleven. This evidence has been replicated in follow up studies. For example, Fogelman (1983) reports from the cohort of children investigated in the National Child Development Study that at seven years of age the girls were significantly ahead of the boys in their reading test scores but that there was no overall difference for boys and girls at the age of eleven. Similar results were also found in the HMI survey of primary education (DES, 1978a). On the basis of a BD reading test given to 5,000 primary school children at the age of nine years 2–6 months, it was found that girls obtained a higher score than the boys – a

TABLE 1: *BD Reading Test. Percentile distribution for boys, girls and all pupils age corrected at nine years 2–6 months (England)*
Possible range of scores 0–44

Percentile	*Boys' score*	*Girls' score*	*Boys' performance compared with girls*	*All pupils*
90	32.9	32.5	(+0.4)	32.7
80	28.5	28.6	(−0.1)	28.5
70	25.0	25.6	(−0.6)	25.2
60	21.9	23.0	(−1.1)	22.5
50	19.2	20.7	(−1.5)	20.0
40	16.6	18.5	(−1.9)	17.5
30	13.5	15.4	(−1.9)	14.4
20	10.6	12.6	(−2.0)	11.5
10	7.2	8.9	(−1.7)	8.0

SOURCE: DES (1978a) p. 165

result that was statistically significant, as shown in table 1.

However, these distinctions have not been sustained in terms of mathematical ability as there has not been such a clear cut difference between boys and girls. Douglas (1964), for example, shows that while girls surpassed the performance of boys at the age of eleven, middle class boys produced better results than middle class girls but manual working class boys did not perform as well as manual working class girls (see Chapter 4 in this volume). In addition, Fogelman (1983) reports that in the National Child Development Study there is no evidence of anything but a small average difference in the performance of boys and girls, with boys being 0.2 years ahead at the age of seven and 0.1 years at the age of eleven. Similarly, the HMI primary education survey (DES, 1978a) found there was no statistically significant difference between the performance of boys and girls in mathematics.

But have these patterns persisted in secondary schools? Much of the statistical evidence that is available to us on gender differentiation in secondary schools concerns examination courses and examination performances. However, this evidence has to be seen in the context of the school experiences of pupils. Sociologists have found autobiographical accounts from former pupils, especially from girls, a useful source of evidence in examining the way in which definitions of gender are established among working class grammar school girls (Payne, 1980), middle class grammar school girls (Garland, 1979) and by girls in independent schools (Okely, 1978). Among the most illuminating accounts is that provided by Irene Payne who highlights the implications of upward mobility for a working class girl who attains a grammar school place. In particular, Payne shows how there was a clash between the school's definition of femininity and that of her own family and her peers. She highlights the ways in which school uniform and the refusal to permit jewellery reinforced an image by which working class pupils were being turned into middle class young ladies – a transition that Moody (1968) has also documented in relation to life in a London comprehensive school. She illustrates how rebellion took a feminine form with challenges to teachers through the adaptation of the uniform and through behaviour in class (cf. Lambart, 1976, 1982). This example has also been considered by Arnot (1983) who argues that it illustrates several issues. First, how gender definitions are not class specific but a form of social control when imposed on the children of another class. Secondly, that there may be discontinuities over the definitions of femininity and masculinity learnt at home and at school with the result that gender socialization may not necessarily be a smooth process. As a result of the disjuncture between the middle class culture of the school and working class culture, Arnot (1983) argues that this may explain why working class girls do not take up all the opportunities available to them.

However, the educational opportunities available to boys and girls

TABLE 2: *Differentiation by sex in craft subjects: by type of school (England)*

Number of schools

	Type of school				*All schools:*	
	Modern	*Grammar*	*FR*[1] *Comprehensive*	*RR*[2] *Comprehensive*	*Nos.*	*Percentages*
Type of differentiation						
Prescribed by sex in mixed schools	28	5	28	8	69	19
Operating but not prescribed	31	2	31	10	74	20
Single sex schools	29	38	18	10	95	26
Wholly open choice	33	7	71	16	127	35
Totals	121	52	148	44	365	100

NOTES: 1. Full ability range comprehensive.
2. Restricted ability range comprehensive.

SOURCE: DES (1979) p. 15

from the same social class background may be very different. For example, in her discussion of life in an independent school, Okely (1978) argues that there are differences in the education provided for boys and girls, as she states:

> The boys' and girls' educations are not symmetrical but they are ideologically interdependent. That considered female is partly defined by its opposite: that which is considered to be male. The characteristics of one institution are strengthened by their absence in the other. Qualities primarily reserved for one gender will have a different meaning in the institution for the opposing gender. The two educations are also linked in practice since, in adulthood, individuals from the separate institutions will be united in marriage, for the consolidation of their class. As members of the same social class the girls and boys may share similar educational experiences, but as members of different gender categories some of their education may differ. (Okely, 1978, p.110)

In such ways, divisions between boys and girls are transmitted within schools. For example, Walford (1982) has found distinctions occur between arts orientated girls' sixth forms and science orientated boys' sixth forms, in co-educational independent schools.

Such subject-based gender divisions have also been found in state secondary schools. For example, an HMI survey of secondary education in England (DES, 1979) found that there were differences in the opportunities to study craft subjects and science subjects. The definition of craft subjects for boys included woodwork and metalwork, while for

TABLE 3: *Science subjects studied by boys and girls in England in secondary schools in the fourth and fifth year*

	Percentages of pupils	
	Boys	*Girls*
Year 4		
Physics	51	13
Chemistry	31	19
Biology	32	60
Integrated & General Science	21	15
Other science	7	4
Year 5		
Physics	48	10
Chemistry	29	16
Biology	31	58
Integrated & General Science	23	15
Other science	7	4

SOURCE: DES (1979) derived from Table 8b, p. 167

TABLE 4: *Attainments of school leavers as a percentage of the relevant population[1] in the United Kingdom, 1970–71 and 1981–82*

	Percentages					
	1970–71			*1981–82*		
	Boys	*Girls*	*Total*	*Boys*	*Girls*	*Total*
As a percentage of the relevant population[1]						
17 years at 31 August						
With 1 or more GCE 'A' levels or SCE 'H' Grades	17.8	15.3	16.6	17.6	17.7	17.7
With 5 or more A to C awards[2] alone at GCE 'O' level or equivalent[3]	6.2	8.0	7.1	8.5	10.4	9.4
15 years at 31 August						
GCE 'O' level or equivalent						
1 to 4 A to C awards[3]	16.2	17.4	16.8	23.8	27.5	25.6
1 or more D to E awards[4]	10.7	8.9	9.8	32.0	30.4	31.2
No GCE/SCE/CSE qualifications	43.9	44.1	44.0	14.3	11.3	12.9

NOTES: 1. Based on population aged 17 for 5 or more 'O' levels and above, and aged 15 for other qualification levels.
2. Including Scottish equivalent – SCE 'O' grade.
3. Equivalent to standard of a former pass and including CSE grade 1 passes.
4. Including CSE 2 to 5 grades

SOURCE: DES (1983a) p. iv

girls it was taken to include home economics and needlework. This particular division was found to occur in 19 per cent of the 365 mixed schools that were studied, while in 20 per cent of the schools such divisions operated but were not prescribed. Overall, differentiation occurred in 65 per cent of the schools in the sample (see table 2). Similar trends were also found in science where there were differences in the number and availability of science courses (DES, 1979, p.166). Furthermore, as table 3 illustrates, more boys than girls took physics courses, while more girls than boys took biology courses – a trend that has implications for examination entries at 16 and 18, entrance to undergraduate science courses and postgraduate courses in higher education. However, the DES survey revealed that while 70 per cent of girls in the fourth and fifth year of secondary school had an opportunity to study physics, only 17 per cent followed a course in the subject. Such patterns demand the attention of sociologists, who need to raise questions about the reasons for these trends (cf. Kelly, 1981a).

However, it is not only course enrolments that need to be studied, but also the pattern of entries in public examinations and the passes that are obtained. Table 4 shows the basic trends in the examination passes obtained by school leavers during the period 1970 to 1982. In interpreting this material, account needs to be taken of the fact that the school leaving age had been raised to 16 in 1972 (DES, 1972) which accounts, in part, for the increase in the percentage of pupils who stayed at school to obtain examination passes. The overall pattern in table 4 shows how girls perform better than boys at 'O' level or its equivalent, but how boys and girls do equally well in terms of obtaining one or more 'A' levels. However, the situation is such that according to data for England (DES, 1981a) more boys than girls attempt and pass three 'A' levels (9.7 per cent of boys compared with 7.4 per cent of girls) while girls were marginally more successful than boys in obtaining two 'A' levels and one 'A' level.

Such trends hold implications for the post-school destinations of male and female pupils. Table 5 outlines the basic trends for pupils in England. In particular, these data indicate that the vast majority of boys and girls do not proceed to any form of further or higher education. However, for those who do proceed to further and higher education it is boys who outnumber girls in degree courses and in higher education, while girls outnumber boys in teacher training and non-degree further education courses.

These patterns recur in universities (cf. Rendel, 1980; Spender, 1981), which have until relatively recently been bastions of the male sex. Indeed, Spender (1981) argues that power in universities is held by men – a situation that is confirmed by statistical evidence which shows that in 1981 women held 2.3 per cent of professorial posts, were 6.4 per cent of readers and senior lecturers and 14.5 per cent of the lecturers (for further discussion see Szreter, 1983). However, this position is hardly surprising

TABLE 5: *Intended destination of school leavers: by sex, 1982–83*

England and Wales — Percentages and thousands

	Boys	*Girls*	*Total*
Leavers intending to enter full-time further or higher education as a percentage of all school leavers-by type of course.			
Degree	8.5	6.6	7.6
Teacher training	0.1	0.7	0.4
HND/HNC	0.4	0.3	0.4
OND/ONC	0.2	0.1	0.1
BTEC	2.0	1.9	1.9
GCE 'A' level	3.3	3.6	3.4
GCE 'O' level	1.5	1.9	1.7
Catering	0.7	1.8	1.3
Nursing	—	1.8	0.9
Secretarial	—	4.3	2.1
Other full-time	6.4	8.9	7.6
Total leavers intending to enter full-time further or higher education			
(percentages)	23.2	31.8	27.4
(thousands)	95.9	126.5	222.4
Leavers available for employment[1]			
(percentages)	76.8	68.2	72.6
(thousands)	317.2	271.4	588.6
Total school leavers (=100%) (thousands)	413.1	397.9	811.1

NOTE: 1. Including leavers going into temporary employment pending entry into full-time further education or whose destination was not known.

SOURCE: Central Statistical Office (1985) p. 50

when we examine patterns of entry and the main trends in undergraduate and postgraduate study. While in the post-Robbins era (Robbins, 1963a) the numbers of students in universities have increased, the proportion of women has remained at about one third of the undergraduate population with some improvement in recent years (see table 6). However, there are sharper differences within subject groupings as women are found to be under-represented in science but over-represented in arts and modern languages at the undergraduate level. In turn, at the postgraduate level there is a further decline in the proportion of women, as, apart from education, there are less women than men and women are particularly absent from the sciences and from engineering (cf. Cockburn, 1985; EOC, 1983a). Accordingly, the pattern of educational differentiation that was revealed in the secondary school is mirrored with a vengeance in the distribution of women among subject groupings in higher education.

TABLE 6: *Full time UK domiciled undergraduate students analysed by sex 1978–79 to 1983–84*

	Thousands *1978–79*	*1982–83*	*1983–84*
Men	136.3	136.7	132.8
Women	82.6	96.0	94.5
Women as percentage of total	37.7	41.3	41.6

SOURCE: University Grants Committee (1984) derived from Table C, p. 6

But how might these patterns be explained? Sociologists who have conducted research on sexual inequalities have asked: Why do boys and girls who are in the same schools and classrooms come out with different experiences, interests, achievements and expectations? To address this question they have turned their attention to accounts of socialization and to differentiation in the school system which we shall briefly examine in turn.

Sex role socialization

Here, the search for explanations for the pattern of girls' educational achievement and underachievement consists of an analysis of the patterns of learning that take place in the home as well as the school. At this point, authors draw on psychological as well as sociological accounts (cf. Arnot, 1983; Ballantine, 1983) to examine the ways in which gender identities and roles are acquired. Arnot (1983), for example, provides an assessment of three theories: the psychoanalytic theory of Freud, social learning theories and cognitive developmental theories. She emphasizes that there is no evidence to suggest that any one theory provides the answer, for, as Alison Kelly (1981b) argues, there is evidence to suggest that 'reinforcement, observation and cognitive processes all play a part in children's acquisition of sex roles' (p.75). As a consequence, it is important to consider the implications of each of these different theories. Within the psychoanalytic theories of Freud there is a tendency to see the acquisition of gender having different consequences for men and women with the result that women are placed in a subordinate position. Nancy

TABLE 7: *Subjects studied by Undergraduates & Postgraduates in UK universities in 1983–84 analysed by domicile and sex*

Subject Group	UNDERGRADUATES % of Total who were:				POSTGRADUATES % of Total who were:			
	Total (000's)	*Home Men*	*Home Women*	*Over-seas*	*Total (000's)*	*Home Men*	*Home Women*	*Over-seas*
Education	3.7	27	61	12	8.1	38	45	16
Medicine, Dentistry & Health	28.1	51	44	5	3.6	35	27	38
Engineering & Technology	35.4	77	8	15	6.9	43	6	52
Agriculture, Forestry, Veterinary Science	4.9	60	38	2	1.1	28	16	57
Biological & Physical Sciences	58.4	64	31	5	11.0	56	17	28
Administrative, Business & Social Studies	57.2	51	42	7	10.4	34	24	42
Architecture & other professional and vocational studies	4.0	56	33	11	1.5	31	24	44
Languages, Literature & Area Studies	31.5	30	67	3	2.7	31	27	41
Arts, other than languages	21.0	44	50	6	2.1	45	25	31
All subjects	244.2	54	39	7	47.5	41	23	35

NOTE: The increase in education students at postgraduate level can be accounted for by the numbers taking a one year postgraduate teacher training course.

SOURCE: University Grants Committee (1984) derived from Table E, pp. 6–7

Chodorow (1978), for example, considers that mothering is crucial in this socialization process and, as a consequence, argues that mothers reproduce in their daughters the acceptance of mothering and in their sons the rejection of femininity. She argues that the way out of this situation is by collective child care and the change of the father role to a role which is interchangeable with mothering.

In contrast, social learning theory argues that gender images are transmitted through books, television programmes and children's toys. Of these three areas it is the sexism in books that has received most attention. In particular, Lobban (1975) has examined the extent to which reading schemes in the infant and junior school transmit sexist images through the characters used, the illustrations, the portraits of men and women and the use of stereotypes (for further discussion of this analysis and also its relationship to other areas of the primary school curriculum, see Chapter 9 in this volume). Meanwhile, in terms of children's toys, Delamont (1980) has provided an analysis of toy catalogues that illustrates how the girls' toys emphasize passive, domestic roles, while the boys' toys emphasize action, adventure and future careers (cf. Ballantine, 1983). In turn, the images presented through television and other materials put the emphasis on subordination and passivity, as McRobbie (1978) found in her analysis of the schoolgirl magazine *Jackie* where stories reinforce the idea of a girl being subordinate to a boy. As a consequence, Arnot (1983) suggests that parents need to campaign for the availability of non-sexist books, magazines and television programmes as well as extending the educational and occupational horizons of their children. Finally, Arnot considers theories of cognitive development which suggest that children construct their own gender classification. As a consequence, Arnot maintains that parents should promote forms of dual role typing. It is this strategy that has also been suggested by Kelly and her associates who argue that science should be given a feminine image and be seen as part of feminine behaviour (cf. Kelly, 1981a). Nevertheless, there are also major elements of the school system that have been used to explain differences in the achievement of boys and girls and it is to these that we now turn.

Differentiation in schooling

We have already noted that there are differences in the patterns of qualifications obtained and courses that are followed by males and females in school and in higher education. At this point it is important to recall that a number of factors need to be considered in relation to the schooling process, which include:

1. The distribution of male and female teachers in primary and secondary schools and the availability of senior women teachers as role models for girls (cf. Byrne, 1978) (a topic that is considered in Chapter 6).

2. The expectations that teachers have of boys and girls and the way in which this is transmitted in the process of interaction in schools and classrooms (cf. Delamont, 1980) (a topic which is considered in Chapter 7 on schools and in Chapter 8 on classrooms).
3. The content of the curriculum and the ways in which different images of the social world are successfully communicated through the school curriculum (cf. Wolpe, 1978) (a topic which is considered in Chapter 9).

Drawing on historical evidence, Delamont (1978a) suggests that the notion of class control can be used to account for the similarity of working class education for boys and girls in the nineteenth century. Meanwhile, Davin (1979) has argued that schools imposed the family form of the bourgeoisie with a male breadwinner, dependent wife and children – a view that influenced the pattern of girls' schooling (cf. Purvis, 1981a; 1981b). Indeed, Purvis has identified two models of femininity that were used in schools: 'the perfect wife and mother' among the middle classes and the 'good woman' among the working class. Such influences have been traced through the school curriculum in the nineteenth century by Dyhouse (1977) and in the twentieth century by Wolpe (1974) who makes detailed reference to reports published by the Norwood Committee in 1943, the Crowther Committee in 1959 and the Newsom Committee in 1963. In the case of these reports Wolpe (1974) illustrates how they included a set of assumptions about women and marriage with the result that they were able to perpetuate an educational system that does not open up new opportunities for most girls. In a similar vein, Miriam David (1985) has illustrated how courses on family life and parent education within the Youth Training Scheme and other post-school programmes emphasize education for motherhood. Such evidence from the nineteenth and twentieth centuries has therefore been used to illustrate the way in which education maintains patriarchal relationships in society.

One area that has been considered central to the study of women and education is the relationship between sex and social class (cf. Delamont, 1978b). This topic has been considered by King (1971) in discussing access to education. He argues that it is impossible to use 'conventional' theories to explain the sex gap that occurs in the access that male and female students have to 'O' Level, 'A' level and degree courses. As far as a sex-differential ability theory is concerned, he argues that this would propose that girls are less able than boys – a position that conflicts with the evidence. Similarly, he shows how this is the case if a sex-differential access theory or a sex-differential provision theory, or a sex-cultural discontinuity theory were to be advanced. Accordingly, he argues that what is required is a theory that explains not only class differences in education but also the educational experiences of middle class boys, middle class girls, working class boys and working class girls. On this basis, he advances a model that brings sex and social class together, which can be expressed in the typology shown in figure 1. Here, a distinction is made between the symbolic value of education where it is seen as a means of social status, and the functional value of education where it is seen as a means of entering an occupation. On the basis of this model, King argues that middle class boys place a high value on the symbolic and functional aspects of education, while middle class girls place a high value only on the status aspect of education. Similarly, the differences between working class boys and girls are explained in terms of the way in which the boys see the occupational worth of education, while the girls do not see its worth either in terms of occupation or status.

Figure 1: King's model of sex and social class

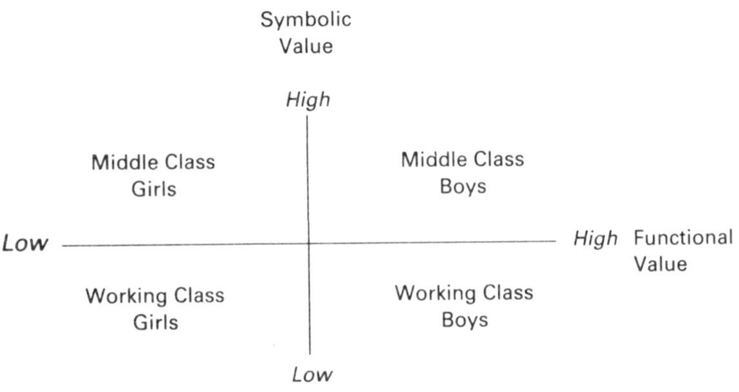

SOURCE: King (1971) p. 173

As Delamont (1980) remarks, this model maps patterns of inequality and raises several sociological questions:

1. How does education confirm middle class status in women if it is not allied to career success?
2. Is it realistic to view the middle class as a united force with one dominant ideology, concerning the education of girls?
3. Why does education have no instrumental value for working class girls?
4. Are working class boys *actually* undifferentiated?

(Delamont, 1980, p. 48)

An alternative explanation to that of King is provided by Byrne (1978) who links class and gender together. Indeed, she suggests that

> there are five major indices of potential inequality which, where two or more are aggregated create a cumulative cycle of under-achievement which can only

be overcome by positive affirmative, interventionist programmes aimed at increasing resources, counteracting cultural and social banners, and adding to the skills and experience. (Byrne, 1978, p.20)

The factors that Byrne considers are: sex, lower social class, low intelligence, residence in regions with a history of underachievement and residence in rural areas. It is on this basis that she argues that working class girls from rural backgrounds in the north of England are quadruply disadvantaged. But we might ask: what about the influence of race? Mary Fuller (1984a) has suggested that race could be added as a further potential indicator of inequality, but she also points out that the empirical evidence from Epstein (1973) in the USA and from her own work (Fuller, 1980, 1983) in Britain highlights how the double subordination of pupils who were female and black is related to their greater desire for higher educational and occupational attainment than black men or white women. Similarly, she also shows how we have relatively little knowledge of the interrelationship between gender and race, as much of the literature focuses on boys rather than girls. Such themes suggest that work on race and education follows some of the dominant trends in the sociology of education. Accordingly, we now turn to a review of the literature, focusing once more on patterns of achievement and underachievement, as it is important to understand how sociologists have examined differentiation by race in education.

Patterns and processes of racial differentiation in education

There is now a voluminous literature on race and education which has recently been well summarized in a wide ranging review by Tomlinson (1983). Her analysis suggests that work concerning race and education has been conducted in all the central areas that have been identified within the sociology of education. As a consequence, a major theme concerns itself with achievement and underachievement.

As with discussions of gender, terminology is important as writers have attempted to distinguish between 'race' and 'ethnicity' (cf. Bulmer, 1986; Cohen and Manion, 1983; Moore, 1986). As Bulmer (1986) indicates, 'race' and 'ethnicity' are among the most difficult concepts for a researcher to define. He suggests that both concepts can be defined with reference to the meanings that they have for members of a particular society. The result is that the definitions adopted are a product of the societies in which they are used. However, this holds implications for empirical studies as Bulmer (1986) demonstrates the lack of consistency in the way in which these terms are used in research reports. Nevertheless, there has been some consistency in educational studies devoted to underachievement in terms of race, as much of the British material has been concerned with West Indian pupils compared with pupils of Asian origin and with members of the indigenous population.

Much of the available evidence focuses on the concept of underachievement, but as Troyna (1984) has recently shown there are a number of conceptual and methodological flaws in the data that are available. First, there is the question of what we understand by 'underachievement'. Robert Jeffcoate (1982) maintains that underachievement among working class children refers to situations where

> the *mean* attainment of working class children is below what would have been predicted on the standardized tests of ability or aptitude, or that the *mean* attainment of working class children is below the *mean* attainment of middle class children. (Jeffcoate, 1982, p.15, emphasis in original)

He argues that the second meaning (where it is assumed that the same distribution of aptitude and ability occurs in both groups and where comparison is made between groups) is used to demonstrate black underachievement. However, Troyna (1984) maintains that such comparisons between groups cannot be sensitive to the qualitative difference in the relationship that black and white pupils have to schooling. Indeed, Troyna also suggests that, when interpreting research on black underachievement, special note should be taken of the period when the research was conducted, as work reporting on situations in the 1960s cannot automatically be generalized to the 1980s. Furthermore, note should be taken of the size of the samples that have been used, as much of the evidence is based on samples of less than 600 pupils (cf. Tomlinson, 1983 especially pp.27–59). In turn, as with research on gender, there is very little evidence available that examines social class in relation to ethnic origin (although this has been done by Craft and Craft, 1983 and will be reviewed below). The evidence that is available on underachievement among black pupils therefore requires careful interpretation.

TABLE 8: *Percentage of immigrant pupils fully educated in the United Kingdom placed in the upper band on transfer to secondary school in the Inner London Education Authority*

	Verbal Reasoning	*English*	*Mathematics*
1966	12	13	14
1968	10	12	12
1971	13	12	12

SOURCE: Little (1981) p. 136

Despite all these criticisms and reservations about the data that are available, it is important to examine the main trends in the educational performance of ethnic minority pupils (especially black pupils) compared with white indigenous pupils in both primary and secondary schools and in turn their access to higher education. Much of the evidence on primary education comes from surveys conducted by Alan Little and his associates in the Inner London Education Authority in the 1960s (cf. Little, 1975, 1978, 1981; Little and Mabey, 1972), although more recent data have been reported in Mabey (1981). These studies compared the performance of white and black children at the end of their primary schooling. Little found that the children of new commonwealth immigrants had a reading age one year below the national norm for their age group. In addition, Little's investigations also examined the percentage of 'immigrant' pupils fully educated in the United Kingdom who were placed in the upper quartile of pupils who transferred to secondary schools in 1966, 1978 and 1971 (see table 8). Here, he found that the percentage of immigrant pupils in the upper quartile was half of what should be expected, and half what indigenous pupils achieve. Furthermore, of those that had been fully educated in the United Kingdom, Asians did as well as the indigenous white population (see table 9).

TABLE 9: *Percentage of pupils fully educated in the United Kingdom placed in the upper band on transfer to ILEA secondary schools in 1968*

	English	*Mathematics*	*Verbal Reasoning*
West Indian origin	9.2	7.4	7.2
Asian origin	19.3	20.2	21.1
Indigenous	25.0	22.9	19.8

SOURCE: Little (1981) p. 137

A further survey by Christine Mabey, again working in Inner London, followed pupils who were monitored at the age of eight (in October 1968), when they were eleven (in June 1971), at the age of thirteen in autumn 1973 and at the age of fifteen in January 1976. This survey was concerned with literacy and had several characteristics. First, it was concerned mainly with reading skills, but at the age of eleven verbal reasoning, English and mathematics scores were also collected. Secondly, the children selected for this study were all those born between September 1959 and September 1960. Originally, this included a group of over 30,000 pupils, although subsequently pupils were lost through school leaving, non-attendance at school and the non-co-operation of schools they attended. On the basis of the survey evidence it was found that the reading attainment of black British pupils was very low compared with other groups. The reading scores are summarized in table 10.

TABLE 10: *Mean reading scores at eight, ten and fifteen years by ethnic group*

Age in Years	*UK*	*Eire*	*WI*	*IND*	*PAK*	*GC*	*TC*	*O*
8	98.1	94.8	88.1	89.6	91.1	87.3	85.4	93.2
10	98.3	97.9	87.4	89.6	93.1	87.8	85.0	93.9
15	97.8	96.6	85.9	91.4	94.9	87.6	84.9	95.4
N	12,530	229	1,465	137	74	194	139	502

NOTE: UK=United Kingdom; WI=West Indies; IND=India; PAK=Pakistan; GC=Cyprus, Greek speaking; TC=Cyprus, Turkish speaking; O=All other immigrants.
SOURCE: Mabey (1981) p. 85

In particular, it was found that black British attainment was lower at the age of eight and by the time of leaving was relatively lower still compared with white children. Furthermore, Mabey found that black British attainment was only marginally affected by the length of education that pupils had received in Britain. In addition, social deprivation together with restricted education and attendance at an Educational Priority Area school accounted for about half the difference of the scores of the white and black British pupils.

At the secondary school level there has also been a range of evidence available concerning the achievement of Asian and West Indian pupils in public examinations compared with the indigenous white population (for a review of small-scale studies see Tomlinson (1983)). However, the most wide ranging British survey was conducted in 1978/79 and discussed in the Rampton report (1981). This survey attempted to establish the extent of West Indian pupils' academic underachievement by collecting data on the ethnic origin of school leavers in six local education authorities that included approximately half the school leavers from ethnic minorities in England. It had been hoped that this study could be replicated for the Swann Committee in 1981/82. However, the Swann report (1985a) indicates that only five local authorities agreed to participate in the second study. Accordingly, all the data presented in the Swann report that compares 1978/79 and 1981/82 concentrates on five LEAs. Indeed, the original material presented in the Rampton report has

TABLE 11: *'O' level and CSE achievements*

	Asians		*West Indians*		*All other leavers*		*Total school leavers from 5 LEAs*		*All maintained school leavers in England*	
	1978/79	*1981/82*	*1978/79*	*1981/82*	*1978/79*	*1981/82*	*1978/79*	*1981/82*	*1978/79*	*1981/82*
	%	%	%	%	%	%	%	%	%	%
No Graded Results (including those who attempted no examinations)	20	19	17	19	22	19	21	19	14	11
At least 1 Graded Result but less than 5 Higher Graded Results	63	64	80	75	62	62	64	63	66	66
5 or more Higher Graded Results	17	17	3	6	16	19	15	18	21	23
Total Leavers (number)	466	571	718	653	5,012	4,718	6,196	5,942	693,840	706,690

SOURCE: Swann (1985a) p. 114

been carefully reworked on to the five LEA basis so that comparability is possible.

The evidence with respect to 'O' level and CSE achievements is summarized in table 11, while 'A' level achievements are shown in table 12 and the progress of pupils into further and higher education is shown in table 13. The main trend at 'O' level and CSE was that 6 per cent of West Indians obtained five or more higher graded results compared with 17 per cent of Asians and 19 per cent of all other leavers. However, it was also found that there was some statistically significant improvement in the performance of the West Indian leavers obtaining five or more higher graded results in 1981/82 compared with 1978/79. In turn at 'O' level and CSE it was found that 15 per cent of West Indians obtained higher grades in English Language compared with 21 per cent of Asians and 29 per cent of other leavers, while in mathematics 8 per cent of West Indians obtained higher grades compared with 21 per cent of Asians and 21 per cent of other leavers. These results showed a statistically significant improvement from 9 per cent to 15 per cent for West Indians in English Language and from 5 per cent to 8 per cent in mathematics between the survey conducted for the Rampton Committee in 1978/79 and the survey in 1981/82.

At Advanced level the main trends are shown in table 12. This table shows that at 'A' level 5 per cent of West Indians gained one or more passes compared with 13 per cent of Asians and 13 per cent of all other leavers. In turn the percentage of West Indians obtaining one 'A' level has increased from 2 per cent in 1978/79 to 5 per cent in 1981/82 – a figure that represents a statistically significant improvement. Accordingly, the Swann Committee indicates that they are encouraged by the narrowing of the gap in performance between these groups (cf. Fogelman, 1983; Tomlinson, 1983) but they point out that there is no cause for complacency.

This becomes evident when we turn to an analysis of the West Indian pupils who proceed to university and to degree courses. The Swann Committee report that 1 per cent of West Indians compared with 4 per cent of Asians and 4 per cent of other leavers went to university and that only 1 per cent of West Indians went on to a full time degree course compared with 5 per cent of Asians and 5 per cent of other leavers, as shown in table 13. The main trends in table 13 indicate that the numbers of West Indians who were to enter degree courses were low compared with all other leavers. However, these trends, like those reported by the Rampton Committee, still do not take account of social class (cf. Reeves and Chevannes, 1981), although a recent study by Craft and Craft (1983) conducted in an Outer London Borough showed that, *irrespective of social class*, West Indian children are under represented among high achievers. The main trends found among fifth form pupils according to ethnic origin and social class are shown in table 14. A further dimension to this

TABLE 12: *'A' level achievements*

	Asians		*West Indians*		*All other leavers*		*Total school leavers from 5 LEAs*		*All maintained school leavers in England*	
	1978/79	*1981/82*	*1978/79*	*1981/82*	*1978/79*	*1981/82*	*1978/79*	*1981/82*	*1978/79*	*1981/82*
	%	%	%	%	%	%	%	%	%	%
No 'A' level Pass	88	87	98	95	88	87	90	88	87	86
At least 1 'A' level pass	12	13	2	5	12	13	10	12	13	14
Total Leavers (number)	466	571	718	653	5,012	4,718	6,196	5,942	693,840	706,690

SOURCE: Swann (1985a) p. 116

TABLE 13: *Further education courses (full-time)*

	Asians		*West Indians*		*All other leavers*		*Total school leavers from 5 LEAs*		*All maintained school leavers in England*	
	1978/79	*1981/82*	*1978/79*	*1981/82*	*1978/79*	*1981/82*	*1978/79*	*1981/82*	*1978/79*	*1981/82*
	%	%	%	%	%	%	%	%	%	%
Degree	5	5	—	1	4	5	4	5	6	6
'A' level	5	8	1	2	1	2	1	3	2	3
Any other course	11	21	15	24	7	10	8	13	11	17
No course (including unknown destination)	80	67	83	72	88	83	87	80	81	74
Total Leavers (number)	466	571	718	653	5,012	4,718	6,196	5,942	693,840	706,690

SOURCE: Swann (1985a) p. 113

TABLE 14: *Fifth form examination performance by ethnicity and social class*

Examination Performance	*White* (%)		*Asian* (%)		*West Indian* (%)		*Other* (%)		*All* (%)		*Totals* (%)
	MC	*WC*	*MC*	*WC*	*MC*	*WC*	*MC*	*WC*	*MC*	*WC*[1]	
High[2]	31	18	32	16	20	9	26	16	30	16	21
Medium	55	62	58	64	49	51	59	63	56	61	59
Low	14	20	10	21	31	41	16	21	14	23	20
Total (number)	445	786	165	359	31	176	114	155	761	1,476	2,237[3]

NOTES: 1. MC=Middle Class. WC=Working Class. These categories are based on OPCS classification.
2. High, Medium, Low. These categories are based on number of GCE 'O' level and/or CSE passes.
3. Excludes social class 'don't know' pupils.

SOURCE: Craft and Craft (1983) p. 14

evidence concerns gender but, as we have already noted, many studies illustrate how West Indian girls do better than West Indian boys. However, as Pilkington (1984) indicates, this evidence needs to be carefully interpreted as it suggests that West Indian pupils are performing on average at a lower level than their indigenous counterparts. Secondly, he argues that much of this evidence is based on small samples. In addition, many of the surveys have been conducted over different periods of time and hence the explanations are somewhat speculative (cf. Troyna, 1984). Accordingly, we now turn to some of the explanations that have been provided by researchers writing from a sociological perspective.

Intelligence

The debate about the role of the intelligence in educational performance has been well summarized by a number of writers but especially by Lee and Newby (1983). We shall therefore concentrate our attention on the debate as far as race is concerned. Much of the debate has focused around the work of the American psychologist Jensen (1969) who argued that the difference in intelligence test scores between blacks and whites could be accounted for because genetic factors are strongly involved in the average intelligence difference between races. In turn, Eysenck (1971) also supports this view arguing that genetic factors account for intellectual differences between various racial groups. As Mackintosh and Mascie-Taylor (1985) indicate, there are several questionable assumptions here. First, that intelligence can be measured by means of intelligence tests. Secondly, that an intelligence test score measures innate ability. Thirdly, that intelligence tests can provide a fair measure of the ability of working class children and those from ethnic groups. Indeed, these writers go on to argue that few conclusions can be drawn, as much of the material is based on preconception and prejudice rather than detailed evidence. The conclusions of these writers are similar to those of Squibb (1973) who highlighted the importance of critically examining the concept 'intelligence' as its definition has varied at different times, in different social locations and among different groups.

Much of the British evidence suggests that poor performances on intelligence tests, particularly among Asians, are due to the fact that they are relatively recent immigrants, while for West Indian pupils the difference between them and indigenous pupils is related to parental occupation, income, size of family and the material conditions to which they are exposed. However, Mackintosh and Mascie-Taylor do indicate that many of these factors are not unique to West Indians. Nevertheless, they do argue that it is the social and economic circumstances of the families that need to be examined. It is evidence such as this that turns us away from hereditary factors towards those that are environmental.

Home and family background

One of the most wide-ranging literature surveys in this area of study has been done by Tomlinson (1984) who indicates the importance of distinguishing between different ethnic groups. This point is also reinforced by Lashley (1981) who comments that even the term 'West Indian' may refer to a person from a variety of different backgrounds in 1000 miles of separate islands in the Caribbean. It is the range of different backgrounds, Tomlinson argues, that results in West Indian family structures being misunderstood in a situation that contributes to the misunderstanding of parent–child relations (cf. Cross, 1978). In turn, she argues that it is also important to understand the situations of Asians, Pakistani and Sikh Indian migrants who have a wide variety of cultural and religious backgrounds. However, we also need to look at the material conditions of family life among ethnic groups as it has a bearing upon the underachievement of pupils. For example, almost twenty years ago Rex and Moore (1967) in their study of Sparkbrook in Birmingham were able to show discrimination in terms of housing faced by Pakistani immigrants. It is this problem that was also identified in a survey conducted in the 1970s in another part of Birmingham, as Ratcliffe (1981) reports that ethnic minority groups still faced difficult housing problems. In turn, Smith (1977) together with many other researchers has shown how Asians face discrimination in terms of employment. As a consequence, ethnic minority groups are often found in lower paid employment and among the unemployed. It is the employment possibilities that are open to ethnic minorities which reinforces them into situations where only low housing stock is available to them. Furthermore, it also underlines how they are disadvantaged relative to the white population. Such evidence holds implications for the relationship between home circumstances and achievement (see also Chapter 4 in this volume). For example, Pilling, (1980) reviewing research on minority groups in the National Child Development Study, indicates that immigrants have relatively poor attainment but when compared with children of similar financial and material circumstances it is found that they do as well as non-immigrants. In addition, he also shows that the poor school performance which generally occurred among first generation immigrants was short term and language specific.

Language

As we saw in the previous chapter, the main contributor to this area of study is Basil Bernstein, whose ideas have been considered to apply to pupils who do not speak standard English. However, standard English involves a very narrow definition of the kind of language that is appropriate for school success. Furthermore, Labov (1972) has argued that the notion of linguistic deprivation is misleading as he maintains that non-standard English has a logical structure and contains complex ideas that may be presented in a style that is not immediately recognized. He illustrates several of these features in the following extract.

JL: What happens to you after you die? Do you know?
Larry: Yeah, I know.
JL: What?
Larry: After they put you in the ground, your body turns into – an' – bones an' shit.
JL: What happens to your spirit?
Larry: Your spirit – soon as you die, your spirit leaves you.
JL: And where does the spirit go?
Larry: Well, it all depends . . .
JL: On what?
Larry: You know, like some people say if you're good an' shit, your spirit goin't'heaven . . . 'n' if you bad, your spirit goin' to hell. Well, bullshit! Your spirit goin' to hell anyway, good or bad.
JL: Why?
Larry: Why? I'll tell you why. 'Cause, you see, doesn't nobody really know that it's a God, y'know, 'cause I mean I have seen black gods, pink gods, white gods, all color gods, and don't nobody know it's really a God. An' when they be sayin' if you good, you goin't'heaven, tha's bullshit, 'cause you ain't goin' to no heaven, 'cause it ain't no heaven for you to go to.

(Labov, 1972, pp.193–4)

Here, the speaker (Larry) uses non-standard Negro English which some commentators consider is unsuitable for educational purposes. However, Labov argues that the speech that is used in the passage illustrates the way in which a complex argument can be summarized in non-standard Negro English which includes a set of interdependent propositions. On this basis, he maintains that the language is different rather than deficient.

Non-standard English may include dialects such as creole. This dialect lacks formal properties and is regarded by some people as deficient as a medium of education. However, Edwards (1976) has argued that creole works according to regular rules; it is different, not deficient, as it has its own internal structure and coherence and can be used to express logical ideas and abstract thought, as can other languages. Indeed, Edwards (1979) shows how teachers may find such speech patterns unfamiliar, with the result that stereotypes of low ability and lack of potential may be associated with children who use this language. In turn, the children feel threatened and perform badly, thus reinforcing the teachers' ideas. On this basis, it is the attitudes of members of the school rather than the language itself that appears crucial in explanations of underachievement (cf. Stubbs, 1983).

Experiences of schooling

At the present time we have relatively little direct evidence of what happens when white teachers meet black pupils. Instead, we have a number of statements that researchers have taken from staff rooms and meetings that refer to pupils. In these settings West Indians are portrayed as slow, lacking in concentration, volatile, disruptive and riotous (cf. Rex and Tomlinson, 1979). However, the question that remains is whether these views are transferred to the classroom. Some researchers have used attitude scales in an attempt to address this question (cf. Brittan, 1976) but their results have to be treated with some caution. While the rating scales indicate that teachers see West Indians as 'lazy/passive/withdrawn' and 'boisterous/aggressive/disruptive', we need to consider whether pupils accept such teacher judgements, make fewer efforts and confirm the 'correctness' of these judgements. In these circumstances, ethnographic data are required to help us understand the meanings that are attached to interactions between teachers and pupils in multi-cultural classrooms. The only detailed study of the interactions between white teachers and black pupils is reported by Driver (1977, 1979), who worked in a West Midlands secondary school. Driver's data indicate that the teachers lacked cultural competence and insisted that pupils act according to the standards they stipulated – a situation that heightened conflict and added to the ethnic awareness of those involved. He also argues that these factors, together with external pressures, contributed to the relative lack of educational success among West Indians. It is research that is conducted in this way that Jeffcoate (1984) sees as a way forward as there is not a search for a 'guilty' party, but for an explanation of underachievement.

However, as we noted earlier, we cannot generalize from research on West Indian boys to all pupils. Certainly, the dangers of doing so are apparent when we review Fuller's work (1980, 1983, 1984b) on West Indian girls in a comprehensive school. She is able to demonstrate that the girls' achievement was not related to teachers' perceptions but rather to their own perceptions of race and gender. It would seem, therefore, that researchers need to conduct more detailed ethnographic studies in schools to see the ways in which gender and race relate to patterns of achievement.

Conclusion

At this point, we have come back to looking at the relationship between gender and race, but we also need to consider class and race and to ask the question: class, gender and race . . . (how) do they interrelate? Here we confront the central question of sociology concerning patterns of social inequality. Overall, the evidence in this chapter and in Chapter 4 points to disadvantage in education among subordinate groups. However, in common with many research studies the evidence has been reviewed separately, yet in reality individuals experience the interaction of class, gender and race as the product of their membership of different social groups. As Anthias and Yuval Davies (1983) indicate, researchers have yet to come to terms with bringing together evidence on the relationships between all these divisions. However, some researchers have started to explore the interrelationship between class and race and gender and race. A key question that is debated in the literature concerns whether black people form an underclass beneath the white working class (Rex and Tomlinson, 1979) or whether they are an underprivileged group within the working class. But how does gender fit alongside class and race? As we have seen, this area is underdeveloped in terms of evidence. Accordingly, it can be argued that the interrelationship between class, gender and race is one of the great unsolved mysteries, which sociologists need to examine both theoretically and empirically if they are to reach a satisfactory explanation of these variables – variables that have a marked influence on people's lives and their educational experiences.

Suggestions for further reading

There is now a voluminous literature on gender and education (for wider reference see Acker *et al*, 1984) and on race and education (see Megarry, Nisbet and Hoyle, 1981). Indeed, readers will find that reference is made to some of this material elsewhere in this volume (see, for example, the chapters on teachers, schools, classrooms and the curriculum). This list of suggested reading therefore focuses on material that relates to achievement and underachievement.

ON GENDER

Byrne, E. (1978) *Women and Education*, London, Tavistock provides an extensive commentary on the different phases of education with special reference to women.

Deem, R. (1980) (ed) *Schooling for Women's Work*, London, Routledge and Kegan Paul contains a series of papers that deal with various aspects of women's education. See especially the papers by Clarricoates (1980) on primary education, by Shaw (1980) on secondary education and by Rendel (1980) on higher education.

Deem, R. (1984) (ed) *Co-Education Reconsidered*, Milton Keynes, Open University Press provides fascinating insights into the co-education versus single sex debate.

Payne, I. (1980) 'A working class girl in a grammar school', in Spender, D. and Sarah, E. (eds) *Learning to Lose: Sexism and Education*, London, The Women's Press is an autobiographical account of one girl's schooling. It is one of the most fascinating articles available to sociologists of education and is strongly recommended. For comparative material on experiences in an independent school see Okely (1978).

Spender, D. (1981) 'Sex bias', in Warren-Piper, D. (ed) *Is Higher Education Fair?* Guildford, Society for Research in Higher Education provides a useful commentary that challenges sex bias in higher education. This is taken further in Acker and Warren-Piper (1983).

Empirical studies

McRobbie, A. (1978) 'Working Class Girls and the Culture of Femininity', in Centre for Contemporary Cultural Studies, *Women Take Issue*, London, Hutchinson includes a useful discussion of femininity.

Sharpe, S. (1976) *Just Like a Girl*, Harmondsworth, Penguin provides useful material on the education of girls.

Walden, R. and Walkerdine, V. (1982) *Girls and Mathematics*, Bedford Way Papers No. 8, London, University of London Institute of Education is a fascinating study of infant children and the mathematics curriculum.

ON RACE

Little, A. and Robbins, D. (1981) 'Race bias', in Warren-Piper, D. (ed) *Is Higher Education Fair?* Guildford, Society for Research into Higher Education provides a useful review of British and American material.

Tierney, J. (1983) (ed) *Race, Migration and Schooling*, New York, Holt, Rinehart and Winston contains a collection of papers that challenge many of the conventional myths associated with race as well as race and education.

Tomlinson, S. (1983) *Ethnic Minorities in British Schools*, London, Heinemann provides a review of articles written on race, education, achievement and underachievement.

Tomlinson, S. (1984) *Home and School in Multicultural Britain*, London, Batsford provides a useful review of recent research on home and school and ethnicity. This book is included in a series on multicultural education. See also Lynch (1981) and Edwards (1981).

Troyna, B. (1984) 'Fact or artefact? The "educational underachievement" of black pupils', *British Journal of Sociology of Education*, vol. 5, No. 2, pp.153–166 contains a challenge to conventional wisdom about differential performance among white, Asian and Afro-Caribbean pupils.

Empirical studies

Fuller, M. (1980) 'Black girls in a London comprehensive', in Deem, R. (ed) *Schooling for Women's Work*, London, Routledge and Kegan Paul provides one of the few ethnographic studies that brings together a discussion of gender and race. This evidence is extended in Fuller (1983) and for a commentary on the research see Fuller (1984b).

Rampton, A. (1981) *West Indian Pupils in Our Schools*, London, HMSO is an official report that includes data from one of the most comprehensive surveys on race and achievement in six local authorities in England.

Swann, M. (1985) *Education for All: The Report of the Committee of Inquiry into the Education of Children from Ethnic Minority Groups*, London, HMSO is an official report that contains much research evidence. There is a chapter on achievement and underachievement pp.58–183 that contains specialist research appendices. There are also specialist chapters on the education of the Chinese, Cypriots, Italians, Ukrainians, 'Liverpool blacks' and Vietnamese. This extensive report has been discussed in a brief guide (Swann, 1985b). For a critique see Troyna (1986).

6 Teachers and teaching

In a recent survey of the world of work, Richard Brown (1984b) has argued that asking individuals what they do is among the most illuminating questions that can be posed by a sociologist, as he indicates that a man or woman's work, or that they need not work or are unable to work, is 'indicative of so much else about their social situation and their likely life experience' (Brown, 1984b, p.129). Yet, despite the centrality of this question for the sociology of work and occupations it is relatively rare to find sociologists of education asking questions about the work experience of teachers. Indeed, there have been relatively few empirical studies of teachers and teaching as an occupation with the result that we know relatively little about the occupational culture of this group (cf. Woods, 1983).

It was over fifty years ago when Willard Waller (1932) raised questions concerning what teaching does to teachers and the determinants of this occupation. However, his questions remained unanswered as there was little work conducted on these issues in subsequent years. This situation has been accounted for by David Hargreaves (1980b) in terms of subsequent theoretical developments in sociology and the sociology of education that were concerned with role theory and the influence of symbolic interactionism. As a result of these developments he argues that research on teachers and teaching has predominantly focused on professionalism and the work of beginning teachers, although in recent years there has been some interest shown in teachers as workers and debates about proletarianization (Ozga, 1981). There have also been a number of empirical studies and commentaries based upon empirical evidence that have focused on teachers using historical data (cf. Bamford, 1967; Tropp, 1957), using demographic data (Burgess, 1984c; Byrne, 1978; Deem, 1978; Wainwright, 1984) and using evidence from field-based studies concerned with professional socialization in the early years of teaching (Lacey, 1977), new teaching posts in middle management (Burgess, 1983) and headship (Burgess, 1983, 1984g; Morgan, Hall and Mackay, 1983). In addition, there has also been a number of recent studies concerned with the impact of falling rolls, redeployment and equal opportunities legislation on teacher careers and teacher employment (Ball, 1984b; Equal Opportunities Commission, 1985; Sikes, 1984). There has also been some research conducted on teachers and teaching in higher education (cf. Startup, 1976, 1985; Szreter, 1983). However, the bulk of work has been done on school teachers. This chapter will, therefore, provide a commentary on some of the basic sociological questions that can be raised about school teachers and school teaching, especially by reference to data drawn from contemporary Britain.

Teaching has always been a diverse occupation covering a range of institutions: schools, colleges and universities, a variety of age ranges and numerous disciplines. The word 'teacher' can, therefore, refer to individuals in very different circumstances from the nursery school through to the university where different roles are performed. In turn, there are also numerous social differences in terms of age, sex, status, qualifications, payment and membership of unions or professional associations. Indeed, Lacey has remarked that teaching is divided

> by the expertise and understanding that the professionals bring to the classroom; it is divided by the status and function of the institutions in which they serve; it is divided by the training, professional and social origins of its members; and, of increasing importance, it is divided by the aims and purposes attached to that element they hold in common, their teaching (pedagogy). In addition, it is the only major profession that deals almost exclusively with children. The age specialisation of teachers (infants, sixth form, etc.) provides another set of divisions that are not related to major areas of concern outside teaching, for example in research or academic disciplines. Finally, it has a high proportion of women among its members. (Lacey, 1977, pp.31–2)

Many of these divisions do not just apply to contemporary teachers but are rooted in the social and historical context in which the occupation developed.

In the first half of the nineteenth century the teacher in the public schools had to be 'acceptable both to the parents and to the headmaster on academic and personal grounds, and his background was a matter of some importance' (Bamford, 1967, p.120). As a consequence, teachers in public schools were male graduates from Oxford or Cambridge who were often clergymen who had been to public schools themselves. Indeed, Bamford indicates that a significant number of lay appointments did not occur in Eton, Harrow and Rugby until the 1850s. Accordingly, public school masters were predominantly of middle class professional origin with high status that had been achieved through education and through their position in the Church. Meanwhile, in the state elementary school the position was very different. Tropp (1957) reports that with the decision to provide education for the poor in the early nineteenth century came questions about the supply of teachers. It was argued that in elementary schools 'the main need was for a supply of efficient, religious and humble teachers' (Tropp, 1957, p.8). In these schools, individuals were recruited through the pupil teacher system which provided the bulk of teachers in the nineteenth century. The Minutes of the Committee of Council for 1846 highlight the background and qualifications of pupil teachers as follows:

> Pupil Teachers – Qualifications of Candidates
>
> The following qualifications will be required from candidates for apprenticeship:
>
> They must be at least thirteen years of age, and must not be subject to any bodily infirmity likely to impair their usefulness as pupil teachers.
>
> In schools connected with the Church of England, the clergymen and managers, and, in other schools, the managers must certify that the moral character of the candidates and of their families justify an expectation that the instruction and training of the school will be seconded by their own efforts and by the example of their parents. If this cannot be certified of the family, the apprentice will be required to board in some approved household.
>
> Candidates will also be required –
>
> 1. To read with fluency, ease, and expression.
> 2. To write in a neat hand, with correct spelling and punctuation, a simple prose narrative slowly read to them.
> 3. To write from dictation sums in the first four rules of arithmetic, simple and compound; to work them correctly, and to know the tables of weights and measures.
> 4. To point out the parts of speech in a simple sentence.
> 5. To have an elementary knowledge of geography.
> 6. *In schools connected with the Church of England* they will be required to repeat the Catechism, and to show that they understand its meaning, and are acquainted with the outline of Scripture history. The parochial clergyman will assist in this part of the examination. *In other schools* the state of the religious knowledge will be certified by the managers.
> 7. To teach a junior class to the satisfaction of the Inspector.
> 8. Girls should also be able to sew neatly and to knit.
>
> (1846 Minutes quoted in Hyndman, 1978, p.162)

Such qualifications point to a stark contrast with teachers in the public schools. Indeed, the only education beyond the elementary school that was given to pupil teachers was to those who gained scholarships for a period of further education at a training college which awarded certificates to those candidates who completed the course. It was these certificated teachers who were regarded as the elite, as they had higher salaries than pupil teachers, and often held headships of elementary schools. However, the colleges could only admit 1600 individuals each year and there was a shortage of places for women. As a consequence, by the end of the nineteenth century many elementary school teachers were untrained. For example, in 1898 it was reported that 50.9 per cent of women teachers and 28.1 per cent of men teachers had no college training. In this respect, women suffered a lack of training places, and lack of qualifications meant a lower salary in an occupation where men were already paid at a higher rate than women – a situation that continued until 1955 when equal pay was phased in over seven instalments.

This brief examination of teachers in the nineteenth century is sufficient to highlight the sharp divide that existed in the occupation. However, such divisions have not easily been broken down in the twentieth century, although this century has witnessed the early abolition of the pupil-teacher system. In addition, there has been the establishment of Training Colleges (later to become Colleges of Education and subsequently Colleges of Higher Education) that were more closely integrated with the universities, and the replacement of Teachers' Certificates by Bachelor of Education degrees. Nevertheless, there is evidence which suggests that there are still distinctions between teachers depending on their qualifications and the schools within which they work (cf. Hargreaves, 1980b).

Many sociologists have turned to demographic data to examine the extent to which these divisions are represented in different sectors of the educational system. We turn, therefore, to examining the social characteristics of school teachers in contemporary society, drawing on statistical data from England and Wales and the United Kingdom.

The social characteristics of teachers

School teaching is often regarded as a female occupation – a situation that has resulted in some commentators arguing that this accounts for the low status accorded the contemporary teacher (for a critique see Acker, 1983). However, to overcome stereotypes and gross generalizations, we need to know something about the distribution of teachers, their qualifications and their salaries together with other basic social attributes such as whether they are full-time or part-time and their status.

TEACHER NUMBERS AND THEIR DISTRIBUTION

The evidence that women have entered teaching in large numbers is shown clearly in table 1 which provides details of the number of teachers in primary and secondary schools in England and Wales in 1983.

Yet despite the number of women teachers in primary and secondary schools, it is apparent that they are concentrated in the lower status positions in the schools. Men are proportionately more likely to hold positions such as headteacher than women. This becomes more apparent when we look at the sex balance in the primary and secondary sectors respectively.

TABLE 1: *Full-time teachers in maintained primary and secondary schools, grade of post by sex, 1983 (England and Wales)*

	Primary		*Secondary*	
	Men	*Women*	*Men*	*Women*
Headteachers	12,405	9,918	4,187	780
Deputy Head	7,460	11,529	5,460	2,317
2nd Masters/Mistresses	173	276	1,250	1,664
Senior Teachers	17	8	5,532	1,303
Scale 4	90	115	22,434	6,363
Scale 3	4,909	10,286	34,671	20,395
Scale 2	11,275	57,692	31,910	32,140
Scale 1	3,845	45,808	27,162	45,346
Total	40,174	135,632	132,606	110,308

SOURCE: Derived from Department of Education and Science (1983c) Table B129, pp. 24–27

Within the primary school sector in England and Wales women constituted 77 per cent of the teaching force but more men were headteachers in 1983 (see tables 2(a) and 2(b)). Indeed, only 44 per cent

TABLE 2 (a): *Distribution of Full-time Teachers in Maintained Primary Schools in England and Wales 1983*

	Men	*Women*	*Total*
Nursery	10	1,664	1,674
Infants	396	25,108	25,504
First Schools	2,425	17,467	14,892
Junior with Infants	20,108	57,236	77,344
First and Middle	1,187	3,433	4,620
Junior	12,216	22,975	35,191
Middle deemed Primary	3,271	5,999	9,270
Unattached & Visiting	561	1,750	2,311
Total	40,174	135,632	175,806

NOTE: Primary includes Nursery
SOURCE: Derived from Department of Education and Science (1983c) Table B129, pp. 24–25

TABLE 2 (b): *Sex Balance in Each Sector*

	Men %	*Women* %
Nursery	0.6	99.4
Infants	1.5	98.5
First Schools	12.2	87.8
Junior with Infants	26.0	74.0
First and Middle	25.7	74.3
Junior	34.7	65.3
Middle deemed Primary	35.3	64.7
Unattached & Visiting	24.3	75.7
Total	22.9	77.1

of the available primary school headships were held by women in England and Wales in 1983 and only 7.3 per cent of women primary teachers were heads. In contrast, men held 55 per cent of headships yet they only constituted 23 per cent of the primary school teaching force. Furthermore, 31 per cent of men in primary schools were headteachers. Indeed, despite the predominance of women in primary schools it is men who hold the most powerful positions and have a greater proportion of posts from scale 3 upwards relative to their numbers.

Similar patterns can be seen in the secondary school sector in England and Wales (see table 3(a) and 3(b)). The number of teachers employed in state secondary schools in England and Wales in 1983 was such that men were more likely to hold senior posts. As in the primary sector, men were proportionately more likely to hold senior posts. Yet while women constituted 45 per cent of the teaching force they held only 16 per cent of the headships and only 0.7 per cent of women teachers were heads. If we turn to statistical evidence on further education we find similar trends. In further education in England and Wales in 1983 women constituted only 22 per cent of the teachers (see table 4). In addition, women are underrepresented in senior posts. Further evidence of the under-representation of women in teaching posts is also the case in higher education (Burgess, 1984c; Startup, 1976; Szreter, 1983). Here, the majority of posts at each level are held by men who are also more likely to occupy senior posts – a situation that reflects patterns of student recruitment by sex in higher education (see Chapter 5 in this volume). But how have these trends been explained?

It is not only sociologists who have turned their attention to the

TABLE 3 (a): *Distribution of Full-time Teachers in Maintained Secondary Schools in England and Wales 1983*

	Men	*Women*	*Total*
Middle deemed Secondary	5,812	6,919	12,731
Secondary Modern	5,792	5,352	11,144
Secondary Grammar	3,971	3,000	6,971
Secondary Technical	265	222	487
Comprehensive	112,203	88,553	200,756
Other Secondary	1,134	743	1,877
Unattached & Visiting	2,665	4,403	7,068
Divided Service & Miscellaneous	764	1,116	1,880
Total	132,606	110,308	242,914

SOURCE: Derived from Department of Education and Science (1983c) Table B129, pp. 26–27

TABLE 3 (b): *Sex Balance in Each Sector*

	Men %	*Women %*
Middle deemed Secondary	45.7	54.3
Secondary Modern	52.0	48.0
Secondary Grammar	57.0	43.0
Secondary Technical	54.4	45.6
Comprehensive	55.9	44.1
Other Secondary	60.4	39.6
Unattached & Visiting	37.7	62.3
Divided Service & Miscellaneous	40.6	59.4
Total	54.6	45.4

presence of women in teaching. Teachers themselves have also commented on trends in employment and career profiles. In a central text on school headship (Peters, 1976), Alan Coulson (himself a primary head) argues that since women combine teaching with family life they are less committed and lack long term career ambitions. He also argues that women find the traditional authority patterns, where they are required to play much more submissive roles, acceptable (Coulson, 1976). Such explicit sexist remarks from an individual who selects teachers will contribute to a situation where women are not only underrepresented but

TABLE 4: *Full-time teachers in Maintained, Assisted and Grant Aided Establishments of Further Education[1] in England and Wales 1983*

Grade	*Men*	*Women*
Principals	624	29
Vice Principals[2]	632	62
Heads of Departments	3,122	332
Readers	87	4
Principal Lecturers	5,691	508
Senior Lecturers	22,123	3,899
Lecturers Grade 2	13,953	4,642
Lecturers Grade 1[3]	16,794	8,895
All Teachers	63,026	18,371

NOTES:
1. Includes former Colleges of Education.
2. Includes Vice Principals who were heads of departments.
3. Includes Lecturers 1A and 1B in Agricultural and Horticultural Establishments.

SOURCE: Derived from Department of Education and Science (1983c) Table B140, p. 35

also undervalued in high status positions in the primary school sector. Even the Plowden Committee (Central Advisory Council for Education, 1967) entitled one section of its report 'The Head Teacher and his Staff' (Central Advisory Council for Education, 1967, p.332). Such a title reflects the dominant image of the male headteacher – a situation that has been discussed in a project on the selection of secondary headteachers (the POST project). In this study Morgan, Hall and Mackay (1983) discuss the selection procedures adopted in relation to male and female candidates, and conclude:

> In the current procedures, where non-explicit, non-job-related factors dominate, women are bound to be relatively disadvantaged, even if they receive positive discrimination at the beginning of the appointment. Many more models of men headteachers are available to selectors as a basis for stereotypes. (Morgan, Hall and Mackay, 1983, p.77)

In a similar way, the formal investigation of selection procedures in a Coventry secondary school by the Equal Opportunities Commission (1983b) has revealed that when women do apply for senior posts the selection procedures favour men.

However, it is not only sexism by male heads and selection procedures that influence the distribution of women in senior positions in school. Traditionally it has been argued that the position that women hold in teaching is a reflection of the pattern of their careers and the age at

TABLE 5: *Full-time Teachers in Maintained Schools in England and Wales 1982–3: Wastage[1] by Graduate Status and Age*

Teachers' Age	*Male*	*% of Age Group*	*Female*	*% of Age Group*
Under 25	195	7.3	875	9.2
25–29	1,208	5.2	5,822	11.9
30–34	1,185	3.0	4,416	11.2
35–39	837	2.5	2,399	7.2
40–44	455	2.1	1,394	4.2
45–49	359	1.9	1,144	3.3
50–54	834	4.8	1,935	6.4
55–59	1,629	13.3	2,802	16.7
60 and over	2,426	36.9	2,278	41.6
Total	9,128	5.2	23,065	9.2

NOTE: 1. Wastage is defined as 'transfers to other sectors of education and other leavers'.
SOURCE: Derived from Department of Education and Science (1983c) Table B125, pp. 12–13

which they break their service after only a relatively short period of teaching (see table 5).

In the years between the ages of 25 and 34 a higher proportion of women than men appear to leave teaching. Some commentators suggest that this means that women are not available for promotion, but this overlooks the fact that almost 90 per cent of their contemporaries are still in schools. A further argument advanced by traditional commentators is that these patterns reflect the life cycle and child rearing patterns of women, but this still does not account for the position of those women in teaching who are single and those who are childless. Indeed, Rosemary Deem (1978) argues that if teaching 'does provide an occupation for women, which has good pay, career prospects and high status, it does so only in comparison with other jobs for women, which also reflect the existing sexual division of labour in society' (p.115). Men who become teachers have a greater chance of higher salaries than their female colleagues, as shown in table 6.

In terms of salaries, we find divisions not only between male and female teachers but also between graduates and non-graduates and between those who work in the primary and secondary sectors. However, there are numerous other divisions that exist between teachers based on their status, to which we now turn.

TABLE 6: *Average salary for Full-time Teachers in Maintained Schools in England and Wales 1983*

Type of School	*Qualification*	*Men*	*Women*
Primary	Graduate	£9,144	£7,912
Primary	Non-Graduate	£9,870	£8,476
Primary	All Teachers	£9,682	£8,375
Secondary	Graduate	£9,721	£8,363
Secondary	Non-Graduate	£9,362	£8,464
Secondary	All Teachers	£9,577	£8,411

SOURCE: Derived from Department of Education and Science (1983c) Table 130, pp. 28–29

TEACHER STATUS

The social origin of any occupational group reflects the status of that group and is a reflection of its status. Teachers are not easily grouped in terms of their class position, which is in part due to the diversity of the group (cf. Harris, 1982). We have already seen that teachers who were recruited to the elementary schools and to the independent schools in the nineteenth century were of different social origins. Of the few studies that are available on the social origin of teachers, a study by Floud and Scott (1961) that was carried out with a sample of teachers in England and Wales in 1955 confirms the general impressions of many commentators that teachers are recruited from all levels of the status hierarchy but are drawn predominantly from the lower middle and skilled working classes. As table 7 indicates, there were major differences found between teachers in different schools and between men and women. However, these data are taken from a study that was conducted at a time when equal pay had yet to take effect. Nevertheless, sociologists still tend to argue on the basis of this evidence that the broad trends shown here are also supported by smaller studies such as that which was conducted by Ginsburg, Meyenn and Miller (1980) among a sample of middle school teachers in the Midlands. However, these writers do argue that teachers occupy an ambiguous and contradictory position in terms of their economic position. Clearly this is an area in which further basic data are required.

However, the status of teachers does not merely depend on their social origin. Status may be attributed to teachers depending on whether they work full-time or part-time, in a primary or a secondary school, in an academic, non-academic or practical subject. For as Ball and Lacey (1980) have demonstrated in their studies of student teachers and departments in secondary schools, subject subcultures do influence the status of teachers. Indeed, pupils themselves make such distinctions

TABLE 7: *Social Origin of Teachers in Grant-earning Schools, England and Wales 1955*

(A) Men

Father's occupation when teacher left school	*Type of school*			
	Primary %	*Modern* %	*Maintained grammar* %	*Direct-grant grammar* %
Professional and administrative	6.0	7.5	12.5	19.8
Intermediate	48.3	45.9	55.1	61.9
Manual, Skilled	32.5	36.5	25.3	14.6
Manual, semi- and unskilled	13.2	10.1	7.1	4.0
All	100.0	100.0	100.0	100.0
(N)	1,251	1,178	1,209	544

(B) Women

Professional and administrative	8.8	11.4	17.8	30.4
Intermediate	52.2	54.8	63.1	57.4
Manual, skilled	29.6	28.1	16.4	10.4
Manual, semi- and unskilled	9.3	5.7	2.7	1.8
All	100.0	100.0	100.0	100.0
(N)	1,449	1,083	1,100	733

SOURCE: Floud and Scott (1961) p. 540

between teachers. For example, White with Brockington (1983) provides a consumer's view of education which highlights the distinctions pupils make between teachers of academic and practical subjects. Furthermore, pupils show an awareness of the distinctions between teachers on the basis of subjects taught and qualifications held, as illustrated by the following remark:

The games teachers were the worst. I think they had an inferiority complex because they had a diploma and not a degree and they were always trying tae prove themselves tae other teachers (Maureen McLaughlin, aged 18, Edinburgh). (White with Brockington, 1983, p.60)

Such distinctions between teachers based on subjects taught and qualifications held is also illustrated by Burgess (1984f) in his study of pupils on Newsom courses designed for the less willing and less able in a co-educational comprehensive school. Burgess was a part-time teacher in the school he was studying and reports the following conversation between himself and pupils in his Newsom classes which were designed for non-academic pupils:

> Terry: What subjects do you teach besides this (the Newsom course)? What qualifications do you have?
>
> R.B.: I'm qualified to teach sociology and geography.
>
> Terry: It's not important to have these qualifications to teach Newsom.

At this point the conversation was joined by another boy who remarked:

> Peter: What's the sense of teaching Newsom with these qualifications? You don't have to be clever to teach Newsom.
>
> (Burgess, 1984f, p.183)

In these extracts, pupils are not only making comments on the status of this non-academic course but also about the status of the teachers involved in it. As far as they were concerned, teachers did not require qualifications to teach the course. Furthermore, they went on to indicate that as far as they were concerned Newsom work was 'not proper teaching' compared with subject work in departments such as geography, English and mathematics where 'proper' teaching and learning occurred (Burgess, 1983, 1984f). It is this notion of 'proper' teaching that has also been discussed by Blackie (1977) and Measor (1984) who indicate that the subject areas in which teachers work together with their teaching style influences their status.

Such evidence points to pupils highlighting the role of the teacher – a discussion that has been contributed to by many sociologists including Goble and Porter (1977), Grace (1972), Hoyle (1969), Westwood (1967) and Wilson (1962). For some sociologists such as Coulson (1972) the concept 'role' is redundant in sociology and of limited use when applied to educational settings, as it provides a static view of social action which cannot capture the range of activities with which teachers are involved. Nevertheless, Robinson (1981a) argues that, despite the validity of these remarks, it is not appropriate to argue for the total abandonment of this concept in sociological studies of education given our limited understanding of teachers and teaching.

Of all the accounts of the role of the teacher the article by Wilson (1962) highlights the range of circumstances in which teachers work and examines the diffuseness associated with the teacher role. Unlike many occupations teachers do not have a definable expertise in an objective body of knowledge, with the result that it is difficult to know what limits can be placed on the job. Indeed, Wilson remarks:

> Because of the diffuse, affective character of the teaching role there is in contemporary society a most significant role conflict arising from the divergence of role-commitment and career orientation. (Wilson, 1962, p.29)

Such a statement serves to highlight how teachers are perceived in society and the ambiguity that surrounds the status of teachers and teaching. Indeed, there has in recent years been increasing specialization in the teacher's role with scale posts for management tasks and pastoral care as well as for specialist work in subject departments (cf. Burgess, 1983; Roy, 1983). As a consequence, many questions have been posed by sociologists about the task of teaching and about the extent to which teaching is a profession.

Teaching – is it a profession?

In the language of everyday life teaching is frequently referred to as a profession – a situation that teachers themselves have been quick to capitalize upon. Indeed, the Houghton Report (1974) on the remuneration of teachers indicated that teachers themselves have regularly attempted to claim professional status. Nevertheless, sociologists have come to question such statements and to ask – is teaching a profession?

Sociological studies of professions have a long history in the discipline dating back to the pre-war work of Carr-Saunders and Wilson (1933) who considered that a profession was an occupation that was based on specialized skill and training which allows the individual to provide skilled service or advice to others for a fee or a salary. The assumption behind such statements is that there is an ideal type profession which can be characterized by reference to particular traits. In turn, sociologists have also argued that a process approach can be developed towards professionalism and, finally, that professionalism can be seen as a form of occupational control.

The trait or attribute approach to the study of professions attempts to identify the distinguishing characteristics of a profession. Millerson (1964) has shown how no two theorists agree on the kinds of qualities associated with professional activity. Nevertheless, sociologists have identified the main attributes of a profession as:

1. A group that has a systematic body of theory which helps professionals to understand their own practice.
2. A group that has authority.
3. A group that exercises control over its members.
4. A group that has its own code of ethics which allows it to exercise control.

5. A group that involves a culture and a career.

Such attributes have been adopted and adapted by numerous sociologists in discussions about teaching. However, as Millerson (1964) has argued, the most commonly identified attributes are that a profession:

1. Adheres to a professional code of conduct.
2. Is internally organized.
3. Involves skill based on theoretical knowledge.

Many such lists might easily be identified by those in medicine and law but become open to debate as far as teachers and teaching is concerned. However, this approach is also highly dubious as it assumes that professionals are a homogeneous group with shared values, norms, roles and interests – a situation which, as we have seen from ethnographic evidence, is far from true in teaching.

A second approach to the study of professions was developed by the Chicago School of Sociology who examined the processes through which an occupation has to go if professional status is to be achieved. Once again the stages that have been identified are more readily applicable to medicine and law than to teaching. Nevertheless, Parry and Parry (1974) have used this approach in examining teachers in England and Wales. They begin by examining the teachers' registration movement in the late nineteenth and early twentieth centuries which was central to the struggle for professional status. Here, they reject a functionalist approach to professions and identify professionalism as an occupational strategy. However, in reflecting on teachers and teaching in contemporary society they argue that teacher militancy and teacher unionism are indicators that reflect the failure of teachers to achieve professional status (cf. the studies by Deem, 1976 and by Ginsburg, Meyenn and Miller, 1980).

A third approach to professionalism has been developed by Johnson (1972) who has examined professionalism as a means of occupational control. He begins by criticizing the functionalist and trait theories about professions before advancing an alternative view. He argues that professionalism can be redefined as:

> A peculiar type of occupational control rather than an expression of the inherent nature of particular occupations. A profession then is not an occupation but a means of controlling an occupation. Likewise, professionalisation is a historically specific process which some occupations have undergone at a particular time, rather than a process which certain occupations may always be expected to undergo because of their essential qualities. (Johnson, 1972, p.45)

In turn, Johnson presents a typology of forms of control:

collegiate control: an ideal type form of professionalism when the client is dependent on the practitioner who sells his skills for a fee

patronage: when the demand for occupational service comes from a small and powerful client group

mediative control: when the state intervenes between practitioner and client to define needs and the ways in which they can be met.

It is the third type of control that is most applicable to individuals such as teachers who are employed in the public sector within a bureaucratic organization. Here, the individual is exposed to administrative and professional control – a situation which results in conflicting loyalties to the organization and the client and where autonomy is severely reduced. In circumstances such as these, teaching can only be loosely regarded as a profession or semi-profession (Etzioni, 1969) as teachers work in complex organizations where they are under the control of others.

Some commentators have considered that professions where there is a high incidence of bureaucratic control with hierarchical authority and low autonomy are a consequence of the presence of women (cf. Simpson and Simpson, 1969). Some of these sexist stereotypes have been applied to teaching by several writers (cf. Leggatt, 1970). In particular, Acker (1983) shows how Leggatt (1970) argues that the bureaucratic nature of the work context is compatible with women's traditional characteristics: submissiveness, acceptance of authority, lack of ambition and nurturance (cf. Coulson, 1976). As a consequence, Acker (1983) argues that such studies provide a deficit model of women, a low regard for the intellectual qualities of teachers – especially women – and a persistent tendency to see women in family role terms. Overall, sociologists appear to be uncertain about the extent to which teachers do constitute a profession – a situation that teachers themselves appear to share, as work by Deem (1976) and by Ginsburg, Meyenn and Miller (1980) indicate that teachers had a very diverse set of views about what constitutes a profession. In particular Ginsburg, Meyenn and Miller (1980) highlight the ideological construction of teacher professionalism and trade unionism whereby professionalism was seen in terms of: performance of a task or service, mental rather than manual labour, appeals to reason, an orientation towards clients and individualism. Nevertheless, they do stress that there was much uncertainty about professionalism among their teachers – a situation that is commonly shared by others. For example, a recruiting poster for the NAS/UWT at the end of the 1970s indicated the ambivalence about the status of teaching in its statement 'Reach for true professional status with your feet on solid trade union ground'.

However, the terms 'profession' and 'professionalism' are also ideological concepts as they signify claims to certain kinds of status and suggest a particular form of 'service' orientation. Yet in recent years we have witnessed a situation whereby 'professionalism' has become a double-edged weapon, for as soon as teachers take industrial action they are accused by politicians and by members of the general public of being 'unprofessional'. In this sense they are hoist by their own ideology. Alongside industrial action we also find teachers coping with cuts in public expenditure and facing the effects of falling school rolls. It is these activities, together with the demands made upon teachers by the inspectorate and by central government (see for example the white paper *Teaching Quality* (DES, 1983b)), that expose the teachers to an employer/employee relationship. Indeed, Ozga (1981) rejects the idea of a mental-manual divide between workers and argues that teachers may be seen as members of the working class – an argument that she supports by reference to teacher proletarianization.

As Ozga (1981) indicates, the term proletarianization refers to:

> the process that results when the worker is deprived of the capacity to initiate and execute work. It is, essentially, the removal of any element of skill from the work. (Ozga, 1981, p.40)

This situation results in the erosion of autonomy, the breakdown of employer/employee relations, the decline of craft skills and an increase in management control. While this process has traditionally been discussed in relation to manual workers, it can now be applied to a number of white collar groups, including teachers. Teachers are now encouraged to be more flexible, are de-skilled through retraining and curriculum packaging (cf. Buswell, 1980) and are required to take on management skills which Ozga (1981) argues is analogous to the creation of foremen or supervisors and subdivides the workforce. It is changes such as these that signal important changes in teaching. In addition, there is now teacher redeployment, teacher unemployment and talk of the possibility of teacher redundancy. On this basis, sociologists such as Ozga and Lawn (1981) have criticized the use of the concept of professionalism that has been used to allocate teachers to the middle class. In turn, they argue that the limited use of professionalism has resulted in teachers being separated out from other workers. As a consequence, Ozga and Lawn maintain that teachers need to be perceived as workers who have used professionalism and had professionalism used against them. Much of this discussion is, as these writers indicate, highly speculative and, once again, further basic data are required if this analysis is to be advanced. Nevertheless, in recent years teachers *as well as* sociologists have become less preoccupied with professionalism and more concerned with their conditions of work and with the notion of teaching as a career.

Teaching as a career

Among the members of some occupational groups, reference is often made to the stages involved in a career. Indeed, Purvis (1973) has argued that 'any fully fledged profession offers its practitioners the prospect of a professional career since the latter is an integral part of the term "profession". However, she suggests that teachers do not have a professional career due to the semi-professional nature of the occupation, structural variables such as the flat career structure, the scale of remuneration and the authority structure of schools as well as the attitudes of teachers and of members of the general public towards teachers. Nevertheless, teachers' careers have been the subject of sociological investigation by researchers who have been less concerned with the term 'profession' and more preoccupied with the term 'career', especially when working from the perspective of symbolic interactionism. The main interest has been directed towards the process of becoming a teacher, that is of how the individual acquires the identity of a teacher. The key concept that has been used is 'socialization' and 'secondary socialization' which is concerned with the internalization of institutional norms and values. In turn researchers such as Becker (1964) and Geer (1966) have been concerned with the way in which secondary socialization involves the establishment of an identity and a commitment to teaching. But, we might ask: how are these processes established among teachers?

BECOMING A TEACHER

In Britain this question has been addressed through Lacey's study of the socialization of teachers on initial teacher education courses (1977). The starting point of Lacey's study was the view that in our accounts of teachers we have little understanding of the process of induction into teaching. In particular, he was concerned with the following questions:

> What does this process mean for individuals? How do they perceive it? What does it feel like to go through it? . . . What can an individual or group do to obtain some control over certain features of the process? (Lacey, 1977, p.56)

In order to address these questions, Lacey conducted a case study of student-teacher socialization among students on the postgraduate certificate of education course at the University of Sussex. He argues that when students begin their course they have already identified with and internalized a view of their subject. The consequence is that there is a strong subject sub-culture which influences the subject teacher perspective of the students. Lacey summarizes these influences when he states:

> The effect is to equip him (the teacher) with a knowledge of special meanings (language), special preoccupations (view of the world), analytical and conceptual frameworks and ways of posing questions and directions in which to look for answers (a methodology). (Lacey, 1977, p.75)

Lacey, therefore, argues that the subject discipline provides intending teachers with a range of social strategies to negotiate their way through their initial training and into teaching.

In addition, Lacey also examines the process of becoming a teacher, which he maintains passes through four phases:

1. *The honeymoon period* which is characterized by a period of euphoria and heightened awareness when students were excited by the practical work in which they were engaged in classrooms, were adjusting to the idea of being called 'Miss' or 'Sir' and were optimistic about overcoming future difficulties.

2. *The search for material and ways of teaching* when students have to prepare material for the classroom, deal with classroom control and work out ways of performing their roles. Here, the student teacher has to search for teaching materials in order to respond to classroom problems. However, this period is marked by failure and rejection which Lacey argues paves the way to the next phase which he calls 'crisis'.

3. *Crisis* occurs when students feel they are not in control of the situation, are failing to get through to pupils and failing to teach them. Here, the students wished to find some solution as their careers were perceived to be at stake. Lacey demonstrates that these problems are often displaced by blaming the system or the children or both – a process that is central to the final phase he identifies.

4. *Learning to get by (and failure)* is a phase when students discuss problems (collectivize them) with friends or are guarded about problems and do not speak about them (privatize them). Three strategies are used:
Strategic compliance whereby the student goes along with how things are managed but subscribes to a personal view;
Internalised adjustment where the student accepts the prevailing view;
Strategic redefinition where the student uses teaching strategies to challenge the existing view of the curriculum in the school. Change is brought about by enabling those with formal power to alter their interpretation of situations.

For many of the students that Lacey studied strategic compliance was the strategy most often involved in learning to get by. However, this model was used by Lacey to examine the way in which student teachers are socialized into teaching. But we need to consider what patterns apply to more established teachers. For example, Woods (1981) examines the strategic redefinition orientation of two teachers. Here he follows Hammersley (1977) in making a distinction between paradigmatic and pragmatic strategies; for, as Hammersley writes:

> By paradigm I mean views about how teaching ought to be, how it would be in ideal circumstances . . . The pragmatic component of teacher perspectives is concerned with what is or is not possible in given circumstances and with strategies and techniques for achieving goals. (Hammersley, 1977, p.38)

Woods (1981) identified two teachers (Tom in his early 50s, a head of art, and Dick in his 20s who taught social studies). Both these teachers were similar in their values and beliefs about teaching. However, Woods found that Dick embodied the paradigmatic orientation and Tom the pragmatic orientation. As far as Dick was concerned, ideals and principles were most important and there was little adjustment to the situation. In contrast, Tom, who took a pragmatic orientation to teaching, had privatized his problems, adapted to near-conformity in terms of career and acquired power within the framework of the school. However, Woods indicates that this teacher was involved in a degree of compromise. Here, the orientation involved opportunism, testing out of chances and taking up situations to further his aims. However, as Woods suggests, we need further studies of teacher socialization and teacher careers if this model is to be developed.

While Lacey's case study illuminates the fundamental processes involved in student teaching and becoming a teacher, it has been shown by Burgess (1983) to have some relevance for our understanding of the way in which established teachers take on new teaching tasks. Burgess argues that whenever teachers take up new posts where they are faced with new classes, colleagues, books, equipment and ideas they are placed in the role of novices and have to orientate themselves to new tasks. In discussing work within the Newsom Department at Bishop McGregor School, Burgess demonstrates how teachers had to learn how to teach in the department – a process that he identifies as becoming a Newsom teacher.

In McGregor School the Newsom Department was not concerned with a subject area as such and therefore the teachers had no clearly defined syllabus. Instead, they were required to construct their own syllabus which new teachers found had to be considerably modified in the light of their experiences with actual pupils. In order that Newsom teachers could handle crises and learn to get by, they had to redefine the aims and objectives of their abstract curricula and redefine the work norms that had been established for pupils. In these terms, Burgess (1983) demonstrates how established teachers who were new to Newsom work with the less willing and the less able had to learn new sets of norms and new teaching strategies if they were successfully to get by in the classroom. Accordingly, Burgess argues that Lacey's model is not directly applicable to all situations in which individuals become teachers but has to be modified depending on the task in which teachers are engaged. Indeed, becoming a teacher may well be different for men and women (cf. Acker, 1983), and for those who work in academic, non-academic and practical subjects. In addition, those teachers who take on managerial and administrative tasks as heads of departments, heads of house or year, deputy heads and heads, have to learn how to become managers in situations where new norms have to be acquired.

MIDDLE MANAGEMENT

Studies of secondary schools (Burgess, 1983; Lacey, 1970; Richardson, 1973) have shown how many teachers are engaged in middle management as heads of departments and heads of house and year. In his study of Hightown Grammar, Lacey (1970) considers those teachers who were socialized into careers as grammar school teachers. On joining the school young teachers were allocated to positions in the department structure.

and in the house system. The structure of these two systems were as follows:

Figure 1: Academic Organization of Hightown Grammar School

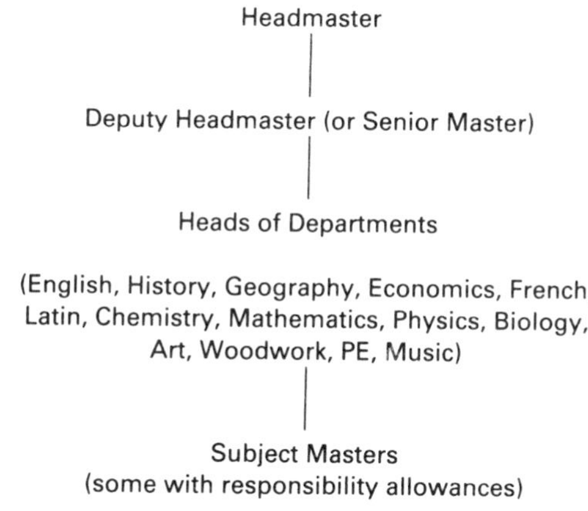

SOURCE: Lacey (1970) p. 159

Figure 2: Social or House Organization of Hightown Grammar School

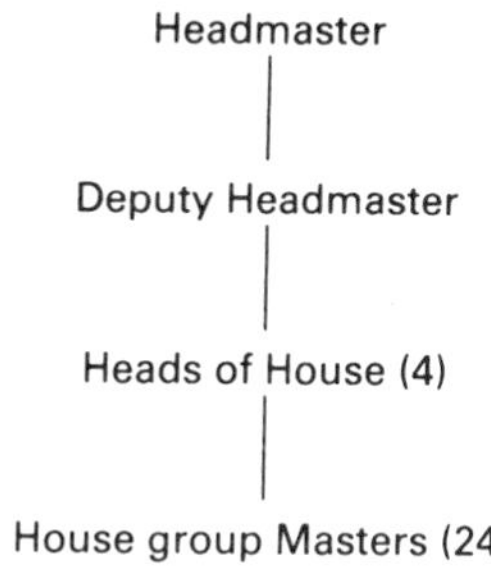

SOURCE: Lacey (1970) p. 159

At Hightown, housemasters were usually selected from those who were deputies in departments or heads of small departments. In return for taking on responsibilities, the teachers concerned were given responsibility allowances but also gained status and seniority in the school which influenced the kinds of teaching that they were given, for, as Lacey (1970) shows, heads of departments received more non-teaching time and more sixth form work than either their deputies or other members of their departments. Furthermore, they were not allocated bottom stream pupils or required to take games. Teachers within the school gradually took up responsibilities which increased their level of seniority, with a portfolio of duties which might include organizing school trips, editing the school magazine and taking other kinds of additional responsibility. This career structure and the process of establishment as a teacher was graphically described to Lacey by the deputy head of a department, in the following terms:

> This school is like a sandwich with a soft top, a soft bottom and a hard core or filling. On the top you've got the Head and Mr. Price wanting to be loved, Mr. Tonkins – he's all talk and Mr. Wright, a very nice man but too soft. (All the teachers mentioned here were in their fifties or sixties). You can't carry on like a benevolent, pipe-smoking Mr. Chips. He's much too soft, his Chemistry results are terrible. You've got to be prepared to drive them like Mr. Wood, thumping them through History. Wright has let many a boy down in this way. The hard filling contains people like Mr. Wood, Mr. Lawless, Mr. Werk, Mr. Stevens and myself (all, including himself, were in their thirties) and the soft bottom is made up of people like Mr. Cook, Mr. Harris and Mr. Robin, where all hell breaks loose in the classroom (these three teachers were all in their first or second year of teaching). (Lacey, 1970, p.167)

This view, we are told, accords with the views of other staff and charts the stages of a teacher's career: as a new teacher joining the 'soft bottom', as a teacher taking on extra responsibility, contemplating promotion and moving into the hard core. However, Lacey (1970) indicates that the new teacher was not socialized into a stable structure, as internal reorganization resulted in a new house system which meant that teachers had the opportunity to decide whether to put their energies and career opportunities into the department structure or the house system. Such a choice confronts many teachers in comprehensive schools where house and departmental systems co-exist. But how are teachers recruited to work in comprehensive schools and what work are they given?

In a school studied by Riseborough (1981) that involved a move from secondary modern to comprehensive, the former secondary modern staff found themselves displaced by subject centred staff who were exam-orientated. Two of the former secondary modern teachers perceived the situation in the following terms:

> I got angry about seeing these new people getting the plums we were considered not good enough for. All the teachers he [the head] appointed were youngish with bloody degrees (Age 39).
>
> The head's idea of a good teacher is everything I'm not. Just look at the ones he's appointed. That's what he thinks a good teacher is. The rating really is on academic qualifications and examination record. This man has a tremendous fear that he has to show results. From the beginning I realised the writing was on the wall. He'd looked up my record and saw someone who'd matriculated at

> sixteen, been emergency trained etc. He told me in an argument once that I was more a schoolteacher than master. He meant that I could cope with children much better that I teach, I suppose (Age 56). (Riseborough, 1981, p.359)

In these circumstances, the headteacher was a critical reality definer for the teachers' careers. The former secondary modern school teachers were stigmatized by the head, and lost all career prospects with the result that they opposed all that the head stood for or attempted to introduce. Overall, those who had worked in the tradition of the secondary modern school lost out to those who had worked in the grammar school tradition – having 'less good' career prospects and 'less good' classes to teach. However, this is not the only 'career map' (Lyons, 1981) that has been found among teachers working in comprehensive schools.

Figure 3: A Pattern of Formal Organization at Bishop McGregor School

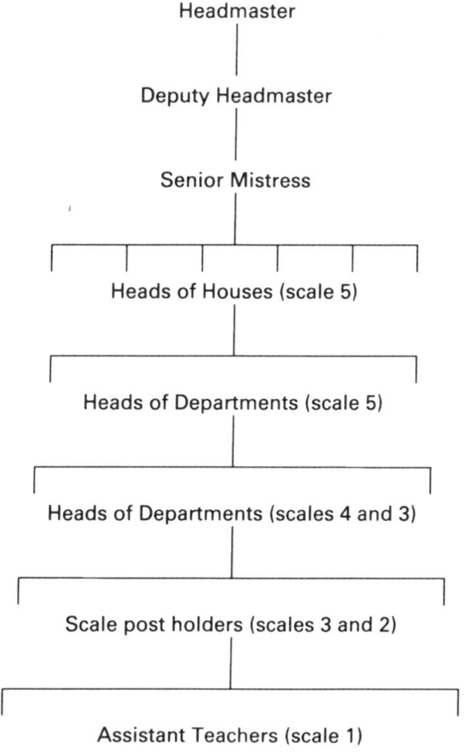

NOTE: This research was conducted in 1973–4 when scale posts were 1–5.
SOURCE: Burgess (1983) p. 56

In studying Bishop McGregor School, Burgess (1983) demonstrates how the internal organization of the school based on a house system influenced the structure of the staff, as shown in figure 3. This structure was based on salaries which teachers used to allocate their colleagues to positions in the staff hierarchy. Although there were more heads of departments than heads of houses, it was the latter who held most power in the school and were regarded as having higher status, despite the fact that three heads of departments were paid on the same salary scale. The heads of houses were seen as being responsible for discipline and good order in the school without which curriculum development work in departments could not successfully take place. House heads were responsible for groups of teachers and pupils that were similar in size to that of a small school. Furthermore, they were seen as being part of the senior management group in the school. As a consequence there was a sharp division between house heads and heads of departments within this school. In turn, it was from among house heads that teachers were recruited to be deputy heads and heads of other schools.

HEADSHIP

As we have seen in the previous section, the head of a school is seen to be at the pinnacle of the school hierarchy. Indeed, Banks (1976) has commented:

> Traditionally the headmaster or headmistress of an English school is expected to function as a leader rather than as part of an administrative bureaucracy. All the teaching methods and procedures, all matters relating to curricula, the relationships with parents and the control of teachers and their duties are recognised as matters for the head to decide and education committees will rarely try to interfere. (Banks, 1976, pp.134–5)

However, this model of headship evolved in an educational system with schools whose maximum size was 400 children (cf. Baron, 1955). Accordingly, some shift of role was demanded with the increased size of comprehensive schools (cf. Secondary Heads Association, 1983) for changes in school size carried implications for the role of the head in terms of interpreting, initiating and managing. In these circumstances, Burgess (1983, 1984g) has raised questions about the extent to which headteachers define and control their schools. Drawing on evidence from Bishop McGregor School, he argues that the head was the key reality definer who was a manager, co-ordinator, decision-maker, organizer and teacher (cf. Sharp and Green, 1975). On this basis some heads have suggested that they have the freedom to develop their schools in whatever directions they wish (cf. Boyson, 1974; Dawson, 1981). However, if heads are viewed in relation to the local education authorities for whom they work, local education officials, governors, unions, parents, pupils, teaching and non-teaching staff, we begin to see the constraints within which they operate. Critical case studies of Risinghill School in London (Berg, 1968), Summerhill School in Aberdeen (Mackenzie, 1977) and William Tyndale Junior School in London (Auld, 1976; Gretton and Jackson, 1976) are illustrative of the limited power of headteachers. In each case the heads of the schools concerned attempted to innovate but in the end were removed from their positions by the local education authorities. Furthermore, in the light of financial restrictions, falling rolls, teacher redeployment and the amalgamation of schools there may be even greater control over heads and in turn teachers and teacher careers (see for example the POST project on the appointment of heads, Morgan, Hall and Mackay, 1983).

Conclusion

Sociologists have only recently begun to conduct basic research on teachers, teaching and teacher careers. This chapter has attempted to examine some of the main issues and basic data that are available on teachers in the English school system. Clearly, there is much work to be done especially at a time when contraction and redeployment has followed on quickly from a period of rapid and extensive expansion. In a recent study, Sikes (1984) has indicated that teachers are dissatisfied as their careers are no longer meeting their expectations in terms of job security, working conditions, job satisfaction and status. She quotes teachers as saying that they were dissatisfied with teaching because of:

> – cuts in educational spending; promotion prospects; the inevitable wrangle each year over pay; the brain washing of the public by the media and politicians that many of the problems in society are due to problems in school (male, age 30, scale 2)
> – changing attitudes within society; a decline in parental support for schools (male, age 40, scale 4)
> – the difference in attitude and behaviour of the children (who are) far more likely to question discipline and who are more aware of what they consider to be their rights (female, age 35, scale 1)
> – change over to comprehensive education from selective (male, age 33, scale 1)
> – comprehensive reorganisation; mixed ability teaching; larger schools (male, age 40, scale 4). (Sikes, 1984, p.247)

Such a list clearly generates a number of issues and questions for sociologists to explore in empirical studies which could concern themselves with teacher status and employer-employee relations. Such studies will, hopefully, take us away from arid debates about 'professionalism' and 'professional careers' to the central question of what teaching does to teachers that Waller so clearly identified over fifty years ago.

Suggestions for further reading

Acker, S. (1983) 'Women and teaching: a semi-detached sociology of a semi-profession', in S. Walker and L. Barton (eds) *Gender, Class and Education*, Lewes, Falmer Press, pp.123–139 provides a critique of key issues and debates on women as teachers from a feminist perspective.

Blackstone, T. and Crispin, A. (1982) *How Many Teachers? Issues of Policy, Planning and Demography, Bedford Way Paper No. 10*, London, University of London Institute of Education examines the responsibilities and powers of central and local government concerning teacher supply.

Deem, R. (1978) *Women and Schooling*, London, Routledge and Kegan Paul contains a useful discussion of women and teaching.

Hannam, C. *et al* (1976) *The First Year of Teaching*, Harmondsworth, Penguin provides a useful set of comments from probationary teachers.

Hyndman, M. (1978) *Schools and Schooling in England and Wales*, London, Harper and Row contains an historical discussion on the training of teachers.

Ozga, J. and Lawn, M. (1981) *Teachers, Professionalism and Class: A Study of Organised Teachers*, Lewes, Falmer Press provides an analysis of professionalism and proletarianization in a historical context.

Wainwright, H. (1984) 'Women and the division of labour', in P. Abrams and R. Brown (eds) *U.K. Society: Work, Urbanism and Inequality*, London, Weidenfeld and Nicolson, pp.198–245 discusses women and education and provides useful statistical data on women teachers. For complementary material see Burgess (1984c) in the same volume.

Waller, W. (1932) *The Sociology of Teaching*, New York, Wiley (new edition published in 1967) contains a series of perceptive comments on the teacher role many of which still ring true.

Wilson, B. (1962) 'The teacher's role: a sociological analysis', *British Journal of Sociology*, vol. 13, no. 1, pp.15–32 is a major article that has provided a framework for subsequent discussions and studies. See for example Grace (1978).

Woods, P. (1983) *Sociology and the School: An Interactionist Viewpoint*, London, Routledge and Kegan Paul includes material on teacher culture and careers. See also some related papers in Hargreaves and Woods (1984) part three.

EMPIRICAL STUDIES

There are numerous small-scale studies and surveys of various groups of teachers. The following brief list includes studies that relate to key issues and debates in this field.

Ball, S. J. and Goodson, I. F. (1985) (eds) *Teacher Careers and Life Histories*, Lewes, Falmer Press contains a series of papers that provide detailed studies of teacher careers together with an analytic essay from the editors.

Burgess, R. G. (1983) *Experiencing Comprehensive Education: A Study of Bishop McGregor School*, London, Methuen. Part one of this ethnographic study looks at the head and teachers concerned with pastoral and academic work. Part two looks at the process of becoming a teacher of the less able.

Lacey, C. (1977) *The Socialization of Teachers*, London, Methuen contains a review of material on teachers together with empirical data on student teachers. The volume is based on case study material.

Lortie, D. (1975) *School-teacher: a sociological study*, Chicago, University of Chicago Press is a detailed ethnographic account of school teaching in the USA.

Partington, G. (1976) *Women Teachers in England and Wales*, Slough, NFER provides an account of the fight for equal pay.

Tropp, A. (1957) *The Schoolteachers*, London, Heinemann. The classic study of teachers from a socio-historical perspective. It is important to consider what Tropp's conclusions might be today in the light of recent developments in teacher unionism.

7 The social organization of schools

Although schools are institutions with which most people are familiar, it has taken some time for sociologists to ask questions about the ways in which they are organized, about the social processes of schooling and the effects of schools on the educational performance of pupils. For many years, sociologists of education were only interested in the input and output processes that were concerned with schools and schooling. As a consequence, the school as an institution was regarded as a 'black box' whose activities could be taken as 'given' in any analysis of the schooling process.

At the beginning of the 1970s there was relatively little material that could be described as a sociology of the school (cf. Shaw, 1969). However, we now find a massive change has taken place with numerous analyses examining different aspects of schools and schooling. There is now much research on elements of school organization, on teacher and pupil subcultures, the effects of schooling and the activities that occur in classrooms (cf. Hammersley and Woods, 1984; Hargreaves and Woods, 1984). Some of these topics are centrally examined in other chapters and therefore the focus of this discussion will be upon sociological analyses of school organization. In particular, two broad trends will be examined. First, the work of some sociologists who have considered the applicability of organizational theories to schools, and secondly, those who have studied certain facets of school organization (especially concerned with secondary schools) and posed sociological questions about them. Accordingly, the focus of this chapter will be upon the internal structure of schools.

Schools do not exist in a social and administrative vacuum, for the ways in which schools are established, organized and structured may vary with the time they are established (cf. Andrew, 1985; Gordon and Lawton, 1978 on school design in the nineteenth and twentieth centuries). Secondly, the structure of schools may also vary with the society in which they are located (cf. Stebbins, 1976 on the architecture of schools in the West Indies and their influence on social processes). Thirdly, school size may be different according to geographical location with large schools in urban areas (Grace, 1978) as opposed to small village schools in rural locations (Nash, 1980). In addition, state schools in England and Wales may vary with the local authority in whose area they are located. For example, grammar schools and comprehensive schools may co-exist within one local authority and differences may occur in the structure of comprehensive schools within and between authorities (cf. Fairbairn, 1971; Mason, 1957 on Leicestershire and Firth, 1963, 1977 on Coventry – for commentary on the UK see Burgess, 1984c).

It is, therefore, against this background that we might ask: what is a school? In attempting to respond to this question, sociologists have tended to generalize far too broadly with the result that numerous assumptions are made. In particular, little account has been taken of the differences between state schools and independent schools, between voluntary (church) schools and local authority schools and between primary and secondary schools. Furthermore, sociologists have also assumed that schools are client-serving organizations involving the socialization of the young. However, this overlooks patterns of teacher socialization (cf. Lacey, 1977 also reviewed in Chapter 6 in this volume) and the fact that schools and community colleges are as much concerned with adults as they are with children (cf. Fairbairn, 1979; Fletcher and Thompson, 1980; Poster, 1982). Finally, it is assumed that schools have as their major goal the organization of teaching and learning. However, this overlooks the diverse set of goals that can be associated with schools and which are well summarized by Corwin, who writes:

> . . . there is little consensus among the many constituents of schools on what their primary goals should be. Many social scientists, educators, parents, and politicians assume that scholastic achievement ('cognitive' outcomes) is the primary goal of schooling. They measure the effectiveness of schools by the readily available standardized achievement measures. Other writers, noting that the correlation between academic achievement in school and subsequent occupational success is far from perfect, insist that the outcomes of schooling must be measured by later occupational success. Still other writers see, as the primary objective of schools, their ability to influence the student's conception of himself, that is, to instill self-esteem and self-confidence and help him discover his talents. Others stress the need of schools to develop 'healthy' (usually meaning conservative) political attitudes, good 'citizenship', or to teach people constructive uses of leisure time. (Corwin, 1974, p.13)

It is, therefore, apparent that there are numerous goals and different sets of expectations that schools and their members are expected to attain. In this respect, we need to consider the different ways in which schools are organized to attain their objectives. Accordingly, we now turn to an examination of the sociology of organizations with a view to considering the extent to which different theories are applicable to the study of schools.

The sociology of organizations and the study of schools

There are now several extensive reviews of organizations that have been developed by industrial sociologists in the course of studying factories. However, there is not a single sociology of organizations but several different sociologies as different perspectives have been used in relation to organizations. It is this situation that King (1983) has identified in relation to the sociology of school organization where sociologists have used several different perspectives when studying the organization of schools. Among the perspectives that King identifies are functionalist, Marxist and symbolic interactionist theories as well as material derived from the work of psychologists and those engaged in the study of administration and business management (for a detailed review see King, 1983, pp.12–35). Following Hoyle (1965), King identifies a theory of approach – that is a method of examining schools and explaining the ways in which they are organized as opposed to other perspectives that provide prescriptions about how schools *should* be organized. As far as sociologists are concerned, the emphasis is upon the ways in which schools are organized, as it is relatively rare for researchers working from a sociological perspective to engage in prescriptive discussions. While there are many different approaches to the study of organizations, we shall focus on three models: bureaucracy, an open systems approach and the total institution. Each of these models will be examined in order to consider the main theoretical elements involved before considering the way in which researchers have attempted to apply a particular theory to the study of school organization.

THE SCHOOL AS A BUREAUCRACY

As Davies (1981b) has noted, within the organizational literature there has been a persistent interest among sociologists in establishing the extent to which schools and school systems are bureaucracies. The starting point of such work is Weber's writing on rational/legal authority where he outlines the major elements of a bureaucracy (cf. Gerth and Mills, 1948 and for commentary see Albrow, 1970; Collins, 1975). Within bureaucratic organizations Weber identified the following characteristics:

(a) An administrative hierarchy with a structure of command.

(b) Specialized training and a clear career structure.

(c) Areas of expertise with a division of labour among experts.

(d) Specific rules and procedures according to which the bureaucrat completes tasks.

(e) Formalized and impartial methods of dealing with clients.

However, the question that arises for sociologists of education is the extent to which such a model is applicable to schools.

Figure 1: Structure of Burns Road Infant School

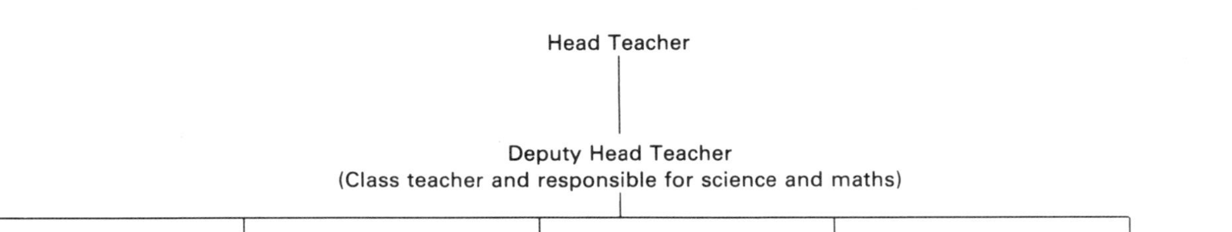

NOTE: Burns Road Infant School had 140 children on the roll aged 4–7 years.
SOURCE: Pollard (1985) p. 120

In recent years there have been several studies of primary schools which deal with the organization of staff (cf. Campbell, 1984, 1985) and the organization of staff and pupils (Pollard, 1985). Within Pollard's analysis of the primary school, he discusses several elements of school organization which he considers in relation to the characteristics that Weber identified in a bureaucracy.

All schools (including many free schools – see Swidler, 1979) have a hierarchy of positions and a formal structure of authority. As we saw in the previous chapter with regard to studies of secondary schools by Burgess (1983) and by Lacey (1970), the teaching staff are organized in a formal hierarchy. It is this kind of organization that Pollard identifies in a school he calls Burns Road Infant School where the staff structure is as shown in figure 1. In this school, Pollard identifies formal authority being vested in the head and deputy head but he points out that this was cut across by the fact that the deputy head was a class teacher responsible for special areas of the curriculum, as were three of the teachers who held scale posts with special responsibilities.

It is this element of primary school organization that has also been identified by Campbell (1984) in his discussion of curriculum postholders in middle schools. However, he argues that there is a degree of uncertainty, conflict and strain for individuals placed in such positions as the postholders that he studied experienced a wide range of demands (including co-ordination and class teaching responsibilities) and were required to initiate curriculum development under the constant scrutiny of peers. A major problem that Campbell identifies (and which is also apparent from Pollard's discussion) is that there is a mismatch of power and authority for curriculum postholders over curriculum matters, as they lack the power to initiate change on a school-wide basis, and, in turn, any attempt to influence curriculum matters in other classes might be perceived as an attack on the autonomy of class teachers. In this way, the evidence from the studies by Pollard and Campbell indicates that the idea of a clear hierarchy of formal authority in primary schools needs to be modified in the light of the actual situation that pertains in many schools.

As far as specialized training is concerned, it can be argued that primary school teachers are provided with specialist courses for the age range that they teach – a situation that is increasingly being demanded by central government in respect of teacher education (see especially *Teaching Quality* (DES, 1983b)). However, as Pollard indicates, much subsequent training will include 'on the job' learning and in-service education. Such a position gives rise to a clear career structure, but it is very short, as shown in Pollard's example of Burns Road Infant School where the staff pyramid is very flat with few status distinctions (cf. Purvis, 1973). It is this flat career structure, together with the general requirement that primary school teachers should be able to teach a range of subjects to all children, that also casts doubts on the idea of being able to identify clearly areas of expertise. Furthermore, there is little division of labour among experts (apart from exchanges between teachers working in highly specialized areas such as music and computer studies).

Further qualification can be entered about the use of fixed rules and procedures, for, as Pollard indicates, this does not take account of the autonomy that is traditionally granted to the classroom teacher. Furthermore, other researchers (Berlak and Berlak, 1981) have indicated that teachers in the primary school face a number of dilemmas in the course of their work concerning control and the curriculum, as well as societal dilemmas over the position of children. Finally, Pollard questions the extent to which Weber's final point on impartiality can be identified in primary schools where much of the work is based on a close relationship between teacher and taught. In addition, many schools attempt to establish close links with parents as well as pupils.

The evidence that has been produced by various researchers working in primary schools indicates that, while Weber's model highlights certain aspects of school structure, it does not provide a perfect match with the organization of a primary school, which is characterized by a degree of structural looseness – a feature that militates against rigid bureaucratization (cf. Bidwell, 1965; Goslin, 1965). Accordingly, Pollard develops an interactionist approach to school organization based on the concepts 'negotiation' and 'institutional bias' which, he argues, assists us to analyse dynamic developments of social understandings in a school as well as the power relationships involved. Yet it might be argued that such an analysis focuses on internal relationships in a school and fails to come to terms with the relationship between the school and the social and educational context in which it is located. Accordingly, some sociologists have utilized an open systems approach to school organization in an attempt to focus on the relationship between school and society.

AN 'OPEN' SYSTEMS APPROACH

A systems approach to the study of organizations has been discussed by Parsons (1968) as referring:

> both to a complex of interdependencies between parts, components and processes that involves discernible regularities of relationships, and to a similar type of interdependency between such a complex and its surrounding environment. (Parsons, 1968, p.458)

Such an approach raises the idea of the relationship between the various parts of an internal structure and the relationship of an organization to the society in which it is located (see figure 2).

At first glance the model referred to in figure 2 appears to have some merit when applied to schools. It can be argued that schools take in raw materials (pupils) and process them through classes (teaching and

Figure 2: A Systems Approach to Schools

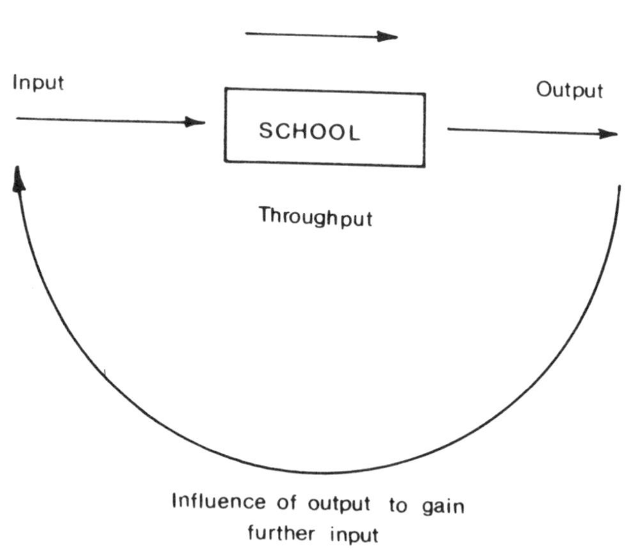

learning) with the result that an 'educational product' emerges at the age of 16 or later. However, in such circumstances it is essential for sociologists to raise questions about the 'processing' that occurs within schools and the extent to which the organizational structure and the content of the curriculum influences teaching and learning and the pupil product. Nevertheless, the advantage of this approach is that it does not merely examine the internal structure of the school, but demands that sociologists focus their investigations on the relationship between the school, the society and the educational system within which it is located. However, the question that once more confronts the sociologist is: to what extent is this model applicable to the study of schools? One writer who has used an open systems model in the course of her work is Elizabeth Richardson (1973, 1975) who engaged in a study of Nailsea School – a comprehensive school in Bristol.

Between 1968 and 1971 Richardson worked as a consultant to the staff of Nailsea School where it was her intention to study:

(i) the nature of authority and leadership in the school community;
(ii) the stresses under which teachers and pupils at different levels of the organizational structure have to work in carrying out their tasks;

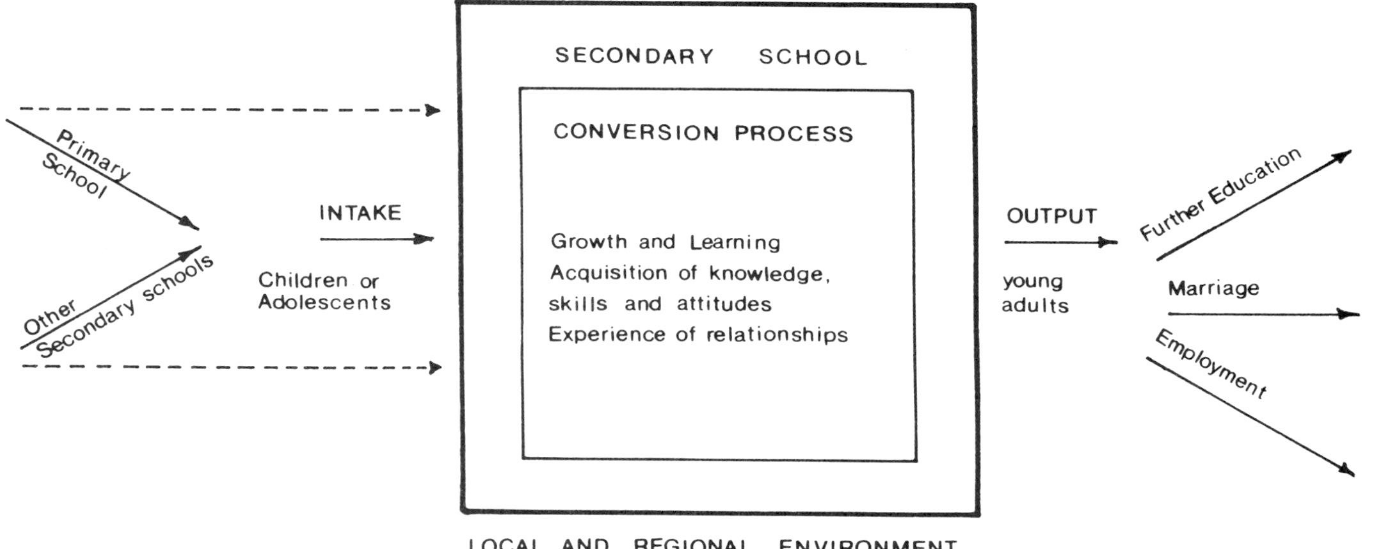

Figure 3: The Secondary School as an Open System

SOURCE: Richardson (1973), p. 18

> (iii) the roles taken, both consciously and unconsciously, by different individuals and groups in the school;
> (iv) the difficulties encountered in implementing change – for example in introducing new methods of teaching, in structuring or restructuring the curriculum, in reorganizing the system of management within the institution. (Richardson, 1975, p.131)

For the purposes of this study, Richardson (1973; 1975) perceived of the school in terms of an import-conversion-export model as shown in figure 3. However, Richardson indicates that there are several problems associated with this model. First, the school is not the child's only educational contact. Secondly, children, unlike raw materials in factories, cannot be simply moulded by those individuals who operate schools. Thirdly, pupils, unlike materials used in factories, are interacting with teachers and with others in order to define their education. Accordingly, it would appear that, rather like Weber's notion of bureaucracy, the open systems model cannot simply be detached from an industrial setting and used directly to understand the organization of schools. Nevertheless, Richardson does use this model to explore the ways in which boundaries are created, developed, sustained and changed within the school with special reference to the management of authority. The open systems model is, therefore, adopted in the course of analysing the staff structure of this secondary school.

While it might be argued that such a model (with some modifications) is appropriate for a state school, questions could be raised about the extent to which it is applicable to schools in the independent sector. In considering models that are appropriate for the study of independent schools, sociologists have turned to Goffman's model of the total institution with a view to assessing its usefulness for the study of school organization.

TOTAL INSTITUTIONS AND THE STUDY OF SCHOOLS

The idea of the 'total institution' is advanced by Goffman (1961) in his essay 'On the characteristics of total institutions' in which he discusses the key features of different establishments including mental hospitals, prisons, monasteries and schools. Automatically we need to consider the extent to which schools can be equated with other institutions and ask: are schools total institutions?

As far as Goffman is concerned a total institution is:

> a place of residence and work where a large number of like situated individuals, cut off from the wider society for an appreciable period of time, together lead an enclosed formally administered round of life. (Goffman, 1961, p.11)

In turn, Goffman briefly outlines some of the central characteristics of life in a total institution in the following terms:

> First, all aspects of life are conducted in the same place and under the same single authority. Second, each phase of the member's daily activity is carried on in the immediate company of a large batch of others, all of whom are treated alike and are required to do the same thing together. Third, all phases of the day's activities are tightly scheduled, with one activity leading at a prearranged time into the next, the whole sequence of activities being imposed from above by a system of explicit formal rulings and a body of officials. Finally, the various enforced activities are brought together into a single rational plan purportedly designed to fulfil the official aims of the institution. (Goffman, 1961, p.17)

At first glance, some of these features would appear to be appropriate for schools. However, phrases such as '. . . cut off from the wider society . . .' might suggest that this model is more applicable to boarding schools than to schools in the state sector, as the former are often geographically and socially isolated (see the essays in Walford, 1984). However, we need to explore Goffman's model in greater detail to see if it can be applied to the study of independent schools.

Within the total institution it is argued that there is a breakdown of all the barriers of life (between work, sleep and play). In turn the assumption is made that each member of the institution is required to engage in the same activities that are imposed by staff on the 'inmates' of the institution. Yet such an approach does not allow for autonomy on the part of the individual teacher and does not appear to allow for the way in which pupils and some teachers interpret the instructions that come from those members of the staff hierarchy.

As far as staff are concerned, Goffman takes into account the fact that they are integrated into the outside world, but the limitations of his model are highlighted by the fact that he considers the 'inmates' to be cut off from the outside world. When this approach is applied to the world of independent boarding schools, the evidence that is available from sociologists who have conducted research in these schools (cf. Lambert *et al.*, 1975; Wakeford, 1969; Walford, 1984; Wober, 1971) indicates the shortcomings of this model. Any schools (including boarding schools) are part of the educational system and, as such, their internal activities are, in part, governed from beyond the school gates. For example, Heward (1984) in a study of Ellesmere College highlights the way in which the impact of war and the demand for school places influenced the way in which the headmaster established school fees. Secondly, independent secondary schools utilize sets of text books and other teaching materials that have been generated beyond the school itself (cf. Rudduck *et al* 1983). Thirdly, independent schools participate in a system of public examinations that are set on a nationwide basis. Similarly, just as the educational activities are in part determined from beyond the institution so in turn are the activities associated with pupils. Pupils maintain contact with the world beyond the school through letters and visits from parents and friends (cf. Lambert *et al.*, 1975) and from their engagement with the adolescent subculture and the mass media (cf. Delamont, 1984c). This situation has been neatly summarized by Wober, who remarks:

> There is much evidence that the girls (in independent schools) are very interested in the world outside school – they miss their parents, their pets and their boy-friends at a later age; they listen to pop music and attend to its stars; they use the jargon of teenage cultures rather than developing intensive vocabularies special to the school community. (Wober, 1971, p.148)

It would, therefore, appear that not even the independent boarding school is 'cut off from the wider society' and that pupils are not and cannot be systematically stripped of all their links with the outside world. Furthermore, this model is not able to take into account the particular circumstances of schools and schooling where there is an intense relationship between staff and pupils who engage in a variety of tasks with a specific content that is directed towards teaching and learning. On this basis, sociologists need to consider how this model, like the others we have considered, may be adapted in studies of schooling.

It is the particular characteristics of schools, with groups of teachers and pupils, with their style of organization, together with various patterns of teaching and learning, that make it particularly problematic for any sociological or managerial model of organizations to be systematically applied to them (cf. Bell, 1980; Davies, 1973, 1981b). For example, Bell (1980) has indicated how educational goals are ambiguous in schools and, as case studies have shown, do not always have a central position in school life (cf. Burgess, 1983, especially part two). In such situations, Bell argues, the fundamental processes of teaching and learning are not necessarily understood by the participants, with the result that there is a range of situations between teachers and pupils where

> rules and procedures cannot be operated with bureaucratic consistency, impartiality and predictability because the various parties involved do not perceive with any degree of clarity what is expected of them and what may justifiably be expected of others. (Bell, 1980, p.188)

In turn, Bell argues on the basis of his own research on mixed ability grouping in schools (Bell, Pennington and Burridge, 1979) and the work of Turner (1969) that schools are open to diverse sets of demands and a degree of ambiguity concerning membership. As a consequence, he considers that schools are unpredictable organizations where teachers need to be adaptive, creative and flexible to react to changing circumstances. In turn, he argues that schools are places where individuals are accorded discretion and given power to manage. In such situations Bell maintains that:

> For such responses to be understood the traditional notion of the school as a hierarchical decision-making structure with a horizontal division into departments and a vertical division into authority levels needs to be abandoned. (Bell, 1980, p.190)

Such a remark, as Davies (1981b) indicates, accords closely with the problem that confronts the sociologist investigating the structure of contemporary schools. The sociologist has to come to terms with the fluidity of membership, the problematic nature of educational goals, the pattern of organization that exists in schools and the ideological differences that exist in the ways in which different members of the organization define education. It is, therefore, appropriate that at this point we should turn our attention to some of the investigations that have been conducted by sociologists who have examined some of the central features of school organization.

Investigating school organization

Alongside the theoretical models that have been developed, sociologists have also worked on examining some of the main ways in which teachers have subdivided schools into organizational units. While some research has been done in primary schools where attention has focused on the classroom (cf. Galton and Willcocks, 1984; King, 1978; Pollard, 1985 and the reviews in Chapter 9), the bulk of work has been conducted in secondary schools where attention has focused on the pastoral and academic structures of schools with houses, year groups, streams, sets, bands and mixed ability groups. It is, therefore, to a review of some of this material that we now turn.

THE ORGANIZATION OF PASTORAL CARE

As Hughes (1980) has shown, the term 'pastoral care' has only passed into common currency in educational vocabulary in the last decade. Nevertheless, the areas of schools organization to which it refers have been with us for some time, as it includes house systems (which were originally established in the independent schools (cf. Stanley, 1903 writing on Thomas Arnold's house system at Rugby School in the nineteenth century)), year systems, systems for guidance and counselling together with teams of house or year heads and their associated tutors (cf. Best, Jarvis and Ribbens, 1977). It is systems such as these that have been developed in many secondary schools as a means of handling administrative tasks, breaking down the school into smaller, more manageable units and supporting new innovations in the areas of curriculum and examinations (cf. Best, Jarvis and Ribbens, 1977; Burgess, 1983; Corbishley and Evans, 1980; Lang and Marland, 1985).

Surveys of comprehensive secondary schools have shown how large schools have been subdivided on either a vertical (house) or horizontal (year basis). For example, a survey by Monks (1968) found that the most popular form of internal school organization was the house system, while Benn and Simon (1972) found that 122 (17 per cent) of the schools they surveyed adopted a house system. More recently a survey of 384 secondary schools by Her Majesty's Inspectors in the mid 1970s found that 189 schools employed year systems, 59 employed house systems and that about one third of all schools in the survey had mixed systems. For a sociologist, the interesting questions that concern house and year systems relate to the ways in which they are used by educational personnel.

A major feature of Burgess's study of Bishop McGregor School (Burgess, 1983) concerns the significance of the house system. Burgess indicates how this school was established with a house system as a physical entity which the local authority considered would help pupils to 'belong' in a large school of 1500 pupils. Accordingly, when the head established Bishop McGregor School he was constrained by local authority policy to establish a system of pastoral organization based on houses which were part of the school's physical plant. As a consequence there was a major physical division of the school structure into houses and departments which influenced patterns of formal and informal relationships between teachers and between teachers and pupils.

In particular, Burgess found that those teachers who worked in the pastoral structure were quick to redefine rules and routines that had been established by the headmaster, with the result that the different houses within the pastoral structure operated with different sets of social and academic criteria. McGregor School was, therefore, defined, divided and subdivided into a number of different units where teachers and pupils were confronted with a variety of definitions about the institution and the education it provided. In turn, there were several conflicting accounts of what constituted 'education' and 'schooling' which had to be resolved by pupils and teachers on a day-to-day basis. For example, Burgess shows how each house in Bishop McGregor School had a different ethos and how one house head considered that her house was a 'mini-school'. Meanwhile, others saw the importance of the pastoral structure in terms of superiority over the academic and departmental structure. Accordingly many houses were concerned with elements of social control: discipline, rules, punishments and moral standards (cf. Best, Jarvis and Ribbens, 1977). Similar situations have also been reported by Corbishley and Evans (1980) in their account of two secondary schools. Here, some evidence is presented on the way in which teachers in the pastoral system may have conceptions of the pupils that are different from those teachers engaged in work in the academic departments.

However, sociologists have also found that pastoral structures may have some links with the academic structure, as some pupils might be sponsored through the academic structure, while others are 'cooled out'. For example, Burgess (1983) indicates how teachers in the pastoral structure influenced the allocation of pupils in the academic structure. This clearly supports the work done by Cicourel and Kitsuse (1963) in a study of Lakeshore High School in the USA where they found that the school's counselling system classified pupils so that they could be allocated to positions in the academic structure. In particular, Cicourel and Kitsuse were able to conclude on the basis of their investigation that the pupil's progress was not merely based on ability and performance but also on judgements made by counsellors about the pupil's biography, appearance, demeanour and social class position. Such evidence leads us to ask what happens to pupils in the academic structure of schools, what social processes surround their allocation to particular groups and to what extent this influences patterns of teaching and learning.

TABLE 1: *Organization of teaching groups in the third year: by type of school*

	Numbers of Schools				
	Type of secondary school				
	Modern	*Grammar*	*FR Comp*[1]	*RR Comp*[2]	*All schools*[3]
Forms of organization					
Mixed ability (including individual withdrawal)	11	16	4	3	34
Banding only	18	2	20	3	43
Streaming only	25	3	8	1	37
Schools with some setting	67	31	116	37	251
Total	121	52	148	44	365

NOTES:
1. FR Comp – Full ability range Comprehensive School.
2. RR Comp – Restricted ability range Comprehensive School.
3. Only 365 out of 384 schools surveyed could be used for this table.

SOURCE: DES (1979) p. 16

THE ACADEMIC ORGANIZATION OF SCHOOLS

The HMI Survey (cf. DES, 1979) of a sample of secondary schools in England and Wales indicated that there are now a number of different arrangements for allocating pupils to different groups (see table 1). The main ways in which the schools in the survey differentiated pupils into teaching groups was by streaming, setting, banding and mixed ability grouping. However, combinations of these patterns were frequently adopted and modifications were made to the predominant pattern by setting in some subjects and by withdrawing pupils regarded as less able for special tuition. The main forms of school organization can be defined as follows:

Streaming is the subdivision of pupils of the same age into different classes according to ability which may have been determined by a series of tests and by the assessment of teachers. Such a system results in broad subdivisions of a year group, as in Hargreaves's study of Lumley Secondary Modern School where pupils were subdivided into groups A to E (Hargreaves, 1967) and in Lacey's study of Hightown Grammar (Lacey, 1970).

Setting is the allocation of pupils to a specific group based on their ability in a particular subject. As the HMI Survey (DES, 1979) indicated, this has been predominantly used in the teaching of mathematics, English, modern languages and science. While pupils should be allocated to different groups, several researchers (Ball, 1981; Burgess, 1983; Lambart, 1976, 1982) have shown how similar pupils often populate bottom sets.

Banding is a system where pupils are subdivided into broad ability groups such as the above average, the average and the below average. Within these broad groups, parallel classes are established which contain pupils of similar ability. Such a situation is reported by Ball (1981) in Beachside Comprehensive School where out of ten classes in each year group, four classes were in Band 1 for the most able, four classes in Band 2 and two classes in Band 3 for the least able.

Mixed ability grouping consists of a series of classes where pupils may be distributed randomly or where classes contain an assortment of different abilities. Such grouping is discussed in Ball's study of Beachside (1981), in the study by Brian Davies and his associates on mathematics teaching (Corbishley *et al*, 1981), in a study of Inner London by John Evans (1985) and in a series of papers (cf. the contributions to Davies and Cave, 1977).

For the sociologist working in schools, such patterns of organization have been examined with a view to explaining the social mechanisms and social processes within schools and their effects upon teaching and learning and teacher and pupil subcultures. It is, therefore, to a review of this evidence that we now turn.

Streaming

Much of the early work on streaming was conducted within larger sociological studies whose concern was to explore the relationship between social class and educational attainment, especially in relation to the selection examination at eleven for allocation to secondary education. Accordingly, the focus of several studies was upon the influence of streaming on education in the primary school. The longitudinal study by

Douglas (1964) found that, on the basis of performance in ability tests, it was middle class children who had the greater chance of being allocated to the upper streams of a primary school and less chance of being allocated to the lower streams. Similar evidence was also reported by Brian Jackson (1964) in his study of streaming in the primary school. His findings revealed that the child from a professional or managerial background had only five chances in 100 of going into a D stream class. A further study conducted in primary schools by Barker-Lunn (1970) also followed up the relationship between streaming, ability and social class. In a longitudinal study conducted in streamed and non-streamed classes, she pointed to the extent to which streaming occurred in non-streamed schools in a covert way, as it did to some extent within streamed classes. It is this kind of process that has also been identified by Nash (1971, 1973) in relation to pupil grouping in primary classes where supposedly covert streaming by teachers was recognized by pupils who could identify ability ranges among those who sat at tables which were overtly labelled in terms of colours.

Many of the schools in these studies appear to follow a different form of school organization to that which was advocated by the Plowden Committee (Central Advisory Council for Education, 1967) in the late 1960s. Indeed, studies conducted in the 1970s by Bealing (1972) and by Boydell (1981) have shown that streaming had been abolished and replaced by mixed ability grouping. However, there was also evidence of tight teacher control and an emphasis on the traditional curriculum (cf. Barker–Lunn, 1982; Galton, Simon and Croll, 1980).

Within many of the studies on the primary school there is a gradual shift towards researchers identifying the social processes associated with the academic organization of schools and its impact upon the achievement of pupils. It was this issue that was also taken up in studies of secondary schools by Hargreaves (1967) and by Lacey (1966, 1970). Both of these studies involved detailed analyses of the internal organization of schools in Greater Manchester. In his study of Hightown Grammar, Lacey identified social processes associated with streaming which he developed into a model of differentiation and polarization among pupils. Here, he uses the term differentiation to refer to the ways in which teachers categorize pupils on the basis of their behaviour and academic ability. Meanwhile, Lacey argues that polarization among pupils is a subcultural formation where pupils oppose the normative culture of the school and form an 'anti-group' culture. He found that those pupils who conformed to teacher expectations and demands and who valued academic success were rewarded, while those who did not were perceived in negative terms.

For the teachers in Lacey's Hightown Grammar and Hargreaves's Lumley Secondary Modern School these processes were related to the streams to which pupils were allocated. For example, David Hargreaves

Figure 4: Subcultural Differentiation in Lumley Secondary Modern School

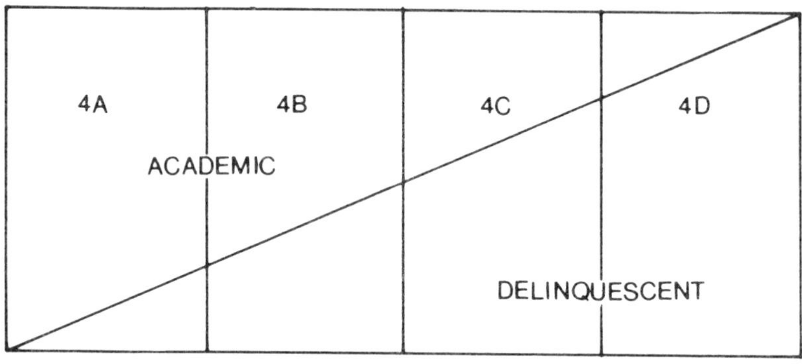

SOURCE: Hargreaves (1967) p.163

reports that in Lumley School the teachers considered that the higher the stream in which pupils were allocated the better their behaviour. Furthermore, the 'anti-group' culture manifested itself within the lower streams where pupils could gain status through a negative response to the values of the school. Within his study, Hargreaves focuses on the fourth year groups in streams A to D, but omits 4E from the study as they formed a separate friendship group and had special teachers allocated to their classes. On the basis of his observations, he reports the subcultural divide shown in figure 4.

On this basis, Hargreaves also proposes an ideal type model which suggests ways in which the school's cultural structure is related to the streaming process in the fourth year. Here, the dominant values of the A and B streams are academic, while those of the C and D streams are delinquescent; although, as Hargreaves is quick to point out, this is not synonymous with delinquency. In turn, Hargreaves also enters further caveats concerning the B stream, where he feels that academic values are not so dominant, and the C stream, where delinquescent values do not predominate. Accordingly, he demonstrates how the A and D streams become the poles of normative differentiation.

The studies by Hargreaves and Lacey outline a differentiation-polarization model in streamed schools that were organized under the tripartite system. While such research highlights fundamental processes in schools, it nevertheless poses a number of questions. First, to what extent are such processes present in schools organized in terms of sets, bands and mixed ability groups? Secondly, to what extent are these processes present in comprehensive schools? It is on these questions that we focus as we examine further evidence on the internal organization of schools.

Setting

Among the school studies that report on setting is Audrey Lambart's analysis of Mereside Grammar School – an unstreamed girls' grammar school in Greater Manachester where research was conducted in parallel with the studies of Hargreaves and Lacey. Within the school, setting occurred in particular subject groups. In the course of her study, Lambart (1976) focuses on patterns of friendship among a group of third year girls which she calls the Sisterhood. This group was composed of girls of varying achievement but who were of above average ability. Members of the Sisterhood were often put on report and were adversely criticized by their teachers. As far as the origins of this group were concerned, one girl relates it to the internal aspects of school organization when she states:

> It (the Sisterhood) grew when we were put in sets. We used to be all in twos and threes before that. (Lambart, 1976, p.156)

As far as Lambart is conerned, her account does provide evidence to show that the Sisterhood's subgroups were in fact related to the internal organization of Mereside School. Such an account, as Ball (1984c) has noted, does not automatically relate to the work of Hargreaves and Lacey and their model of differentiation-polarization, nor is it directly comparable because the evidence is based on the study of a school where setting rather than streaming occurs and where there are girls rather than boys. Nevertheless, Lambart's work highlights the relationship between low status and the internal organization of schools as well as contributing to our knowledge of unstreamed situations in schools such as Beachside (Ball, 1981) where mixed ability groups existed alongside bands.

Banding

One of the clearest ethnographic examples of the ways in which the system of banding has an impact upon processes of schooling is provided in Stephen Ball's study of *Beachside Comprehensive* (1981). Ball reports that, during the period in which he conducted his study between 1973 and 1976, the school was changing its internal organization from banding among pupils in the first three years to mixed ability grouping. Accordingly, the evidence from his study can be used to assess the effects of two different forms of organization upon schooling.

As far as Ball is concerned, the banding system at Beachside had the effect of separating pupils into a number of groups that were provided with different kinds of subject knowledge and different teaching methods, and where the main characteristics of teacher-pupil relationships were different. Ball reports that the banding had a direct influence on curriculum content, teaching styles and patterns of friendship choices among pupils. In particular, he found that pupils tended to make friendships predominantly within their own bands and were to some extent hostile to pupils from other bands. The evidence available to Ball suggested that an anti-school culture, similar to that found by Hargreaves and Lacey, was prevalent among band 2 pupils, who were regarded by many teachers as 'disciplinary blackspots' in contrast to band 1 pupils, who fulfilled the 'ideal pupil' role in terms of academic achievement and behaviour. For many Beachside teachers, therefore, a shift towards mixed ability grouping was seen as a means of 'improving' the social atmosphere in classrooms and eradicating discipline problems. But what evidence do we have on mixed ability grouping?

Mixed ability grouping

The basic pattern of mixed ability organization was defined by HMI as one where:

> at least up to the end of the third year of the normal secondary course, the curriculum was taught wholly or mainly (i.e. with not more than two subjects excluded) in classes in which the span of ability ranged from significantly below to significantly above the average. (DES, 1978b, p.1)

This definition focuses on comprehensive schools and is supported by the evidence that is available not only in Ball's ethnographic study of Beachside, but also in Newbold's study of mixed ability grouping in Banbury School (Newbold, 1977). It is studies such as these that can be used to evaluate the arguments concerning the extent to which mixed ability grouping affects patterns of teaching and learning and pupils' social development.

In reporting the findings of his study in Banbury School, Newbold was concerned to urge caution in attributing pupil achievement to patterns of grouping in the school. In particular, he concludes that there *may* be some advantage for less able pupils in mixed ability classes, but that it is the role of the teacher and teacher-pupil interaction that is of paramount importance in secondary school progress rather than the particular grouping. Similarly, Ball found that even though mixed ability grouping was used, academic achievement continued to be of importance in the school and was reflected in patterns of teacher–pupil interaction in the classroom.

Similarly, both studies provide evidence on social mixing. Newbold argues that the Banbury study took place in a 'natural' setting where two halls worked with a streamed organization and two halls had a mixed ability organization. Accordingly, the study attempted to establish the differences that emerged between these two patterns of grouping. By the end of the first year in which pupils were in the school, Newbold found that mixed ability grouping provided more effective integration between pupils of different abilities and different backgrounds than did the streaming process. However, by the time pupils reached the fourth year, patterns of friendship appeared to be little affected by the grouping pattern to which the pupils belonged. Similarly Ball (1981) found that the mixed ability experiment in Beachside Comprehensive allowed him to make an assessment of polarization and the influence of mixed ability grouping on friendship choice. While mixed ability grouping did appear to prevent the development of an anti-school culture, it did not prevent the sharp divisions among friendship groups based on ability and social class. Indeed, he found that there were several sharp divisions among pupils in the mixed ability groups and that the academic aspirations of working class pupils within these groups were reduced as they could no longer be 'top of the class' and adopt success roles in the way in which they could in the banded groups – a situation that held implications for subject choices and the long-term plans of pupils (cf. Woods, 1976). However, for some sociologists, such evidence on the way in which the internal organization of schools influences pupil performance has generated questions about the *effects* of schooling and the broader processes of social reproduction and the distribution of life chances.

Do schools make a difference?

In addressing this question in the last 20 years, researchers have used evidence that is open to a variety of interpretations. Some commentators argue that schools make no difference to society and that differences between schools only have a minimal effect upon their pupils. For example, in producing the report entitled *Equality of Educational Opportunity* (Coleman *et al*, 1966) Coleman collected data on 600,000 pupils and 60,000 teachers in 4,000 schools. While there were substantial differences in the verbal ability levels of pupils it was argued that these were a reflection of the social composition of the pupil body and could not be attributed to the quality of the schools. When these data were reanalysed by Jencks and his associates (1972), Coleman's findings were upheld as it could be argued that resources had virtually no influence on schooling and that 'Qualitative differences between high schools seem to explain about 2 per cent of the variation in students' educational attainment' (Jencks, *et al*, 1972, p.159). However, in interpreting this evidence it is essential to examine critically the way in which the data were collected, for, as Robinson (1981a) remarks, the conclusions to this study indicate more about social research and the use of large-scale surveys to look at schools and school effects, as other writers *have* found school effects influential in confirming and operationalizing differences among pupils. Nevertheless, similar findings to those provided by Coleman have been reported in a variety of studies in the USA. However, these studies have been criticized by Rutter and Madge (1976) on methodological grounds, as the former maintains that only a limited number of measures of the school were used, while the latter argues that only resource based variables were used to measure school quality rather than teacher–pupil relationships, school 'ethos' and school organization. It is some of these issues that have been taken up in Britain by Rutter and his colleagues (1979) in a study of 12 secondary schools in Inner London and by Reynolds and his colleagues (Reynolds, 1975, 1976; Reynolds *et al*, 1976) in secondary modern schools in South Wales.

The work of Rutter and his team was designed to address two questions. First, do different schools have a different effect upon their pupils? Secondly, if schools did have such an effect, what factors within the schools could account for these differences? Four school output measures were used: delinquency, attendance, behaviour in school, and public examination results. It was found that there was substantial variation between the schools in their performance on these measures even after differences in pupil intake were taken into account. In turn, it was found that schools tended to perform consistently 'well' or consistently 'badly' on all these measures of school output. This research team also examined aspects of the internal organization of the school: school processes, school ethos and teacher pupil interaction. The results suggested that school size, age of buildings, formal academic and pastoral organization, pupil–teacher ratio and class size appeared to make little difference to outcomes. However, the importance of within school influences upon school outcome was said to include: the balance of able and less able pupils, the system of rewards and punishments, the school environment, the opportunities for pupils to participate in the running of their school lives, clarity of academic goals, the behaviour of teachers, the management of classrooms and the pattern of leadership. It is on this basis that Rutter, *et al* (1979) are able to conclude that 'the results carry the strong implication that schools can do much to foster good behaviour and attainment and that even in a disadvantaged area schools can be a force for the good' (Rutter, *et al*, 1979, p.205).

Although this work has been the subject of much methodological criticism (cf. Goldstein, 1980; A. Hargreaves, 1980b; Radical Statistics Group, 1982), it has supported findings from research conducted by Reynolds and his colleagues in secondary modern schools in South Wales. Reynolds and his colleagues collected data on pupil inputs, pupil outputs and school processes in secondary modern schools, taking the bottom two-thirds of the ability range in a catchment area within a former mining valley.

Writing in 1975, Reynolds reported considerable variation in the quality of school outputs, as shown in table 2. In particular, the delinquency rate varied from 10.5 per cent to 3.8 per cent, the attendance rate varied from 77.2 per cent average attendance to 89.1 per cent and the academic attainment rate varied from 8.4 per cent proceeding to the local technical college to 52.7 per cent going into further education. However,

TABLE 2: *Secondary Modern School Performance Academic Years 1966/7 to 1972/3*

School	*Delinquency (first offenders per annum)*	*Attendance*	*Academic attainment*
A	10.5%	79.9%	34.8%
B	8.6%	78.3%	26.5%
C	8.3%	84.3%	21.5%
D	8.1%	77.2%	8.4%
E	7.4%	89.1%	30.4%
F	7.2%	81.3%	18.5%
G	5.2%	87.0%	37.9%
H	4.5%	88.5%	52.7%
I	3.8%	83.6%	36.5%

SOURCE: Reynolds (1975) p. 129

as Reynolds (1982) indicates, these variations could not be explained on the basis of intake scores. Further analysis has indicated that within this study the most effective schools were associated with situations where a high proportion of pupils were in authority positions, where there were low levels of institutional control, low rates of physical punishment, and where the schools were small in size, with favourable teacher–pupil ratios and tolerance over rule enforcement. In addition, Reynolds has noted that interpersonal rather than impersonal relationships have developed between teachers and pupils, and that pupils have been incorporated into the life of the school.

On the basis of a review of his own work, together with other British and American studies, Reynolds (1982) asks: what makes an effective school? He concludes that, while resource levels, quality/quantity of plant and class size are of little importance, academic prowess, pupil participation, psychological 'environment', teacher expectation and rewards and punishments are important. Meanwhile, the evidence concerning school size and institutional control appears contradictory in the search for the effective school. Accordingly, Reynolds (1982) concludes that more work needs to be done on school effectiveness in different catchment areas, in primary as well as secondary schools, among boys and girls and among children from different ethnic groups. Such a set of proposals concerning future research should not, however, be restricted to studies of school effectiveness if sociologists are to advance their understanding of schools.

Conclusion

Sociologists have experienced some difficulty in establishing a framework within which to conduct research about school organization. The models which they have used have often been derived from non-educational settings with the result that their applicability to schools and to educational settings is seriously limited. Accordingly, as several commentators have indicated, we still need an empirically based theory of schools. Such a theory, as Tyler (1982) suggests,

> depends on the recognition, not just of the uniqueness of the school as a subject of study, but of the deep inter-connections by which it coheres, evolves and endures. The school's technologies and structures, rituals and rules can only be appreciated properly as a complex pattern of inter-dependencies whose outlines are at present only barely discernible. (Tyler, 1982, pp.64–5)

On the basis of these criteria, studies of the school have only just begun.

Suggestions for further reading

Bell, L. A. (1980) 'The school as an organization: a reappraisal', *British Journal of Sociology of Education*, vol. 1, no. 2, pp.183–192. A critical review of sociological analyses of the school as an organization.

Bidwell, C. E. (1965) 'The school as a formal organization', in J. G. March (ed) *Handbook of Organizations*, Chicago, Rand McNally, pp.972–1022. A standard reference to organizational analysis and its applicability to school. It includes a useful discussion of bureaucracy.

Davies, W. B. (1973) 'On the contribution of organizational analysis to the study of educational institutions', in R. K. Brown (ed) *Knowledge, Education and Cultural Change*, London, Tavistock, pp. 249–295.

Davies, W. B. (1981) 'Schools as organizations and the organization of schooling', *Educational Analysis*, vol. 3, no. 1, pp.47–67. A pair of critical discussions of organization theory. The author provides a guide to the theoretical frameworks and an assessment of their applicability to schools. The articles also chart shifts in areas of research over a decade. Each article has a detailed bibliography.

Hammersley, M. and Woods, P. (1984) (eds) *Life in School: the sociology of pupil culture*, Milton Keynes, Open University Press. The first section of this book reproduces articles from ethnographers who have contributed to our understanding of school organization.

King, R. (1983) *The Sociology of School Organization*, London, Methuen. A brief introductory guide to research and writing in this field of study.

Reynolds, D. (1982) 'The search for effective schools', *School Organization*, vol. 2, no. 3, pp.215–237. An excellent guide to research and writing on school effectiveness in Britain and the USA.

Tyler, W. (1982) *The Sociology of the School: A Review*, London, Social Science Research Council. A review of the literature on the sociology of the school commissioned by the SSRC – brief but comprehensive.

Waller, W. (1932) *The Sociology of Teaching*, Chichester, Wiley (reprinted in 1967). A classic American account that has still not been surpassed by

researchers.
Woods, P. (1983) *Sociology of the School: An Interactionist Viewpoint*, London, Routledge and Kegan Paul. A very good summary of the contribution of symbolic interactionism and ethnography to studies of schools and schooling.

EMPIRICAL STUDIES

Ball, S. J. (1981) *Beachside Comprehensive*, Cambridge, Cambridge University Press provides a detailed account of banding and mixed ability grouping in a comprehensive school.
Burgess, R. G. (1983) *Experiencing Comprehensive Education: A Study of Bishop McGregor School*, London, Methuen provides an ethnographic account of the pastoral/academic divide in a comprehensive school.
Hargreaves, D. H. (1967) *Social Relations in a Secondary School*, London, Routledge and Kegan Paul. A pioneering British study of a secondary modern school in Greater Manchester.
Lacey, C. (1970) *Hightown Grammar, the School as a social system*, Manchester, Manchester University Press. A study of a boys' grammar school which focused on differentiation and polarization that has subsequently been taken up by other researchers. For a discussion of the trends in this research see Hammersley (1985).
Lambart, A. (1976) 'The Sisterhood', in M. Hammersley and P. Woods (eds) *The Process of Schooling*, London, Routledge and Kegan Paul, pp.152–159 provides an account from an unstreamed grammar school for girls; this project was linked to the studies by Hargreaves and Lacey.
Pollard, A. (1985) *The Social World of the Primary School*, Eastbourne, Holt, Rinehart and Winston contains a useful interactionist discussion of school organization.
Richardson, E. (1973) *The Teacher, the School and the Task of Management*, London, Heinemann is an account of Nailsea School using a systems approach.
Rutter, M. *et al* (1979) *Fifteen Thousand Hours*, London, Open Books. A study of 12 Inner London secondary schools. See the reviews of this study especially by the Radical Statistics Group (1982).
Wakeford, J. (1969) *The Cloistered Elite*, London, Macmillan. A study of boarding schools from an interactionist perspective.

8 Life in classrooms

Teachers and pupils spend about five hours each day in classrooms, for the classroom is formally at the centre of the educational stage. It is one of the settings in which teachers and pupils encounter each other and the location where some aspects of schooling occur. On this basis alone we might expect sociologists to be interested in the actions and activities between participants in classrooms. Yet we find that classroom research by sociologists has only developed in the last decade (although social psychologists have worked in classrooms for some years (cf. Lippitt and White, 1943)). As a consequence, sociologists reviewing the state of the art in Britain and in the USA in the 1970s were able to bemoan the dearth of classroom studies (cf. Walker, 1972; Wax and Wax, 1971). Indeed, commenting on British work, Walker remarked that, although

> the interaction of teachers and pupils within the social arena of the classroom is a central element in all educational institutions, . . . it has been left largely unstudied by sociologists. British sociologists of education in particular have been dominated by a concern with an education system that has failed to give social equality of access to different parts of the system. As a result they have concentrated their attention on the analysis of inputs and outputs to different institutions, and tended to assume uniformity in the nature of the educational process. (Walker, 1972, p.32)

While this area was omitted from view by sociologists it was, nevertheless, examined by social psychologists and by teacher educators, many of whom were more concerned with identifying 'good' or 'effective' classroom practice than with a fundamental analysis of the social processes associated with classroom life.

Among the most popular approaches to classroom study has been interaction analysis which is based upon systematic observation schedules. A pioneer of this approach has been Ned Flanders, whose categories for analysing classroom talk are shown in table 1.

This approach involves a researcher coding classroom talk into one of

TABLE 1: *Flanders's interaction analysis categories* (FIAC)*

Teacher talk	Response	1. *Accepts feeling.* Accepts and clarifies an attitude or the feeling tone of a pupil in a non-threatening manner. Feelings may be positive or negative. Predicting and recalling feelings are included. 2. *Praises or encourages.* Praises or encourages pupil action or behaviour. Jokes that release tension, but not at the expense of another individual; nodding head, or saying "Um hm?" or 'go on' are included. 3. *Accepts or uses ideas of pupils.* Clarifying, building, or developing ideas suggested by a pupil. Teacher extensions of pupil ideas are included but as the teacher brings more of his own ideas into play, shift to category five.
		4. *Asks questions.* Asking a question about content or procedure, based on teacher ideas, with the intent that a pupil will answer.
	Initiation	5. *Lecturing.* Giving facts or opinions about content or procedures; expressing *his own* ideas, giving *his own* explanation, or citing an authority other than a pupil. 6. *Giving directions.* Directions, commands, or orders to which a pupil is expected to comply. 7. *Criticizing or justifying authority.* Statements intended to change pupil behaviour from non-acceptable to acceptable pattern, bawling someone out, stating why the teacher is doing what he is doing; extreme self-reference.
Pupil-talk response		8. *Pupil-talk – response.* Talk by pupils in response to teacher. Teacher initiates the contact or solicits pupil statement or structures the situation. Freedom to express own ideas is limited.
	Initiation	9. *Pupil-talk-initiation.* Talk by pupils which they initiate; expressing own ideas; initiating a new topic; freedom to develop opinions and a line of thought, like asking thoughtful questions; going beyond the existing structure.
Silence		10. Silence or confusion. Pauses, short periods of silence and periods of confusion in which communication cannot be understood by the observer.

* There is *no* scale implied by these numbers. Each number is classificatory; it designates a particular kind of communication event. To write these numbers down during observation is to enumerate, not to judge a position on a scale.

SOURCE: Flanders (1970) p. 34

TABLE 2: *The observation categories of the Teacher Record in the ORACLE project*

Conversation	*Silence*
Questions	Silent Interaction
Task	Gesturing
Q1 recalling facts	Showing
Q2 offering ideas, solutions (closed)	Marking
Q3 offering ideas, solutions (open)	Waiting
Task supervision	Story
Q4 referring to task supervision	Reading
Routine	Not observed
Q5 referring to routine matter	Not coded
Statements	No interaction
Task	Adult interaction
S1 of facts	Visiting pupil
S2 of ideas, problems	Not interacting
Task supervision	Out of room
S3 telling child what to do	Audience
S4 praising work or effort	Composition
S5 feedback on work or effort	Activity
Routine	
S6 providing information, direction	
S7 providing feedback	
S8 of critical control	
S9 of small talk	

SOURCE: Galton, Simon and Croll (1980) p.17

these categories during each three second interval. A different schedule that has been devised in Britain for use in junior school classrooms was used in the Observational Research and Classroom Learning Evaluation (ORACLE) project on primary education (see especially Croll, 1986; Galton, Simon, and Croll, 1980). Here, the researcher makes a recording at 25 second intervals – these being pre-recorded on tape and fed to the classroom observer through an ear piece attached to a tape-recorder. To observe teachers, the following teacher record was used as shown in table 2. This record was used to focus on teacher contact with pupils where the researcher was required to note down what the teacher was doing, with whom it was being done and the type of conversation involved or the silent interaction that occurred between the participants.

While these systematic observation schedules are different in terms of their content and the approach that is used, we find that the results which are obtained are broadly similar. Both indicate that classrooms are dominated by teacher talk. Yet we need to consider whether this tells us more about the instrument of data collection rather than patterns of classroom interaction.

There have been several critiques of systematic classroom observation, but the best known is provided by Hamilton and Delamont (1976, revised and updated in 1984). In their critique they argue that such data tell us about 'average' or 'typical' classrooms, rather than about actual situations. Secondly, they maintain that this approach ignores the temporal and spatial context in which data are gathered, with the result that we learn little about physical settings. Thirdly, the focus is upon overt and observable behaviour, with the result that underlying and potentially more meaningful behaviour is lost from view. Fourthly, the prespecified codes relate to what can be measured and fail to make links to global concepts. Fifthly, the categories tend to lean towards particular kinds of explanations; and finally, there is a static representation of classrooms.

To overcome some of the deficiencies associated with systematic observation, some researchers have adopted an ethnographic stance towards classroom investigation. Working from an interpretative perspective, and especially from the tradition of symbolic interactionism, these researchers have focused on the meanings which individuals attribute to their behaviour in the classroom. Accordingly, rather than merely recording that a pupil is 'busy' or 'late', the researcher is interested in the way in which 'busyness' or 'lateness' is constructed by teachers and pupils in the classroom. But how can the researcher conduct ethnographic studies using observational methods in school classrooms?

At first glance it may appear relatively straightforward for a researcher to sit in the back of a classroom and record what occurs. Yet many experienced researchers have commented on the difficulties involved in using such a strategy. For example, the American sociologist Howard Becker has commented that:

> We may have understated a little the difficulty of observing contemporary classrooms. It is not just the survey method of educational testing or any of those things that keeps people from seeing what is going on. I think instead that it is first and foremost a matter of it all being so familiar that it becomes irresponsible to single out events that occur in the classroom as things that occurred even when they happen right in front of you . . . it takes a tremendous effort of will and imagination to stop seeing only the things that are conventionally there to be seen. (Becker, 1971, p.10)

In short, Becker is indicating that there are difficulties associated with attempting to go beyond what is conventionally known about classrooms – a point that is graphically illustrated by George Spindler in relation to his research in elementary school classrooms when he remarks:

> I sat in classes for days wondering what there was to 'observe'. Teachers taught, reprimanded, rewarded, while pupils sat at desks squirming, whispering, reading, writing, staring into space as they had in my own grade school experience, in my practice teaching in a teacher training program, and in the two years of public school teaching I had done before World War II. (Spindler and Spindler, 1982, p.24)

In situations such as this it is the researcher's task to make the familiar 'routines' of school strange so that they are the subject of sociological inquiry. For example, Delamont (1981) has suggested four strategies by which a researcher can render a familiar situation problematic. First, she argues that different kinds of classrooms for pupils and adults and in which different subjects are taught need to be examined, as unfamiliar situations may help to highlight familiar social processes. Secondly, she suggests that comparative studies may provide a stimulus for looking at familiar classroom settings. Thirdly, that non-educational settings can be compared with educational settings; and finally, that familiar aspects of schooling such as the way gender is used to organize classroom activities should no longer be taken for granted but used as a basis for questioning procedures. It is by using strategies such as these that researchers have begun to examine some of the social processes that occur in the classroom (cf. Burgess, 1984a). However, it is not merely a question of looking at the processes which occur in classrooms: it is also essential to consider the settings in which they occur.

The classroom setting

In some studies it would appear that the events which occur in some classrooms exist in a social vacuum, yet classroom events are located within a society, an educational system and a school at a specific point in time. For example, in Burgess's study of Bishop McGregor School (1983) we are shown the way in which events that occur beyond the school and classroom have a bearing upon the actions and activities of teachers and pupils. In this study, Burgess examines different 'crisis' situations that disturb the regular processes associated with classroom life. However, he demonstrates that events that occurred in the classroom need to be set in the wider context of the school, the local education authority, the city in which the school was located and the English educational system. For example, he discusses a series of decisions that were taken outside the school by members of the local education authority who decided not to grant the pupils a special holiday on the day when Princess Anne was married. It was this decision together with the actions of the headteacher and teachers on the wedding day which resulted in a mass walk out of pupils from classrooms. Such situations, Burgess argues, can only be understood in relation to the events beyond the classroom. Similarly, he shows that analyses of classroom encounters between teachers and pupils engaged in the

Newsom programme for the less willing and the less able within this school need to be placed in a wider context. Here, it becomes essential to view teacher–pupil interaction in the context of school and departmental policy and in relation to the curriculum policies advocated by the Newsom Committee (Ministry of Education, 1963), otherwise these interactions become unclear (cf. Burgess, 1983, especially part two).

However, it is not just the temporal setting of the classroom but also the physical setting that is important. For example, there are differences between one room, one teacher classrooms that constitute a whole school in rural localities in Scotland and Wales (cf. Nash, 1980) and classrooms in large inner-city schools (cf. Grace, 1978). The physical location will influence the pattern of classroom interaction. In turn, the relationships between classrooms and their surroundings may have implications for social relationships. Returning once again to Burgess's study of Bishop McGregor School (1983) we find that he demonstrates how physical territory was important for teachers and pupils, as the resources that each department possessed in terms of suites of rooms had some bearing on social status. Furthermore, he indicates how the kinds of rooms available to the Newsom Department had some bearing on patterns of teaching and learning. Newsom teachers were often in rooms that lacked adequate resources and equipment, which in turn impeded the teaching process. In a similar way, Hamilton (1975) has indicated in the course of discussing the implementation of the Scottish integrated science scheme in two schools that the physical setting allocated for science influenced patterns of communication between teachers and, in turn, the style of teaching.

In a similar way, the architectural features of schools can also have an impact upon patterns of teaching and teacher–pupil interaction. Stebbins (1976), in discussing an open plan school in the West Indies, indicates how lack of windows and doors has implications for the way in which pupils define appropriate classroom behaviour. In turn, the provision of open plan designs in English primary schools also has had an impact upon the ways in which teaching and learning are organized (cf. Bennett *et al*, 1980).

Sociologists have, therefore, had to consider the way in which different settings – primary or secondary school – and different architectural designs may influence patterns of interaction. Furthermore, the time at which an event is observed may also provide further insight into the actions and activities that are recorded. For example, Ball (1983a) and Burgess (1983, 1984a) have discussed the way in which the annual cycle of the school year may have some impact upon the activities that are observed. They illustrate how different kinds of activities may be observed at the beginnings and ends of terms, at times of major religious festivals, such as Christmas and Easter, and on special school days, such as the period before 'open evenings' or parents' visits. In recent years, several educational researchers have taken note of the impact of time upon classroom interaction as they have chosen to focus on those events which occur when teachers and pupils initially encounter each other in the classroom.

Initial encounters in the classroom

Initial encounters between teacher and pupil occur in the nursery school (cf. Walkerdine, 1981), in the reception class of the infant school (cf. Hamilton, 1977), in the primary school (Bennett *et al*, 1984), on transfer between first school and middle school (Galton and Delamont, 1980) and between middle school and comprehensive school (Measor and Woods, 1984) and in the secondary school classroom (Ball, 1980; Beynon and Atkinson, 1984). Despite the range of situations, researchers have found a number of similar processes occurring within the classroom when teachers and pupils meet for the first time.

Stephen Ball (1980) has argued that an analysis of such encounters is not only important in its own right but also provides a context within which to view more routine events. In particular, Ball highlights the importance of understanding the ways in which routines are settled through a process of establishment which he defines as

> an exploratory interaction process involving teacher and pupils during their initial encounters in the classroom through which a more or less permanent, repeated and highly predictable pattern of relationships and interactions emerges. (Ball, 1980, p.144)

Ball focuses on this process using data taken from a mixed ability innovation in a comprehensive school and on student teachers' first encounters with classes. On the basis of his data, he argues that initial encounters may be subdivided into two phases. The first is a passive stage where the pupils engage in observational work, which is followed by a more active stage when pupils start to become 'real horrible'. Similar phenomena have been identified by Measor and Woods (1984) in their comprehensive transfer study where they report that pupils entering secondary school go through a 'honeymoon' period when teachers and pupils present their best fronts to each other, and a 'coming out' period which was characterized by greater activity as pupils probed, tested and negotiated the ground rules that had been established. These accounts suggest that pupils need to observe *how* teachers define classroom rules and *how* space is defined so that they may establish a set of hypotheses about their teachers that can subsequently be tested out. On this basis, pupils can predict the ways in which teachers will react to their deviant activities. But we might ask: how do teachers establish routines in the classroom? How do pupils move from observing these routines to testing them out?

Studies that have been conducted in infant, middle and comprehensive schools indicate how, in the initial encounters, teachers are highlighting what constitutes 'proper' pupil behaviour and establishing the rules within which they all work. In an attempt to get close to the initial activity in an infant classroom, Hamilton provides a record of the activities that occurred on the first fourteen days of a school year. The extracts that he provides from his field notes on day one indicate that the focus is upon proper pupil behaviour and the acquisition of classroom conventions. He begins by reporting on the activities in the classroom between 8.20 a.m. and 8.50 a.m. when new pupils arrive with their parents. As the children arrive, the teacher gets them involved in some activity but uses the situation to establish rules, as Hamilton reports:

> Michael gets up from his chair leaving a large wooden shoe (used for learning how to tie laces) on the table. Noticing this, Mrs Robertson shows him how to put it back in its 'proper' place (i.e. on the high table). Meanwhile Nicola is rolling the plasticine on a table instead of on a board. Like Michael she is shown how to follow the correct procedure. (Hamilton, 1977, p.41)

Such actions on the part of the teacher not only establish routines and rules but also help establish a context in which teaching can occur, for at 9.10 a.m. Hamilton reports that Mrs Robertson follows up this theme of tidiness and keeping objects in their correct place when she remarks to the class 'Oh dear, someone doesn't push their chairs in'. Meanwhile, at the end of the first morning, Hamilton reports:

> At 11.35 a.m. Mrs Robertson gathers the children together in the home base and tells them the story of the three bears. Some of the children keep interrupting. Eventually Michael is told that 'When I'm telling a story, you sit very quietly and listen . . .'. Before letting the children return to their individual activities, Mrs Robertson reminds them to bring their pinafores the following day . . . Douglas and Michael become noisy; Mrs Robertson takes them 'for a walk' while the rest of the class continue with their drawing, painting etc. Meanwhile Miss Dean (another primary one teacher) comes into the area to report that the toilets are awash. When she returns Mrs Robertson takes her entire class back into the toilets and reiterates the correct procedures (e.g. 'turn the taps on gently'). At 12.25 the children are asked to find their schoolbags and put on their coats. Peter is sent with Julie to show her how to put off the lights. When the children have gathered in the base Mrs Robertson reminds them about the toilets. Finally, she says a formal 'Good Afternoon' to the children. Their reply is ragged. She asks the children what her name is and then repeats the greeting. Their response is more appropriate. At 12.30 the children pick up their schoolbags and move out into the communal area where their parents are waiting. (Hamilton, 1977, pp.44–5)

At the end of the first morning in the infant school, the children have been introduced to their role as pupils, appropriate pupil behaviour, elements of teacher control and rules surrounding classroom activity.

Similar routines have also been examined in other schools. For example, Galton and Delamont (1980) have shown that, when pupils transfer from first school to middle school, teachers attempt to establish appropriate rules about doing work. Using data that was collected in two middle schools, they report how teachers use the initial lessons to discuss ways in which work should be set out in exercise books, as shown in the following extract:

> Mrs Hind settles them – discussion of storage drawers. 'Notes into your English books'.
>
> These are notes on the presentation of work. Dudley comes wandering out to Mrs Hind's desk, and is sent back to his seat – then he says 'capital letters, full stops', and is ticked off. Mrs Hind says 'I thought you were talking to yourself'. Dudley says 'I was'. They are told to put date on the top left by margin, and a heading *Presentation* underlined 'if you have a ruler' . . .
>
> Rule one is 'Always start your work with the date'. Dudley says he can't see. Moved nearer the board – he pushes his new pencil/geometry case onto the floor.
>
> Rule two is 'Put the heading and underline it'.
>
> Rule three is 'Leave a line after the heading'.
>
> When she asks a question there are several people giving the answer. But she waits for hands to go up, chooses, and says 'Alan' or whoever.
>
> . . . Class are very quiet – noise is fidgetting not talk . . . Mrs Hind checks at each stage to see if the idea is familiar . . . (Galton and Delamont, 1980, p.213)

In these circumstances, the pupils are not only learning about rules for doing work but also about rules for behaviour and they are also learning about their teacher. Similarly, the teacher is making decisions and judgements about pupil behaviour and defining pupil roles. For example, Galton and Delamont report how one child is singled out by the teacher as reliable, competent and eager and as a consequence is allocated to the role of successful pupil. Meanwhile, the teacher also indicates those forms of behaviour which are not approved, as extracts from field notes taken during the second week of the autumn term at Gryll Grange Middle School illustrate.

> 9.00 Miss Tweed is busy mounting the pupils' work on sugar paper. Davina is still the official runner – taking register, dinner numbers, etc. to the office . . .
>
> Break Miss Tweed said in the staffroom she picked Davina for her class when making up the forms. She taught her elder brother, and likes the family. Davina is the kind of pupil she likes because she is good at work, active in games including swimming, plays an instrument, sings, and does a lot of art and craft.
>
> 1.15 Miss Tweed's class have music. Davina gives out music books.
>
> 2.00 Back to their form room, the pupils are told to: 'Finish writing about yourself. Do exercise in book. Do a pattern, based on a closed curve, and colour it.'
> Miss Tweed attacks a table of boys: 'Are you having another rest? You had a long rest all morning.'

A girl takes her work to be marked: 'I like smyming. What's smyming? You've got your w the wrong way up.'

2.10 Dean has spelt rugby so it looks like rabbit. Table of boys near me (Delamont) are not working – their 'essays' so far consist of the name and date . . .

2.20 Dean has been in the lavatory for ten minutes. (Galton and Delamont, 1980, p.214)

It is this process of establishment of appropriate pupil behaviour that has also been reported by Measor and Woods (1984) during the 'honeymoon' period when pupils transfer from middle school to comprehensive school. Here, rules, regulations and procedures that were appropriate in particular classrooms were transmitted to the pupils. Measor and Woods report that pupils were introduced to such practices as queuing outside classrooms before lessons began, entering classrooms in a quiet and orderly manner, waiting for permission to sit down and being discouraged from talking in the classroom. Teachers were also very careful about the way in which they explained instructions concerning new work to pupils. In turn, the authors also demonstrated how, in this initial phase of classroom encounters, pupils were willing to comply with teacher requests. However, they report that teachers could not permanently keep up a 'front', with the result that pupils began to 'come out' and test the ground rules that had been established in each classroom.

It is this process that Beynon and Atkinson (1984) have identified as the phenomenon of 'sussing out' teachers thoroughly, as they argue that the methods that pupils used to 'muck around' in particular classrooms depended on the way in which pupils had perceived the characteristics and weaknesses of teachers. In their report on research in a boys' comprehensive school in South Wales, Beynon and Atkinson provide accounts from pupils on how they collect 'data' on their teachers. For example, two boys explained to John Beynon about their data collection in the following way:

Roland: We sussed out all the teachers at the start of the year, didn't we?

JB: How?

King: Talking, messing about, whistling, funny noises, shouting your head off when they're not looking, firing paper balls through an empty biro pen, bits of rubber an' that. When the teacher's not looking you shout your head off and he turns round and says 'Who's that?' I like firing things around like bits of paper and laughing your head off when other people get into trouble. We started throwing paper aeroplanes around in Union's Maths lessons – old foureyes – but you can't fool with him much 'cos he'd send you out into the corner. You had to be careful of Mr Pickwick as well. When you're in class he's patient, in' he, but he sometimes goes really mad. (Beynon and Atkinson, 1984, pp.264–5)

Here, the pupils indicate how they had established a knowledge of those teachers with whom they could mess around and those with whom they dare not risk it. In particular, the boys found that they needed to engage in verbal and non-verbal collaboration when challenging teachers. For example, Beynon and Atkinson provide illustrations of the ways in which pupils combine with each other to challenge women teachers who they regarded as weak. Some of their activities are portrayed in the following extract from Beynon's fieldnotes:

> Mrs Paint (who teaches Art) is guillotining large sheets of art paper at a side table. Boys are in groups talking and painting. The noise builds up and peaks with an outburst in the far corner, with kids laughing and dodging around the table.
>
> Long (shouting): Sir, Sir, King is throwing water around.
>
> Mrs Paint: I'm Miss. My name is Mrs Paint.
>
> Long (cheekily): Hey, Mrs, King is chucking water around.
>
> Mrs Paint (shouting as she walks to the scene): STOP IT! Stop throwing water around. RIGHT NOW! Look at the mess!
>
> Green: He (Ginger) wet himself, Miss. (Laughter)
>
> Ginger: It's piss, Miss. (All boys collapse into laughter)
>
> Mrs Paint: Get the sponges and mop this lot up, QUICKLY! (She hits King across the head and pushes him, none too gently, towards the door) (Beynon and Atkinson, 1984, p.270)

As in many classroom situations, laughter has a major role in the action. For as Willis (1977) and Woods (1979) have shown, much 'mucking about' in classrooms centres on the activity 'having a laugh'. Peter Woods (1979) has shown how laughter can be used to help develop better relationships as well as being used as a means of reacting against authority. In particular, Woods distinguishes between two types of laughter: natural and institutionalized laughter. In the category of natural laughter he includes laughing and joking with teachers and among friends, while institutionalized laughter includes 'mucking about', using what teachers describe as silly or childish behaviour, and subversive laughter where pupils aim to undermine authority and the status of particular teachers. It is through the use of laughter in the classroom that pupils get to know their teachers.

In the early days in the classroom both teachers and pupils are gathering 'data' about each other. Both groups are establishing the boundaries in which they work, and the ways in which negotiations can occur within those boundaries. Teachers and pupils also establish classroom characters and reputations. In short, both groups begin to understand each other by categorizing and labelling their actions and activities.

So far we have focused on the intense activity that occurs in early classroom encounters, with a view to highlighting the areas that sociologists working from an interactionist perspective have attempted

to understand. In these settings, sociologists have posed numerous questions including:

How do teachers and pupils perceive each other in the classroom?

On what basis do teachers and pupils establish ideas about each other?

What kinds of strategies do teachers and pupils utilize in their attempts to gain control in the classroom?

It is to questions such as these that we now turn by reviewing work on the way in which pupils and teachers categorize each other in the classroom and the strategies used in the context of day-to-day life in classrooms.

Perceptions of pupils and teachers

As we have already seen in the examples taken from research on initial classroom encounters, teachers establish ideas about the kinds of pupils in their classes just as pupils establish information on the characteristics of their teachers. But how do teachers and pupils perceive each other in the classroom? In addressing this question, sociologists have turned to accounts of typification – a process that has been identified by Hargreaves, Hester and Mellor (1975) as the way in which people understand things by naming them, categorizing them and by labelling them. In short, they see categorization as the main way in which teachers and pupils perceive and understand each other.

In a further review of the ways in which perceptions are created through teacher–pupil interaction in classrooms, David Hargreaves (1977) identifies three models for typification. First, an *ideal matching model* which, following the work of Becker (1952), suggests that teachers have an image of the ideal pupil – a situation that results in good pupils being identified as those who come closest to the teachers' ideal image and create few problems, while deviant pupils are those who are furthest from the teachers' ideal image. In this sense, good pupils are typified according to the extent to which they conform to those rules that the teacher establishes about behaviour and patterns of learning; they are pupils who conform to the teacher's moral standards. A second model that Hargreaves (1977) identifies is the *characteristics model* by which teachers and pupils are 'typified as a unique configuration of such characteristics and these typifications are constructed in the form of an Identi-Kit'. However, those researchers working within an interactionist perspective are concerned with dynamic or process models which take account of changes in perception and typification over time and reflect the variations that occur in a particular context. This approach is identified by Hargreaves (1977) as a *dynmaic interactionist model.* This type of model has been used when pupils typify teachers and teachers typify pupils.

Among those researchers who have utilized a dynamic interactionist

Figure 1: An evaluation scheme for teachers

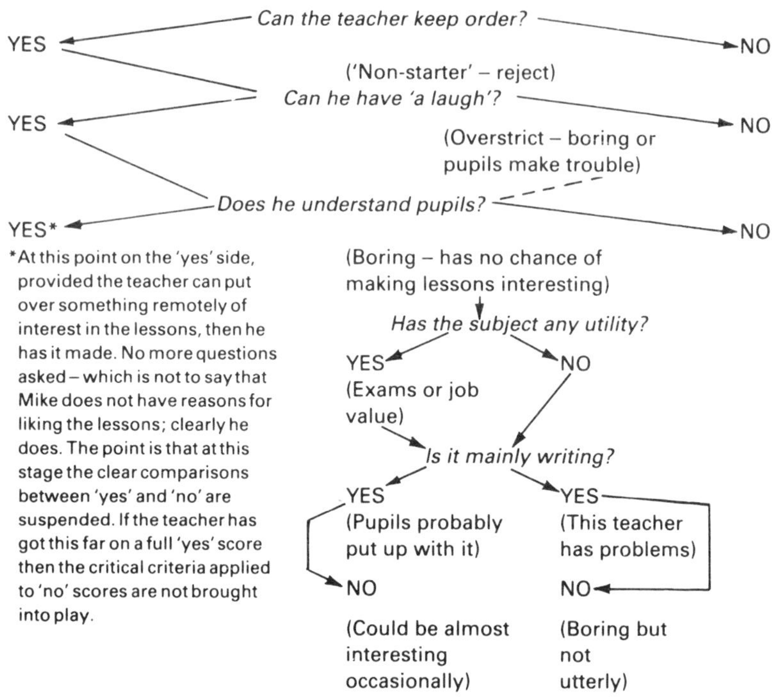

SOURCE: Gannaway (1976) p. 60

model is Gannaway (1976), who examines the way in which teachers are subjected to a series of tests (rather like those whose classroom interaction with pupils was reported by Beynon and Atkinson (1984)). Gannaway suggests that teachers are subjected to three major tests. First, can the teacher keep order? Secondly, can the teacher have a laugh? Thirdly, does the teacher understand pupils? Gannaway's model and the questions contained within it imply that pupils have some expectation that teachers will maintain control, will keep order without being too strict, and will understand the class as a group. The basic features of Gannaway's model are summarized in figure 1. This model illustrates the kinds of tests which teachers have to regularly 'pass' in the classroom and also highlights the way in which sociologists can take account of the long-term career of pupils' typifications.

But to what extent have sociologists arrived at similar models to examine the processes by which teachers typify pupils? Hargreaves, Hestor and Mellor (1975) have advanced a theory of typing which is subdivided into three stages. Firstly, speculation, when the teacher initially meets the pupil and develops a hypothesis about the kind of person the pupil will turn out to be on the basis of what the pupil has done. Secondly, elaboration, when teachers verify their initial impressions and are concerned to confirm their initial view. Finally, stabilization, when teachers have categorized their pupils and are no longer surprised by their actions and activities. It is this process that Burgess (1983) identified not merely in teachers' classrooms but also reinforced through informal discussions in the staffroom and through school reports (cf. Woods, 1979).

A further model concerning the way in which teachers perceive pupils is provided by King (1978) on the basis of observations that he made in three infants' schools. King argues that typification was inseparable from teaching, assessment, learning and classroom control. It was part of the flow of interaction in the classroom. The process of typification (as we saw in the example from Hamilton's work in infant schools and Galton and Delamont's work in middle schools) starts from the first day in the school. King found that there were three important points about the way teachers assessed and typified their pupils. First, teachers drew predominantly on their own experiences with children, as records were seldom consulted. Secondly, three aspects of classroom behaviour were used to typify pupils: compliance with the teachers's rules, relations with other pupils and their learning progress. Thirdly, typifications were not absolute but varied over time. As a consequence, King could analyse the process of typification from the teacher's point of view as:

> Each child possesses a unique, developing personality, which is expressed in his or her compliance with classroom rules, relationships with other children and learning progress each of which may influence the others. Children change naturally as they develop, but changes may also be due to changes in home or family circumstances, or illness. (King, 1978, p.60)

It is this process which is summarized in figure 2. Such a process indicates that the way in which teachers perceive pupils is based principally upon observations that were made in the classroom. In this respect, the processes that occur in each classroom influence teachers' perceptions. For example, Pollard (1984, 1985) has argued on the basis of his research in primary schools that teacher typifications are the means by which teachers achieve the goal of coping in the classroom. In particular, he maintains that teachers establish a partial view of their pupils which is based on processes of interaction, the context that structures the interaction, and the values of the wider culture. Obviously, this is just one of many processes that occur in the classroom.

Figure 2: Teachers' Typifications of Invidivual Children

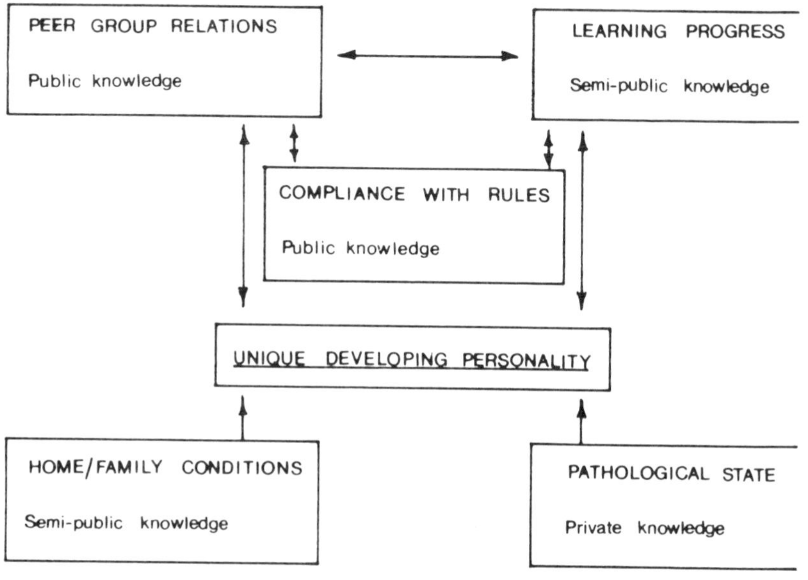

SOURCE: King (1978) p.60

However, several researchers have indicated that routine encounters in classrooms can be characterized in terms of the strategies that are used by both teachers and pupils.

Classroom strategies

Teachers and pupils are seen by researchers to engage in a variety of strategies with a view to gaining control in the classroom. This concept has been clearly specified by Pollard (1985) who writes as follows:

> Strategies . . . are essentially ways of accomplishing interaction in particular situations so that self-interests are protected or enhanced. Strategies thus have a great deal to do with power and control. Each participant in interaction will adopt strategies which best serve their interests in the context of the situation and will actively seek to define or influence that situation. (Pollard, 1985, p.184)

On this basis, he argues that teachers (who generally have more power) are able to pre-structure situations with the result that pupils develop reactive strategies, or what Denscombe (1980) has described as counter-strategies.

Several researchers working in this area have identified different kinds of strategies used by teachers and by pupils. For example, Woods (1979), in his study of a secondary modern school, outlines eight survival strategies that teachers use in order to accommodate to the circumstances that they encounter in the classroom. First, there is socialization, by which teachers attempt to get pupils to conform to patterns of prescribed behaviour. Situations such as those involved in teachers' initial classroom encounters when the rules are established are attempts on the part of teachers to define the situation. However, when these tactics do not work, teachers have to resort to a range of other strategies that include domination, negotiation, fraternization, absence or removal from the classroom, ritual and routine, therapy and morale boosting. For Woods, these approaches are initiated by teachers with a view to gaining classroom control. For example, he reports situations where teachers fraternized with pupils – a situation in which particularly young teachers attempted to identify strongly with the pupils in terms of their style of dress, manner, speech and interests. In particular, he points to the ways in which common interests, discussions about television programmes and jokes are all means by which the teacher attempted to identify with the pupils.

In his study of the primary school, Pollard (1985) identifies four teacher strategies – open negotiation, routinization, manipulation and domination – which, he indicates, are only separated for analytic purposes, as teachers use different strategies over short time periods with the consequence that strategies are often linked together. Pollard argues that it is possible to distinguish between those strategies where the power of teachers and pupils is used unilaterally and those where the power is circumscribed by the understandings constructed by the participants. On this basis, he distinguishes between three strategies. First, unilateral strategies such as domination and rebellion where teachers and pupils confront each other. Secondly, open negotiation where pupils' and teachers' interests are accepted and accommodated and, finally, negotiative strategies such as routinization – drifting and manipulation – evasion which are the product of struggles between the teacher and the pupils. Pollard classifies these strategies in the ways shown in table 3. As far as Pollard is concerned, this model can be used in relation to pupil deviance and teacher censure and to help explain the ways in which teachers and pupils handle situations in classrooms.

Yet not all pupils are treated alike in classrooms, as researchers have found that teachers develop different tactical responses in working with boys and girls. In observing four primary schools, Katherine Clarricoates (1980) found that teacher perceptions of sex differences resulted in different tactics for handling boys and girls. For example, she reports:

> Craig and Edward were involved in a game of plasticine and both are seized

TABLE 3: *Classification of Strategies (by Pollard)*

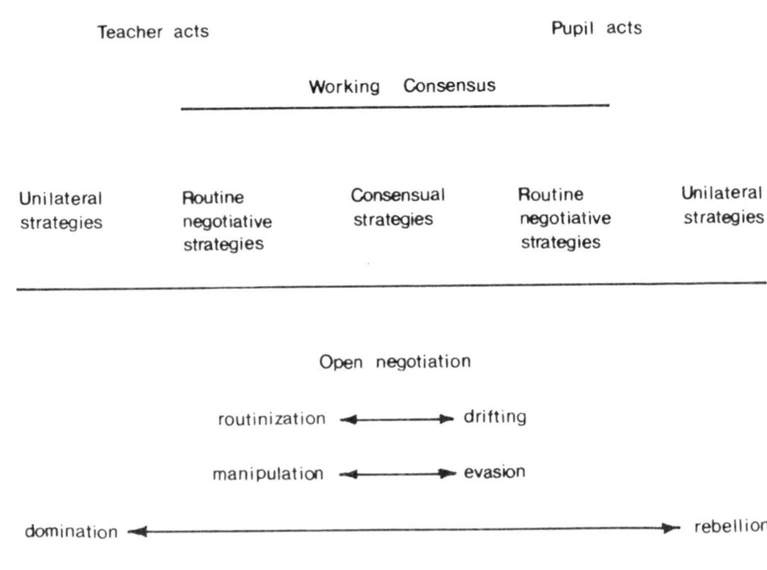

SOURCE: Pollard (1985) p.191

> with a fit of laughter. They are allowed to carry on. But . . . (when) two girls are caught up in a similar game and became noisy the teacher classed it as 'giggling hysterically' and told the girls to calm down. (Clarricoates, 1980, p.31)

Similar evidence about the ways in which boys and girls who are in the same classroom are treated differently by teachers is available in Stanworth's account of pupils in Advanced Level classes (1981). Here, she found that boys received more teacher attention in terms of being asked questions and being praised in the classroom. She also found that teacher's actions were different towards boys and girls. For example, the pupils she interviewed commented on the different ways in which teachers treated boys and girls in the following way:

> Interviewer: Does it make any difference, do you think, that Mr Macmillan is a man and Mrs Wilson is a woman?
>
> Female pupil: I suppose so, because you think he's a bit of a twit, at least I do. Whereas Mrs Wilson, I suppose I relate to her more because she's a woman.
>
> Interviewer: And do you think she feels the same way, that it's easier for her to relate to girls?
>
> Pupil: Possibly . . . No, I think it's equal actually, the way she relates to boys and girls. But take somebody like Mr Macmillan, he tends to relate better to the boys actually. When he's talking about military history or something

like that he says, 'I know you ladies won't like this' or something.

Interviewer: I see what you mean. You might feel a little bit as if you'd been excluded from that discussion.

Pupil: Yes, yes. I had another teacher like that at my old school actually. It was really annoying. He kept saying things like – it was in Physics – and he said, 'Now if you were boys you would understand this.' God, ugh! It really annoys me.

Interviewer: Does it make any difference, do you think, that Mr Macmillan is a man and Mrs Wilson is a woman?

Male pupil: Possibly, yes. I suppose the men sort of tend to . . . be a bit chauvinist, I suppose you could put it, but they do that as a joke really. Particularly Mr Macmillan. He tends to jokingly separate the two teams really. If it's a sort of social rights issue, he'll ask for the point of view of both sexes. Or he'll tease the girls that they won't understand something, say like military history. But he doesn't really concentrate on it. (Stanworth, 1981, pp.36–7)

In this sense the teachers' actions result in discrimination between boys and girls. Indeed, Stanworth argues that the teachers' actions in the classroom have an impact on the way in which pupils evaluate themselves. In addition, she demonstrates how this self-evaluation influences the way in which pupils rank each other in terms of academic ability and how boys and girls perceive each other.

However, many of these strategies appear merely to focus on classroom activity from the teacher's point of view. Accordingly, we need to examine those strategies that are used when teachers and pupils encounter each other in the classroom and which both sides enter into. It is therefore appropriate in these circumstances to look at the ways in which negotiation and bargaining occur in the classroom.

Negotiation is based on the principle of exchange. In classrooms this often results in situations where, in exchange for 'good' behaviour and a 'reasonable' amount of work, teachers relax the demands that are being made. In studying Bishop McGregor School, for example, Burgess (1983) discusses the way in which negotiations, bargains and compromises were made as teachers and pupils worked out the patterns of teaching and learning that were adopted in the Newsom Department for those pupils who were regarded as the 'less willing' and the 'less able'. He reports that some teachers had negotiated a system whereby if pupils worked in their class for one week they were given the subsequent lesson to play games as a reward for their 'work'. However, if in the teacher's view sufficient work was not produced, no games lesson was forthcoming. In a similar way one teacher defined a situation whereby if pupils worked hard they were rewarded by being allowed to make themselves a cup of coffee in the classroom. However, as Burgess notes, the pupils were eager to redefine this situation with the result that many lessons became situations where pupils would only agree to work if they were allowed to make cups of coffee. As a consequence, several classes became little more than extended coffee making sessions.

However, it was not merely over patterns of work but also over rules of behaviour that pupils entered into negotiations and bargains with teachers. For example, Burgess (1983) reports on an exchange between a teacher and a pupil where the pupil indicates he had sworn at a teacher:

John: I told Mr Gear to well . . .

RB: What was this?

John Well we were all supposed to do games last two periods on a Monday, about a couple of months ago. It was really wet so we couldn't go outside and I brought a note in saying I didn't want to do games.

RB: A genuine note?

John: Oh yes, written by me Mam. There was nothing wrong with me though, I just didn't wanna do games and so we all decided we wanted to play table tennis but Mr Gear wouldn't let me play so I said, 'Oh for fuck's sake'. He said, 'Would you mind repeating that?' I said, 'As long as I don't get into trouble'. He said, 'You're chicken' and I said, 'Well as long as I don't get into trouble' and he said 'Go on'. So I said it again and he told me to get out. (Burgess, 1983, p.219)

This account, which was verified by the teacher concerned, involves negotiation, as, in return for repeating the obscenity, the pupil had obtained a guarantee that the teacher would not punish him. Such activity constitutes a bargain over personal behaviour.

However, Delamont (1983) illustrates how bargains also occur between teachers and pupils when a short answer test is marked by pupils in the classroom. She reports as follows:

Mrs Hill: (Announces a firm marking schedule and says there are to be no arguments about it. Then starts asking round the class to get the answers . . .)

Later:
Mrs Hill: Right now what do we call the area of fertile farmland which includes Perthshire?

(Evelyn is giggling hysterically. Mrs H. asks her what the matter is, but Evelyn does not, or cannot manage to answer. Mrs H. sends her out of the room, takes her test paper away from Angela, and makes Angela and Karen swap.)

Jackie: The golden girdle.

Karen bursts out laughing, and Mrs H. asks her what is funny.

Karen: Angela has got 'golden griddle', not 'girdle'.

Mrs H. laughs, and the whole class dissolves into laughter.

Mrs H.: She can have half a mark for ingenuity. Get Evelyn back in will you?

A chorus of protests about the half mark – for the schedule had stated 'no half marks'.

Mrs H. ignores protests. Tells Evelyn she can see why it was funny, but she should have explained why she was laughing. They go on. Another question asked for 'the industries of Glasgow after the American War of Independence'. After the right answers have been given, Karen raises her hand and is asked what she wants . . .

Karen: I had 'the slave trade'. Does that count?

Mrs. H.: That's not an industry.

Karen: Well for modern Scotland we've got 'tourism' as an industry – if tourists are an industry surely slaves are too?

Mrs H. gives in and lets her have a half mark too. Another chorus of 'not fair' breaks out and is silenced . . . (Delamont, 1983, pp.106–7)

In this sense, teachers and pupils are constantly reacting to each other in the classroom. In these extracts pupils are testing out their definition of the situation compared with the definition provided by the teacher. Clearly, teachers cannot expect to be able to prescribe actions that pupils will routinely follow. Instead, negotiation occurs between teachers about rules, and about work. Woods (1983) establishes a model to illustrate the kinds of negotiations that occur in schools. In particular, he illustrates the ways in which different ways of working are linked to pupil adaptation, as shown in table 4.

TABLE 4: *Pupils and Work*

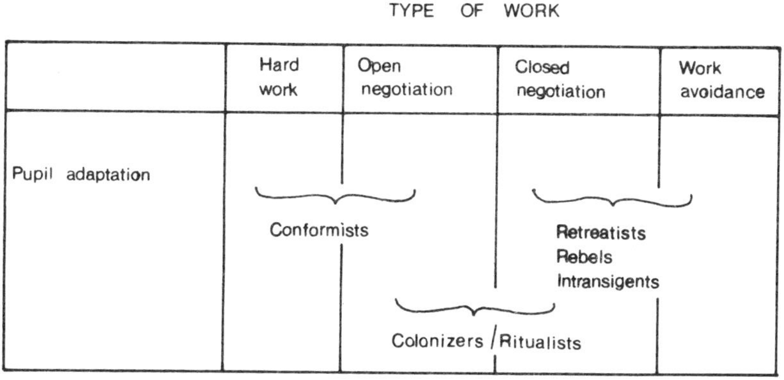

TYPE OF WORK

	Hard work	Open negotiation	Closed negotiation	Work avoidance
Pupil adaptation	Conformists	Conformists		
			Retreatists Rebels Intransigents	Retreatists Rebels Intransigents
		Colonizers / Ritualists	Colonizers / Ritualists	

SOURCE: Woods (1983) p.133

At the extremes 'hard work' is practised by conformists, while 'work avoidance' occurs among school rebels. However, most pupils are involved in some form of negotiation. Here, Woods distinguishes between open negotiation, where consensus is arrived at, and closed negotiation, where conflict occurs between the parties involved. As

Woods remarks, both 'open' and 'closed' negotiation involve mutual agreement, but while the former is made willingly, the latter is made unwillingly.

As we have seen, much of this research focuses on patterns of interaction, but relatively little work has made links between teacher–pupil interaction and curriculum content. Accordingly, we turn briefly to examine some work that researchers have conducted on what happens when teachers question pupils about the lesson content in the classroom. Walker and Adelman (1975) have suggested a typology of teaching strategies to look at the relationship between the teacher, the pupil, the knowledge that is being transmitted and the question strategy. They locate teaching strategies along two dimensions which they call 'high' and 'low' definition, and 'open' as opposed to 'closed' contents. The definition refers to the pupil's role in relation to knowledge, whereby if it is 'open' the pupil is engaged in negotiating knowledge, while if it is 'closed' the knowledge is tightly organized and the pupils have no control over it. Accordingly, this results in three questioning strategies: focusing, the Cook's tour, and freewheeling as shown in figure 3.

Figure 3: Questioning Strategies

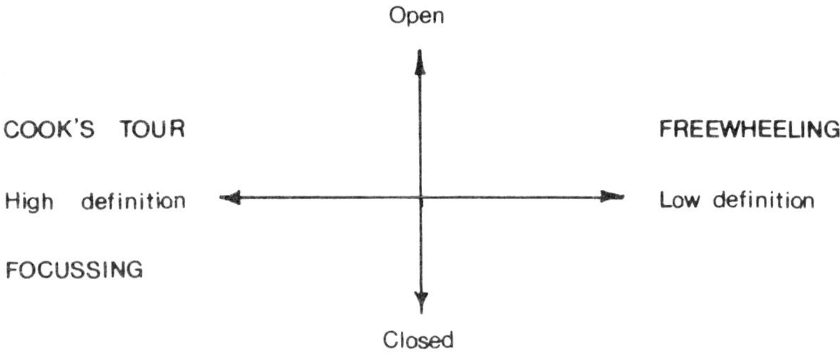

SOURCE: Walker and Adelman (1975) p.47

Within this typology focussing concerns situations where the teacher establishes question and answer sessions in a logical order where there are 'right' answers. The Cook's tour refers to further situations where right answers occur but where the subject moves in an unpredictable way. Meanwhile, freewheeling consists of an unpredictable structure where pupil contributions are not labelled right or wrong by the teacher. Such a typology needs further discussion and development if we are to begin to understand the ways in which teachers and pupils routinely work in classrooms. Clearly, if classroom research is to get close to the teaching-learning nexus it will be important for researchers to examine the ways in which classroom strategies are associated with curriculum content.

Conclusion

Writing just a decade ago, Olive Banks (1976) remarked that classroom research was characterized by its predisposition to use a similar set of research strategies. Indeed, she considered that the adherents to this approach were more concerned with a particular research method (observation and participant observation) than with a common set of problems. Much of the research in this area of study is still small scale and exploratory, but some theoretical as well as descriptive work is being conducted by researchers. At the heart of interactionist studies in classrooms is the way in which strategies, negotiations and bargains are handled in the classroom. Yet as several commentators (Hammersley, 1984a, 1984b; A. Hargreaves, 1978, 1980a, 1984, 1985; Pollard, 1982) have indicated, a central task is to link up microscopic questions in the classroom with macroscopic analyses of the educational system. Certainly, Banks (1978) has indicated that it is important to build bridges between these two approaches but, as Archer (1981) has rightly remarked, it is not simply a matter of adding together incompatible theoretical positions, as it would appear Andy Hargreaves has suggested in his discussions of 'coping strategies' in the classroom. In this respect, there are still numerous problems for classroom researchers to pursue, but the story so far does at least allow sociologists to take issue with Williamson (1979) who suggests that 'the classroom and the lessons are perhaps the least significant aspects of school learning', for classroom researchers have taken us several steps closer to the processes of teaching and learning through their research in the last decade.

Suggestions for further reading

There are now numerous accounts of classrooms that have been provided by sociologists and social anthropologists. The following list gives some guidance on the *range* of material that is available.

Atkinson, P. and Delamont, S. (1980) 'The two traditions in educational ethnography: sociology and anthropology compared', *British Journal of Sociology of Education*, volume 1, no. 2, pp.139–52, provides a comparative guide to the literature available in Britain and the USA.

Burgess, R. G. (1984) (ed) *The Research Process in Educational Settings: Ten Case Studies*, Lewes, Falmer Press contains a series of accounts by researchers on how they have conducted classroom research; see especially the essays by Ball (1984), Delamont (1984b), Fuller (1984b) and Hammersley (1984c).

Delamont, S. (1981) 'All too familiar? A decade of classroom research',

Educational Analysis, vol. 3, no. 1, pp.69–83; a fascinating critique of classroom research that raises important methodological points.

Delamont, S. (1983) *Interaction in the Classroom*, 2nd edition, London, Methuen is a basic guide to the literature. It contains a good bibliography.

Hargreaves, D. H. (1977) 'The process of typification in classroom interaction: models and methods', *British Journal of Educational Psychology*, vol. 47, pp.274–284 discusses the use of the concept of typification in the study of education.

Hargreaves, D. H. (1980) (ed) *Classroom Studies, Educational Analysis*, vol. 2, no. 2 is a special issue which reviews classroom research in the field of systematic observation (McIntyre, 1980), socio-linguistics (Edwards, 1980) and sociology (Hammersley, 1980).

McAleese, R. and Hamilton, D. (1978) (eds) *Understanding Classroom Life*, Slough, NFER consists of a set of multi-disciplinary papers.

Spindler, G. D. (1982) (ed) *Doing the Ethnography of Schooling: Educational Anthropology in Action*, New York, Holt, Rinehart and Winston. A collection of anthropological essays from classroom researchers in the USA. See especially the accounts by Spindler and Spindler (1982), Wilcox (1982) and Wolcott (1982).

Stubbs, M. (1983) *Language, Schools and Classrooms*, 2nd edition, London, Methuen is an excellent guide to classroom language.

EMPIRICAL STUDIES

There are now numerous papers and full-length studies concerned with classroom life. The following British material is especially recommended.

Burgess, R. G. (1983) *Experiencing Comprehensive Education: A Study of Bishop McGregor School*, London, Methuen. The second part of this study includes material on classroom encounters between teachers and pupils who were regarded as 'less willing' and 'less able'.

Chanan, G. and Delamont, S. (1975) (eds) *Frontiers of Classroom Research*, Slough, NFER includes a range of studies conducted in Britain in the early 1970s.

Delamont, S. (1984) (ed) *Readings on Interaction in the Classroom*, London, Methuen complements the text by Delamont. The paper by Beynon and Atkinson (1984) on sussing out teachers is worth careful study.

Edwards, A. and Furlong, V. J. (1978) *The Language of Teaching*, London, Heinemann. A study of humanities teaching which focuses on the use of language.

Hammersley, M. and Woods, P. (1984) (eds) *Life in School: The Sociology of Pupil Culture*, Milton Keynes, Open University Press.

Hargreaves, A. and Woods, P. (1984) (eds) *Classrooms and Staffrooms: The Sociology of Teachers and Teaching*, Milton Keynes, Open University Press. A pair of readers reprinting articles that have appeared in various journals and books predominantly in Britain in recent years.

Hargreaves, D. H., Hester, S. and Mellor, F. (1975) *Deviance in Classrooms*, London, Routledge and Kegan Paul provides a detailed account of typification and the way in which rules are established.

King, R. (1978) *All Things Bright and Beautiful? A Sociological Study of Infants' Classrooms*, Chichester, Wiley is a very readable account of life in infants' classrooms.

Pollard, A. (1985) *The Social World of the Primary School*, Eastbourne, Holt, Rinehart and Winston provides one of the few accounts of primary school classrooms. See especially the chapters in part three.

Stanworth, M. (1981) *Gender and Schooling*, London, WRRC (republished by Hutchinson in 1983) is an excellent study of gender relations in classrooms.

Swidler, A. (1979) *Organization without Authority: Dilemmas of Social Control in Free Schools*, Cambridge, Mass., Harvard University Press is a very good account of a Free School in California.

Woods, P. (1979) *The Divided School*, London, Routledge and Kegan Paul uses empirical material to examine theoretical issues. It contains an interesting chapter on classroom strategies.

9 The school curriculum

Sociologists have a tendency to indicate that the study of the curriculum was 'discovered' and established by Michael F. D. Young and the contributors to *Knowledge and Control* (1971a) in the early 1970s. Yet such a view overlooks the earlier interventions that were made by sociologists and other commentators as well as changes in the school system itself which stimulated teachers' and researchers' interests in the curriculum.

Among sociologists, Floud and Halsey (1961) expressed their disappointment about the lack of sociological work on the curriculum when they stated: 'It is regrettable that this whole question of the fate of the content of education should have been relatively so neglected by sociologists. Many questions suggest themselves to which no answers can as yet be attempted' (p.10). They suggested that sociologists should concern themselves with patterns of cultural transmission in the schools, but another decade was to elapse before this question began to be tackled at a theoretical level by Bernstein (1971a) and by Bourdieu (1971). While Bernstein's work has involved theoretical speculation, Bourdieu has used empirical evidence to illustrate his theoretical arguments (Bourdieu, 1973).

In England, Lawrence Stenhouse (1963) was quick to see the importance of the gap that Floud and Halsey had identified and suggested ways in which a cultural approach could be used to examine the curriculum. He suggested that researchers should develop a conceptual framework which would relate the sociology of the classroom to the content of the curriculum and that would assist in the analysis of both general and specialist education. However, Stenhouse (1983a) has subsequently shown that sociologists in the early 1960s had no interest in the curriculum. As a consequence the ideas developed in his paper were taken no further by British sociologists, yet attracted much interest in Scandinavia. A similar fate seemed to befall the work of other writers who developed research agendas for the study of the curriculum. For example, Musgrove's ideas about the contribution that sociology could make to the study of the curriculum were largely overlooked until the early 1980s when Ball (1983b) and Goodson (1982, 1985) took up his recommendation that sociologists should:

> Examine subjects both within the school and in the nation at large as social systems sustained by communication networks, material endowments and ideologies. Within a school and within the wider society subjects are communities of people, competing and collaborating with one another, defining and defending their boundaries, demanding allegiance from their members and conferring a sense of identity upon them . . . even innovation which appears to be essentially intellectual in character can be usefully examined as the outcome of social interaction. (Musgrove, 1968, p.101)

However, sociological studies of this kind were not started in schools as the content of education was not treated as problematic by researchers in the 1960s. Indeed, Williams (1961) comments that

> We speak sometimes as if education were a fixed abstraction, a settled body of teaching and learning, and as if the only problem it presents to us is that of distribution: this amount, for this period of time, to this or that group. (Williams, 1961, p.145)

Williams suggests that the content of education is developed from basic elements of culture and involves a particular selection from that culture. As a consequence the content of education reflects particular kinds of emphasis. However, much of this discussion was theoretical and speculative as no empirical studies in this area had been conducted by sociologists. As a consequence, sociologists needed to place basic questions on the research agenda concerned with the selection and organization of knowledge and the curriculum.

The 1960s and early 1970s witnessed a number of changes in the structure and organization of English education which called for close scrutiny of the curriculum and curriculum development. The reorganization of secondary schools along comprehensive lines (DES, 1965) is often seen as little more than an organizational change, but it raised issues concerning the way in which groups of pupils could be taught in mixed ability sets (cf. Ball, 1981) and issues concerned with curriculum content in both secondary and primary schools where the demise of the eleven plus selection examination caused teachers to rethink the curriculum. Finally, the proposal to raise the school leaving age to sixteen (DES, 1972) also promoted a number of curriculum developments including the Humanities Curriculum Project (Stenhouse, 1973), the Keele Integrated Studies Project (cf. Shipman, 1974) and Geography for the Young School Leaver (Wheatley, 1976), all of which have attracted detailed discussion and comment (cf. Stenhouse, 1980). As a consequence, the late 1960s and early 1970s could be seen as a period of intense curriculum development (for a detailed discussion and assessment see Stenhouse, 1983b). However, the question that still demands investigation by sociologists is the extent to which curriculum developments influence the organizational structure of education and schools. Nevertheless, such developments did not go unnoticed or unquestioned in public debate as many of the 'new' approaches to teaching and learning were subjected to critical scrutiny in the Black Papers on education (Cox and Dyson, 1969, 1970a, 1970b) which contained an attack on comprehensive education, progressive teaching methods and so on. Among the themes that were raised by contributors to the Black Papers were educational standards and political indoctrination with special reference to the secondary school curriculum.

Alongside this public debate at the beginning of the 1970s came a sociological debate which was initiated at the annual conference of the British Sociological Association and developed by the contributors to Young's volume *Knowledge and Control* (1971a) which focused upon the curriculum. Young maintained, following Seeley (1966), that sociologists had taken the concepts and categories of educators for granted and, therefore, had failed to ask questions about knowledge and the curriculum and the ways in which knowledge became selected, organized and stratified within the educational system. Indeed, the 'major' preoccupation of the contributors to this volume was well summarized by Bernstein who stated that:

> How a society selects, classifies, distributes, transmits and evaluates the educational knowledge it considers to be public, reflects both the distribution of power and the principles of social control. (Bernstein, 1971a, p.47)

In the course of this article, Bernstein outlined a theoretical map for the study of the curriculum which has subsequently been developed in theoretical and empirical studies.

Theoretical perspectives on the sociology of the curriculum

The major focus of Bernstein's work (1971a) was upon three 'message systems' through which educational knowledge is realized. First, he identified the *curriculum* which he defines as what counts as valid knowledge. Secondly, there is *pedagogy* which is concerned with educational transmission and defines what counts as the valid transmission of knowledge. Finally, Bernstein focused on *evaluation* which he regarded as the valid realization of this knowledge by those who are taught.

Within Bernstein's paper, two major concepts were introduced to examine educational knowledge: *classification* and *framing*. The term classification is used to refer to the boundary that is established between school subjects. Accordingly, he distinguishes between *strong classification* which involves subjects being kept separate from each other and *weak classification* where different areas of knowledge are brought together. In turn, Bernstein argues that the curriculum is linked to teaching methods or pedagogy whose basic principles are realized through *framing* which Bernstein defines as the degree of control that teachers and pupils have over the selection, organization, pacing and timing of what is taught. Subsequently, Bernstein (1975) has elaborated on this notion by discussing the factors which regulate teacher–pupil relationships: hierachy, sequencing rules and criteria. Where these are explicit Bernstein argues there will be a form of visible pedagogy, but when they are implicit there will be an invisible pedagogy.

As far as Bernstein is concerned, visible pedagogy involves strong classification and strong framing, while invisible pedagogy involves weak classification and weak framing. Here, Bernstein discusses a number of theoretical propositions which raise questions about curriculum content and teaching style. However, the material that Bernstein presents also deals with the place of education in social reproduction. Meanwhile, other theorists who have worked on the curriculum have been concerned with cultural reproduction (cf. Bourdieu and Passeron, 1977), with economic and cultural reproduction (Apple, 1979a, 1979b, 1982) and with the reproduction of sexual divisions (cf. Wolpe, 1974; MacDonald, 1980a, 1980b).

Much of the theoretical literature has focused attention on the place of schooling in economic reproduction; that is, the way in which the economic base reproduces and is reproduced by the ideological superstructure. However, this omits the analysis of cultural reproduction of class relations and the way in which it recreates the 'cultural capital' of dominant groups. Sociologists concerned with an analysis of the curriculum from this perspective have asked such questions as:

How do schools act as agents of social and cultural reproduction?

What role do schools play in the reproduction of ideas, beliefs, values and meanings through the curriculum?

In addressing these questions it has been argued that schools reproduce the cultural features of a capitalist society with the result that they are seen as serving the interests of dominant groups.

A major contribution to this field which has relevance for the curriculum debate is the work of Bourdieu (1973) who discusses the way in which cultural capital is transmitted between generations. Bourdieu (1973) has argued that the school reproduces the structure of socio-economic groups which are perceived as 'natural'. In turn, he maintains that the school transmits the beliefs and values of the dominant culture with the result that children from families who possess cultural capital can use the school to their advantage as it bestows legitimacy on the ability of powerful groups to use the school curriculum (cf. Anyon, 1979).

In a similar way feminists have demonstrated the way in which the school curriculum has reproduced the sexual division of labour between men and women (see also Chapter 5 in this volume). In particular, Wolpe (1974) takes up the point that has been made by Bourdieu (1971) that schools transmit a 'common code' which, she argues, will result in boys and girls learning about the different forms of behaviour which are expected of them and of men and women. Her analysis of the official reports produced by the Norwood (Board of Education, 1943), Crowther (Ministry of Education, 1959) and Newsom (Ministry of Education, 1963) Committees highlights the ways in which these reports recommended an education for girls that would channel them towards marriage rather than prepare them for waged work. Similarly, Deem (1981) has shown that during the period 1944 to 1981 the main ideas concerned with girls' education involved the preparation of working class girls for marriage and child rearing, as only middle class girls were perceived as having a dual career. In addition, David (1985) has traced the ways in which the notion of motherhood is transmitted in courses on parent education through the Youth Training Scheme and other post school programmes.

These theoretical perspectives have brought a number of curriculum issues, social processes and social mechanisms to the attention of sociologists. But what questions have they suggested? How have sociologists applied theories and concepts to the study of the curriculum?

Among the major questions that have been raised for sociologists are:

How is knowledge structured?

Why is there a status hierarchy of knowledge?

How is knowledge selected and transmitted, to whom and under what circumstances?

However, these questions only relate to that aspect of the curriculum which sociologists have termed the formal, official or manifest curriculum. In turn, they have argued that it is important to raise questions about the way in which the day to day regularities of school life contribute to learning – that is, to focus on the 'hidden curriculum' or 'para-curriculum' of schooling. In the course of examining some of these issues we shall draw on examples from empirical studies.

Studying the curriculum and the hidden curriculum

We have already identified a number of different perspectives that have been used to study the curriculum and the hidden curriculum. Just as much of the theoretical work was at an exploratory stage so are many of the empirical studies. Focusing on the work of Young and his colleagues, Lawton (1975) identified five levels with which their work was concerned:

Level 1: That the present structure and organization of education in our society serves to preserve the *status quo* in an unjust society – this level is particularly concerned with questions such as the *social distribution of knowledge*.

Level 2: That in particular the *content* of education – the selection of knowledge for transmission by schools – should be *made* into a problem for critical examination rather than be taken for granted; this level is concerned with what counts for knowledge in our society, and the stratification of knowledge.

Level 3: That *subject barriers are arbitrary and artificial*, existing largely for the convenience of those in control of education.

Level 4: That *all knowledge is socially constructed*.

Level 5: That not only knowledge but *rationality itself is merely a convention*. (Lawton, 1975, p.58)

While not all these issues are examined in Young's volume, some of them have been taken up in other studies and analyses of the curriculum.

THE STRATIFICATION OF KNOWLEDGE

Just as earlier studies in the sociology of education were concerned with stratification and differentiation so similar trends can be found within the study of the curriculum. Analyses of official reports on schooling indicate how the principles of stratification were embodied not only in the structure of schools but also in their content. For example, the different types of secondary schools that were established in England in the post Second World War period had been advocated in the Spens report (Board of Education, 1938) which argued on the basis of psychological evidence that there should be grammar schools offering an academic curriculum for the more able, and technical schools for the able pupils who were judged to be less academic than those who went to grammar schools and for whom a technical curriculum was considered appropriate. Finally, there should be secondary modern schools whose pupils would need a practical curriculum. These three different kinds of curriculum in different schools for different pupils were justified by the Norwood Committee in 1943 which stated:

> In a wise economy of secondary education pupils of a particular type of mind would receive the training best suited for them and that training would lead them to an occupation where their capacities would be suitably used; that a future occupation is already present to their minds while they are still at school has been suggested, though admittedly the degree to which it is present varies. Thus, to the three main types [of schools] sketched above there would correspond three main types of curriculum, which we may again attempt to indicate.
>
> First, there would be a curriculum of which the most characteristic feature is that it treats the various fields of knowledge as suitable for coherent and systematic study for their own sake apart from immediate considerations of occupation, though at a later stage grasp of the matter and experience of the

> methods belonging to those fields may determine the area of choice of employment and may contribute to success in the employment chosen.
>
> The second type of curriculum would be closely, though not wholly, directed to the special data and skills associated with a particular kind of occupation; its outlook and its methods would always be bounded by a near horizon clearly envisaged. It would thus be closely related to industry, trades and commerce in their diversity.
>
> In the third type of curriculum a balanced training of mind and body and a correlated approach to humanities, natural science and the arts would provide an equipment varied enough to enable pupils to take up the work of life: its purpose would not be to prepare for a particular job or profession and its treatment would make a direct appeal to interests, which it would awaken by practical touch with affairs. (Board of Education, 1943, p.4)

However, it was not just under the tripartite division of secondary schooling into grammar, technical and secondary modern schools that separate curricula were common. As Lawton (1975; 1983) indicates, the advent of comprehensive education did not result in a common curriculum. Instead, he maintains that the comprehensive school has gone through three phases of development as far as the curriculum is concerned. First, the adoption of tripartite organization within the schools with separate curricula for different groups of pupils (cf. the study by Burgess, 1983). Secondly, a phase when different patterns of curriculum arrangements were attempted, with mixed ability teaching taking place in some departments (cf. the study by Ball, 1981). Finally, a phase when concern was expressed that comprehensive schools should adopt a common curriculum which would transmit a common culture (cf. the commentary on particular schools such as Countesthorpe, Watts, 1977).

Some of these trends have become apparent through empirical studies of classrooms in comprehensive schools. For example, Nell Keddie's study of humanities teaching in a comprehensive school (1971) highlights the distinctions between the emphases that teachers gave to the curriculum with different sets of pupils. This was well illustrated by one teacher who distinguished between the different levels at which he taught lessons on the British economy to A stream and C stream pupils when he stated:

> I can streamline it [the curriculum] so it's got various grades of content and I can, I hope, do things which are very useful and valuable to the C child which I don't feel are necessary for the A child. But they're all doing economics, they're all doing certain vital basic studies on how the economy works. (quoted in Keddie, 1971, p.148)

This teacher illustrates how the degree of subject knowledge that is provided for pupils varies with the ability group to which they are allocated – a situation that highlights the ways in which differentiation and stratification occur through the school curriculum.

DIFFERENTIATION IN THE CURRICULUM

In the HMI survey of secondary education (DES, 1979) it was found that special courses were often provided for less able pupils which eliminated subject choice and a choice of options, with the result that the pupils were offered a fragmented timetable. The result was a differential allocation of the curriculum to different groups of pupils in the comprehensive school. This approach had been advocated by the Newsom Committee (Ministry of Education, 1963) who had reported on the education of average and below average children aged 13–16. It had been the view of this Committee that a curriculum should be offered to these pupils based on areas that would be practical, realistic, vocational and would involve some choice. The consequence was that the Committee had recommended courses that they considered were 'relevant' for average and below average children, while others followed examination courses in traditional subject areas – a situation that reinforced the low status given to these courses and to the subject matter. Such an approach attracted criticism from several commentators, including Marten Shipman who labelled it 'a curriculum for inequality', as he remarked:

> The new curriculum, involving topic centred approaches, interdisciplinary enquiry, projects taking the children outside the school and experience of social service and working conditions, will probably increase the motivation of the pupils and give them an insight into the working of the world around them. They are often lacking in real academic discipline and at worst can be a pot-pourri of trivia chosen because they are believed to be of interest to the young. But regardless of their worth, they could separate the education of the Newsom child from that of the future elite as effectively as when these groups were educated in different schools or systems. (Shipman, 1971, pp.103–4)

Further comments from Lawton (1973) indicated that Shipman's remarks were well founded as he argued that these new curricula 'have degenerated into watered-down meaningless outside visits; real experience has degenerated into watered-down life-adjustment courses' which were little more than attempts to keep pupils quiet and prevent them from smashing up school furniture (Lawton, 1973, p.115).

As well as some differentiation occurring between the able and less able pupils in schools, sociologists have also found that subjects have involved further differentiation based on sex. Even within the co-educational classrooms of the infant and junior school, numerous examples occur of the ways in which lesson content is differentiated between boys and girls. In the course of doing research in infants' classrooms King (1978) cites examples where curriculum content involved sexual differentiation. On an occasion when a boy had found a snail, the teacher used this situation to talk to the children about the shape of the snail, but

> When a girl went to touch it she said, 'ug, don't touch it, it's all slimy. One of the boys, pick it up and put it outside.' (King, 1978, p.43)

Such an example would suggest that the teacher is communicating what behaviour is appropriate for boys and girls (see the discussion in Chapter 5 in this volume).

Similarly, in a class lesson devoted to 'christening', King reports on a discussion between a teacher and her class where the teacher uses the curriculum to highlight the distinctions between boys and girls when a pupil volunteers a statement:

> Teacher: Now Karina?
>
> Karina: When you sometimes you got to a christening you can see which is a boy and a girl cause a boy a girl has a long dress and um a boy has a short dress.
>
> Teacher: Either a short dress or a little short suit. What colour do we say for a boy as a rule?
>
> Pupil: White.
>
> Pupil: Blue.
>
> Teacher: Blue for a boy and what for a girl?
>
> Pupils: White.
>
> Pupil: Green! Green!
>
> Teacher: White or?
>
> Pupils: Pink.
>
> Teacher: Pink! Pink! That's right. (King, 1978, pp.45–6)

However, it is not just in incidental classroom teaching where teachers discuss events with pupils that gender differentiation occurs through the curriculum, for the books and schemes of work that are provided for pupils in such basic areas of the primary school curriculum as English and mathematics also reinforce such patterns.

In analysing six well-known reading schemes used in primary schools in Britain, Glenys Lobban (1975) found that the books which were used reinforced sexual divisions, as men were usually portrayed as the central characters, while the women were subordinate to the men and played passive roles or had to be assisted by men. Furthermore, the tasks which were assigned to women and girls tended to focus on domestic roles, while men and boys were often given tasks that involved adventure and innovation. Similar portraits of boys and girls have also been found in 'adventure' stories which have been analysed and discussed by Nightingale (1977).

A further area of the primary curriculum where differentiation occurs is mathematics. In an analysis of the books that are widely used by pupils in many English primary schools, Hilary Burgess has shown how the scheme *Mathematics for Schools* by Harold Fletcher highlights sex differences, as she remarks:

> An examination of the roles in which men and women are placed in the pupils'

> books, quickly reveals that males are depicted as occupation holders in the majority of cases, while women are mainly depicted as mothers and housewives, and only in one instance is a woman shown as an occupation holder. Even here it is a predominantly 'feminine' role; that of waitress, for there are no women factory workers, ticket collectors or youth club leaders as there are men. (H. Burgess, 1983, p.61)

However, it is not only in the illustrations in the text but also in the exercises that children are given, that a differentiated view of the world is presented (cf. H. Burgess, 1983).

Many of these trends are followed up in other curriculum areas which teachers regard as more appropriate for boys than for girls. For example, Clarricoates (1978) reports that in her study of a primary school, subjects involving scientific facts and projects were regarded as more 'natural' for boys, as she reports one teacher as saying:

TABLE 1: *GCE 'O' Level Passes (A to C grades only) and GCE 'A' Level Passes by Sex and Selected Subjects (Summer Examinations) England and Wales 1979*

	'O' LEVEL		'A' LEVEL	
	Boys	*Girls*	*Boys*	*Girls*
Technical Drawing	27670	761	2162	39
Physics	79046	26309	30899	7187
Computer Science	5784	2185	1196	287
Chemistry	56337	31621	23420	10561
Economics	15502	9407	19350	8744
Mathematics	108140	75091	29107	9516
Geography	64578	48449	15073	10562
History	43124	44708	13990	14236
Biology	50456	74272	13553	15272
French	40746	61258	7141	13572
German	12040	18628	2270	4704
English Literature	63940	103779	14604	33651
Sociology	5197	15913	1996	5605
Domestic Subjects	608	33063	21	3977
English Language	126410	171668	—	—

Based upon Department of Education and Science, *Statistics of Education, Volume 2: School Leavers* (DES 1981a) Tables 28 and 29 and figures supplied by the Welsh Office for Wales.
SOURCE: Equal Opportunities Commission (1982) derived from figures 2.1 and 2.2 in the Statistical Appendix.

> I like doing subjects like geography and I do find that this is the area where the lads do come out . . . you know . . . they have got the scientific facts, they've got some geographical facts whereas the girls tend to be a bit more woollier in most of the things.
>
> The (girls) haven't got the imagination that most of the lads have got.
>
> I find you can spark the boys a bit easier than you can the girls.
>
> Boys seem to want more exciting projects to do than girls, whereas girls will fall in with most things. (Clarricoates, 1978, p.357)

Such differentiation continues into the secondary schools where it has been found in surveys by HMI (DES, 1979) and by Kelly and her colleagues (1981a) that differences occur in the number of boys and girls who take science subjects. For example, HMI found that while 48 per cent of fifth year boys took physics, only 10 per cent of girls took this subject, while 31 per cent of the boys took a course in biology compared with 58 per cent of the girls. Furthermore, the passes that pupils obtain in GCE Ordinary and Advanced Level indicate trends whereby girls tend more towards the arts subjects while boys are well represented in the sciences (see table 1 in this chapter but see also the discussion in Chapter 5). But, we might ask, what status do these different areas of knowledge have?

TABLE 2: *Acceptability of 'A' Level Subject Passes to a Sample of University Departments (n=84)*

Pure mathematics	0.92	German	0.63
Pure mathematics w. stat.	0.83	Economics	0.62
Pure mathematics w. mech.	0.82	Greek	0.62
Physics	0.81	Geology	0.61
SMP mathematics	0.78	Nuffield biology	0.60
Further mathematics	0.78	Latin	0.60
Physical science	0.71	British government	0.49
Chemistry	0.70	General studies	0.49
SMP further mathematics	0.69	Engineering science	0.46
History	0.67	Scripture knowledge	0.46
Biology	0.66	Music	0.44
Geography	0.66	Art	0.37
French	0.65	Elements of eng. design	0.27
English literature	0.64	Geom. and eng. drawing	0.24
Nuffield chemistry	0.64	Housecraft	0.15
Spanish	0.64		

SOURCE: Reid (1972) p. 50

HIGH STATUS AND LOW STATUS KNOWLEDGE

In his study of a comprehensive school, Ball (1981) indicates how differentiation between high status and low status knowledge occurs when pupils make option choices in the upper secondary school. He found that many of their choices were based on curriculum experiences in the lower part of the school (cf. Woods, 1979) and the differential status of areas of knowledge in the curriculum, in higher education and in the job market. Such trends are often based on traditional grammar school distinctions between 'academic' and 'practical' subjects (Stevens, 1960) and on the status given to subjects by university departments. For example, Reid (1972) reports how established disciplines were favoured by universities in contrast to the practical and aesthetic subjects as shown in table 2.

However, the subjects that are available in the secondary school curriculum are allocated high and low status not merely by universities and by teachers but also by pupils. For example, Burgess (1983, 1984f) discusses how pupils distinguished between academic and non-academic areas of the school curriculum. His study indicates that pupils tended to see academic subjects as being associated with the transmission of knowledge, with 'conventional' methods of teaching and learning, with standards of discipline, examinations and qualifications (cf. Cooper, 1984).

Such views are frequently shared by teachers. For example, Dodd (1978) has reviewed the development of Heavy Craft – a practical subject which has attempted to gain status and respectability by participating in external examinations. Similarly, Hanson (1971) has indicated that the Society of Art Masters attempted to gain status by means of giving qualifications not only to pupils but to teachers. The Society introduced certification and the Fellowship of the Society (FSAM) based on artistic competence and the ability to pay a fee, as they thought that the initials would carry some weight with local education authorities and boards of governors who appointed teachers.

DEVELOPING SUBJECTS

Such evidence has helped to promote a line of enquiry into the development of school subjects and their establishment as academic disciplines (cf. Ball, 1983b; Goodson, 1982; Layton, 1973). Of all these writers, it is Layton who has suggested a model for the evolution and development of school subjects, based on his analysis of science teaching. First, he suggests, a subject is placed on the timetable due to its relevance to the needs and interests of the pupils, but at this stage it is rarely taught by specialists. Secondly, a tradition of scholarly work emerges with trained specialists who can be recruited to teach, and students are attracted to the subject through its growing academic status. Finally, the teachers become a professional body who, as specialists, are able to select the subject matter. Such a model has resulted in investigations by Ball and by Goodson on the development of Environmental Studies and English respectively using what Ball (1983b) refers to as a social interactionist perspective of curriculum development and change. Goodson's study examines the way in which subjects are not monolithic but comprise shifting sets of sub-groups with a common name. Secondly, he looks at the ways in which school subjects are associated with academic, utilitarian and pedagogic traditions, and finally at the way in which subjects pursue academic status. In concluding his study, Goodson (1982) comments that the dominance of the academic tradition in subject areas bears witness to the view that 'the fundamental structures of the curriculum have withstood comprehensive reorganization' (p.199). Similarly, Ball (1983b), commenting on the development of 'new' English, remarks that it could only make headway in low status areas of schooling: with girls, with the working class and with the lower middle class in state secondary schools. Such evidence suggests a polarity between different subject areas in the school curriculum – a situation that has been clearly revealed in Burgess's study of Bishop McGregor School (Burgess , 1983, 1984f).

In examining this comprehensive school Burgess focused on the Newsom course for 'less able' and 'less willing' pupils. Here he found that pupils made comparisons between subject areas and the Newsom curriculum as shown by the following discussion between three pupils:

> Jenny: My best year here [at McGregor], I thought was my first year. It was really great.
>
> Sheila: Yes. Geography, English, Maths, tutorial, R.E. You learnt loads here you know. It would be great if it went though all the years.
>
> Jenny and Sarah: Yes.
>
> Sheila: Yes you could learn the whole lot, never mind what anybody else wanted to do.
>
> Jenny: I get very fed up when I'm sitting at home and I think well why do I have to do this Newsom?
>
> Sheila: Yes.
>
> Jenny: I sometimes even cry because I get that depressed about it. (Burgess, 1984f, p.191)

These views were supported by other pupils who not only contrasted subject and non-subject areas of the curriculum but drew distinctions between those areas of the curriculum that led to an examination and those that did not. As far as they were concerned, it was examinations and qualifications that gave status to an area of the curriculum. This evidence has also been supported by Measor (1984) who shows how pupils perceive English and mathematics as having high status, especially when compared with needlework, art and music. The pupils in Measor's study considered that examination qualifications in English and mathematics would help them to obtain a job – a situation they did not see arising if they had qualifications in practical subjects.

SELECTING KNOWLEDGE AND CONTROLLING THE CURRICULUM

However, we need to consider who decides on the courses that pupils should follow. The routes that pupils take in making subject choices and the influence of teachers, parents and peers in this programme have been charted by Woods (1979) in his ethnographic study of Lowfield Secondary School. Here, he indicates that curriculum decisions about option choices are not merely made on the basis of pupils' past performances but also on the basis of family background, social class and peer group culture, for, as Woods indicates, pupils make choices that are underpinned by attitudes and values which are derived from the pupils' position in the class structure. But once these decisions have been made, who decides about curriculum content?

In reviewing recent developments in the curriculum, Eggleston (1977b) suggests that it is rather more difficult for headteachers and heads of departments to be aware of all the developments within a curriculum area with the consequence that individual teachers have the authority to interpret what material is appropriate within their classes. Such a perspective suggests that it is the teacher who holds control in the classroom. For example, Keddie (1971) argues that teacher control is established when the teacher's definition of the situation is maintained publicly. Keddie illustrates this phenomenon by quoting a brief discussion between a teacher and a pupil where the pupil asks the teacher about lesson content:

> Pupil: This is geography, isn't it? Why don't we learn about where countries are and that?
>
> Teacher: This is socialization.
>
> Pupil: What's that? I'd rather do geography . . . Metsilik Eskimo – I don't know where that is.
>
> Teacher: (ironically) After the lesson we'll go and get the atlas and I'll show you. (Keddie, 1971, p.140)

Similarly, Delamont (1983) discusses the way in which teachers have access to, and control over, knowledge. In these circumstances the teachers can define what is and is not appropriate material in the classroom. But what mechanisms exist by which this can be done? Delamont provides an illustration from a classroom discussion in a history lesson which is about the Napoleonic wars but follows on from a discussion of British politicians in the period. At the beginning of the class the following situation occurs:

> Evelyn puts up her hand. Mrs Flodden acknowledges it and asks what she wants.
>
> Evelyn: I've got an epigram about Burke – can I read it?
>
> Mrs F. says 'yes of course'. Evelyn reads her epigram and gets laughter from the class.
>
> Mrs F. gets Evelyn to write it on the board so anyone who chooses can copy it down. Then announces 'notes on the Napoleonic wars'. (Delamont, 1983, p.51)

Here it is evident that the teacher has control over lesson content as the pupil offers to make a contribution to the class and the teacher agrees to accept an intervention from a pupil. However, the fact that it is not compulsory to copy down the material that the pupil has written on the board, while the notes provided by the teacher have to be copied, illustrates the degree of control that teachers have over the official curriculum. But what of the unofficial curriculum?

THE HIDDEN CURRICULUM

Those aspects of schooling which carry messages and consequences that are not directly intended or foreseen by teachers are known as the 'hidden' curriculum or the 'paracurriculum'. The term hidden curriculum was identified by Philip Jackson (1968) to refer to situations that:

> each student (and teacher) must master if he is to make his way satisfactorily through the school. The demands created by these features of classroom life may be contrasted with the academic demands – the 'official' curriculum, so to speak – to which educators traditionally have paid the most attention. As might be expected, the two curriculums are related to each other in several important ways . . . Indeed, many of the rewards and punishments that sound as if they are being dispensed on the basis of academic success and failure are really more closely related to the mastery of the hidden curriculum. (Jackson, 1968, pp.33–4)

Accordingly, Jackson argues that the 'hidden' curriculum is essential for pupils to acquire if they are to understand what is being transmitted through the rules, routines and regularities of the school day and to survive in the school and classroom. The hidden curriculum, therefore, has a positive contribution to make to the whole curriculum of a school. Amongst the aspects of the hidden curriculum that pupils quickly acquire are the ability to: ignore interruptions or at least to tolerate them, use time, accept the judgements of teachers and fellow pupils, learn to 'give the teacher what she wants' (cf. Henry, 1963), learn to control the pace of classes, and learn the language of the classroom (cf. Walker and Adelman, 1976).

Another aspect of the hidden curriculum identified by Snyder (1971) he perceives as being closely related to the system of grading, assessment and examinations in the classroom. Indeed, pupils may learn to bargain for marks in the classroom (cf. Delamont, 1983, pp.106–7), may learn when cheating is appropriate and what is essential to pass public examinations. In Glenn Turner's (1983) study of examinations, he indicates how the 'tips' that were provided by teachers were often regarded by pupils as the most important things to learn on an exam course. He reports how pupils make judgements about the relative abilities of teachers in terms of the extent to which they can prepare pupils for examinations.

Nevertheless, David Hargreaves has argued that the term hidden curriculum is inadequate, as he asks 'from whom, one wonders, is the hidden curriculum now hidden?' (Hargreaves, 1978b, p.97). As a consequence, he proposes the term 'paracurriculum' to refer to all that is taught and learned alongside the official curriculum. Accordingly, Hargreaves maintains that the focus of much work and writing in this area has been upon the role of the paracurriculum within the school. Hargreaves extends this view of the paracurriculum by focusing not merely on school-wide processes but also on learning that makes a contribution to socialization outside the school and the years that are spent in formal education. Accordingly, he draws material from neo-Marxist writing on the paracurriculum such as that of Bowles and Gintis (1976) who have argued that hierarchical relationships that occur in schools between teacher and pupils, pupils and pupils and pupils and their work replicate the division of labour in the work place; that there is a degree of correspondence between the social relations of schooling and of the work place and that through educational encounters individuals are taught to accept powerlessness with which they will be confronted at work (see Chapter 2 in this volume). However, it is not merely on the social relations of production that the paracurriculum is focused, for it also communicates messages to pupils about sexual and racial divisions in society.

We have already examined a number of curriculum examples where sexual divisions in society were being communicated, e.g. through the material contained in a series of primary school mathematics books (cf. H. Burgess, 1983). Similarly, Judith Samuel (1981) illustrates how, in secondary schools, the textbooks that are used in many science departments carry illustrations of men and boys in active roles and women and girls in passive roles. She argues that these books are providing material not merely about science but also about gender divisions in society. Furthermore, it is argued that such images may well influence the way in which science is seen as a subject area that might be more appropriate for men and boys. If we turn to reading material and other schemes of work we find that pupils are provided with images of race and ethnicity. For example, in her analysis of the primary school mathematics scheme *Mathematics for Schools*, Hilary Burgess (1983) writes that both in the text and in the illustrations there are very few children who are portrayed as belonging to 'other cultures' beyond Britain. In addition, she found that in all the 17 books that are contained in this mathematics scheme, there is not a single adult who comes from a culture other than what could be described as 'English'. As Hilary Burgess perceptively remarks: 'For an Asian, West Indian or any other child belonging to different ethnic groups, what message is being given concerning their future adult role?' (H. Burgess, 1983, p.63)

Such analyses indicate that the curriculum transmits particular messages to pupils about their own position in society and that of others. Furthermore, it also transmits a particular selection from culture, so much so that some social scientists and sociologists have discussed the relevance of introducing a common culture curriculum, and a multicultural curriculum into our schools (cf. Jeffcoate, 1984). It is, therefore, to a brief consideration of these aspects of the curriculum that we now turn.

The common culture curriculum debate

One of the advocates of a common culture curriculum has been Denis Lawton (1973, 1975, 1983) who bases his argument for it on the view that comprehensive education can only be developed if a common curriculum is adopted for all pupils. Lawton considers that the traditional grammar school curriculum is inadequate as it lacks the coverage and balance that is appropriate for the range of pupils that attend comprehensive schools. Accordingly, he advocates a curriculum based on a coverage of the main elements of common culture which he argues will include: mathematics, the physical and biological sciences, the humanities and social studies, the expressive arts and moral education. An important feature of this type of curriculum is that every child should reach a minimum understanding in each of the five areas. However, he adds that the idea is not to reduce everyone to the same level but to provide an opportunity for each person to have access to the same kind of knowledge.

In advancing this proposal Lawton argues that the idea of a working class curriculum would detract from the idea of a common curriculum. However, on this point he has been challenged by Ozolins (1979) who argues that Lawton overlooks the concepts of class and hegemony, relies too much on working class life style rather than examining wealth and power and overlooks class and culture. As a consequence, Ozolins proposes ways in which schools might begin to come to terms with a working class curriculum that would closely follow the model proposed by Robins and Cohen (1978) which would include: literacy and communication skills, self health, social biology and sex education, the history of working class life and struggle – local, national and international, and studies in applied science and technology.

In response, Lawton (1983) questions the subdivisions that are made within the working class curriculum and argues that these subdivisions could fit into his own categories. Furthermore, Lawton suggests that the criticisms that are advanced are not merely about the curriculum but about the school as an institution, yet he argues that to provide working class pupils with a curriculum that is different from the content provided for middle class children would sell them short. Accordingly, he maintains that it is essential to examine: curriculum content, pedagogy and school organization, including evaluation, in the course of reforming the pattern of schooling and the curriculum.

A further area which has given rise to problems for Lawton's idea of a common curriculum is the provision of curricula for ethnic minorities. Skilbeck's idea (Skilbeck, 1982) that a common curriculum or core curriculum is appropriate for all pupils is now generally endorsed, as the Home Affairs Committee (1981) have argued that curriculum needs for children from different ethnic minorities are the same as for all other pupils. Indeed, Lawton (1983) maintains that a common curriculum would allow an opportunity for cultural differences to be included in programmes on the arts, religious and social values – all of which would be added to the common curriculum. However, sociologists have yet to conduct empirical analyses of the ways in which schools have come to terms with a common culture and with multi-cultural curricula.

Conclusion

This chapter has focused on some sociological perspectives that have been used in analyses of the school curriculum. At the present time, both the theoretical and empirical studies that have been conducted are at a developmental stage. It is only in the last ten years that sociologists have focused in detail on the curriculum using interactionist, feminist and neo-Marxist perspectives. In turn, empirical studies have tended to be of an exploratory kind, examining developments in subject areas, tracing the socio-historical origins of school subjects, examining the ways in which subjects are transmitted in schools and the ways in which the curriculum contributes to stratification and differentiation in the schooling system.

As this chapter has indicated, at secondary school level much curriculum content is closely linked with examinations. Accordingly, with changes in patterns of examining and increased central control (cf. Broadfoot, 1983, 1984) one of the issues that sociologists need to examine is the extent to which teachers and pupils can exercise any control over curriculum content in the schools. Such issues certainly need to be addressed at a time when it is essential to assess the impact of such trends as falling rolls on the content of the curriculum and its transmission in the latter part of the twentieth century.

Suggestions for further reading

There is a vast literature on the curriculum but only a relatively small number of items focus directly on sociological issues or provide material on which sociologists have worked. The following list has, therefore, been restricted to material that deals with sociological questions on the curriculum.

Apple, M. (1979) *Ideology and Curriculum*, London, Routledge and Kegan Paul is a neo-Marxist analysis of the curriculum.

Deem, R. (1978) *Women and Schooling*, London, Routledge and Kegan Paul contains two chapters that deal with the official and the hidden curriculum. The author considers sexism and gender differentiation in relation to these topics.

Eggleston, J. (1977) *The Sociology of the School Curriculum*, London, Routledge and Kegan Paul provides a sociological analysis of the curriculum. It is the only sociological text book at the present time to devote itself entirely to the school curriculum.

Gordon, P. and Lawton, D. (1978) *Curriculum Change in the Nineteenth and Twentieth Centuries*, London, Hodder and Stoughton. A book that combines historical and sociological analyses of curriculum issues in England. The authors provide discussions of curriculum issues together with brief case studies of subjects. There are many excellent examples of curriculum documents reproduced in this volume.

Lawton, D. (1975) *Class, Culture and the Curriculum*, London, Routledge and Kegan Paul includes a discussion and evaluation of some of the main contributions to the curriculum. In the final chapter Lawton develops a proposal for a common culture curriculum together with examples drawn from three schools.

Lawton D. (1980) *The Politics of the School Curriculum*, London, Routledge and Kegan Paul is an analysis of numerous curriculum documents that were produced by the DES and by HMI in the late 1970s. Lawton indicates that they suggest a move towards central control.

Lawton D. (1983) *Curriculum Studies and Educational Planning*, London, Hodder and Stoughton is a useful summary of the main curriculum debates together with a response by Lawton to critics of the common curriculum.

Spender, D. and Sarah, E. (1980) (eds) *Learning to Lose: Sexism and Education*, London, The Women's Press. A collection of essays that contains analyses of the images of women and girls in curriculum materials together with discussions of a feminist model of teaching and learning.

Stenhouse, L. (1975) *An Introduction to Curriculum Research and Development*, London, Heinemann. A challenging text that presents problems and puzzles about curriculum issues. It brings together work that has been conducted from a variety of perspectives. It is an exciting book that is well worth consulting.

Young, M. F. D. (1971) *Knowledge and Control: New Directions for the Sociology of Education*, London, Collier-Macmillan. The first collection of sociological papers on the curriculum. Many are exploratory and those by Bernstein (1971a), Bourdieu (1971), Davies (1971), Keddie (1971) and Young (1971b) are all worth consulting.

EMPIRICAL STUDIES

Many studies are at an early stage of development. There are collections of papers from historians and sociologists, as well as socio-historical and sociological studies.

Goodson, I. F. (1982) *School Subjects and Curriculum Change*, London, Croom Helm is a socio-historical study that focuses on the development of Environmental Studies. A good example of curriculum research from an historical perspective.

Goodson, I. F. and Ball, S. J. (1984) (eds) *Defining the Curriculum*, Lewes, Falmer Press contains histories and ethnographies of the curriculum. The papers by Burgess (1984f) and by Cooper (1984) discuss the criteria associated with non-subjects and subjects respectively.

Hammersley, M. and Hargreaves, A. (1983) (eds) *Curriculum Practice: Some Sociological Case Studies*, Lewes, Falmer Press contains papers on the ways in which the curriculum is transmitted in the classroom. It includes discussions on the development of curriculum subjects, gender and the curriculum and examinations, accountability and assessment.

Kelly, A. (1981) (ed) *The Missing Half: Girls and Science Education*, Manchester, Manchester University Press. A collection of papers that focus on the science curriculum. Sections two and three, which contain discussions of research reports and personal experiences, are especially relevant.

Shipman, M. (1974) *Inside a Curriculum Project*, London, Methuen provides an ethnographic account of the Keele Integrated Studies Project.

Waring, M. (1979) *Social Process and Curriculum Innovation*, London, Methuen provides an account of curriculum change on the Nuffield Science Teaching Project.

10 Sociological enquiry and educational studies

This book has focused upon the research evidence that has been made available through sociological studies in education. A particular concern has been with the kinds of research questions that have been formulated by researchers and the ways in which the evidence that has been made available reflects the kinds of questions that were posed. In each chapter, examples have been taken from major studies to sensitize the reader to the main issues that appear on the research agenda for sociologists engaged in the study of education.

In this sense, this book follows what Davies (1981a, 1983) has called a 'topic' based approach to sociological study rather than theoretical concerns in the sociology of education (cf. Demaine, 1977) or with the methods that are used in educational studies (cf. Cohen and Manion, 1980) or with the processes involved in research that is conducted in educational settings (cf. Burgess, 1984d, 1985a, 1985c, 1985d). Yet this does not mean that these subject areas are neglected, as a research focus brings together a concern with problems, theories and methods in the sociology of education. However, the discussion of theory and method has been much more implicit, while the problem areas have been our central concern.

A brief comparison with earlier texts that use the 'topic' approach to examine the sociology of education (cf. Banks, 1976; Musgrave, 1979; Reid, 1978) indicates that the main subject areas have remained much the same. However, some shifts are worthy of note. First, studies devoted to education and the economy have now to concern themselves with the way in which there is a relationship not only between schooling and occupations but also between schooling and unemployment, a situation that has been discussed in a recent collection of papers entitled *Schooling for the Dole?* (Bates *et al*, 1984). Secondly, while many sociological studies in education have continued to be preoccupied by social division, we should note that they are no longer exclusively concerned with social class as they now include discussions of gender

TABLE 1: *Numbers of pupils in maintained nursery, primary and secondary schools, England (thousands)*

	1976	*1981*	*1986*	*1991*	*1996*	*Birth Projections*	
Under 5			310	390	410	High	
	370	333	300	360	380	Upper	Central
				330	340	Lower	range
			290	290	300	Low	
5–10				3,888	4,537	High	
	4,484	3,851	3,350	3,749	4,229	Upper	Central
				3,654	3,877	Lower	range
				3,434	3,468	Low	
11–15					2,878	High	
	3,405	3,476	3,027	2,500	2,803	Upper	Central
					2,761	Lower	range
					2,630	Low	
16+	259	310	322	279	265		
All ages			7,009	7,057	8,090	High	
	8,522	7,970	6,999	6,888	7,677	Upper	Central
				6,763	7,243	Lower	range
			6,989	6,503	6,663	Low	

SOURCE: Walsh *et al* (1984) p. 2

and race. Thirdly, studies in the sociology of education are concerned not only with the relationship between education and other social institutions but also with the way in which education is defined by participants in schools and classrooms. Finally, sociologists have taken up questions that relate to the content of education which can be examined through analyses of the school curriculum.

Much of this research has been conducted through an analysis of state secondary schools and schooling, although in recent years there have been some studies of infant and junior schools (cf. King, 1978; Pollard, 1985) and analyses of the primary school curriculum (Campbell, 1985). Sociologists have also turned their attention to special education (Barton and Tomlinson, 1981, 1984; Tomlinson, 1982), to aspects of education in the independent sector (Walford, 1984) and to higher education (cf. Startup, 1976, 1985). Yet we should note that much of this research takes up some of the familiar themes and debates that have been at the centre of the sub-discipline and applies them to specialist fields. For example, discussions still continue about equality and inequality and about equality of educational opportunity. In turn, sociologists of education have also been concerned with contemporary issues such as in-school evaluation (Shipman, 1978) and patterns of assessment (cf. Broadfoot, 1979, 1983), and have contributed to debates about pastoral care (Lang and Marland, 1985), and the shape and substance of community education (D. Hargreaves, 1982, 1984).

Some gaps in our knowledge

Recent developments in English education, such as the significance of the Manpower Services Commission, the introduction of the Technical Vocational Education Initiative, the demise of the Schools Council (cf. Plaskow, 1985) and its replacement by two new bodies – the Secondary Examinations Council and the School Curriculum Development Committee – demand sociological attention. An analysis by sociologists of these developments would not only contribute to our understanding of contemporary issues but would also help to develop and test sociological theories and explanations about the place of education in contemporary society.

A further development that we have witnessed in recent years concerns changes in the school population, with falling rolls and the redeployment of teachers, which have implications for the size and structure of schools (cf. Walsh *et al*, 1984). The main trends in the demographic data on pupils and teachers in England is provided in tables 1 and 2. These data on pupils suggest that sociologists should direct their attention not only to the provision of primary and secondary schooling but also to a range of questions about such topics as: education for the under fives, pupils' participation in the independent sector and the proportion of pupils staying at school beyond the age of 16. For it is on the basis of the number of pupils in the school population that projections have been made concerning the number of teachers that will be required in the school system over the next decade. The main trends in demand for primary and secondary teachers are shown in table 2.

TABLE 2: *Primary and secondary teacher numbers as projected by ACSET*[1]

	Primary	*Secondary*
1981	189.0	244.0
1982	180.0	242.5
1983	171.5	238.0
1984	163.5	231.5
1985	160.5	223.5
1986	161.5	215.5
1987	162.5	207.5
1988	165.0	198.0
1989	169.5	189.0
1990	175.5	181.5
1991	180.5	178.0
1992	185.0	178.0
1993	190.5	179.5
1994	196.5	183.5

NOTE: 1. Advisory Committee for the Supply and Education of Teachers
SOURCE: Walsh *et al* (1984) p. 27

These projections have important implications for the ways in which local education authorities implement their policies and, in turn, have further implications for the structure of the teaching force, patterns of employment and redeployment among teachers, teacher morale, the implementation of teacher assessment and bargaining over teachers' pay and conditions of service. Such topics focus on politics and policy-making – a subject that has been on the educational research agenda of political scientists (cf. Kogan, 1975, 1978) but has remained relatively undeveloped in sociological work. Indeed, in a recent survey of sociological evidence Salter and Tapper (1981) went so far as to remark that:

> There is a severe danger that important educational change will take place in Britain unbeknown to many educational sociologists. Preoccupied as they are with how and why the working class remain working class or the way in which the social relations of capitalist production are reproduced, they deal only indirectly with the political and administrative specifics of educational change. (Salter and Tapper, 1981, p.221)

It is on this point that several sociologists of education are agreed (Archer, 1981, 1984; Burgess, 1984b; Davies, 1981a) – namely that we lack the ability to provide explanations about educational domination, power and control. Indeed, Archer has argued that this situation has arisen because sociologists have not developed the study of educational politics.

As far as Archer (1981) is concerned, the term 'educational politics' can be used broadly to refer

> to the attempts of different social groups to influence the inputs, processes and outputs of education, whether by legislation, pressure group and union activities, experimental, traditional or sectional movements, private or collective investment, propaganda or public debate. (Archer, 1981, p.267)

For Archer, the study of educational politics would provide a theory that would give a detailed specification of the processes of educational change in different educational systems and a theory that would specify the conditions under which different social groups can influence the definition of instruction. Such a project would involve, in her view, a sociology of educational systems where decision-making is the focus of study, for she argues (Archer, 1984) that sociologists cannot understand the decision-making processes by treating educational influence as if it were the equivalent of osmosis. Instead she maintains that

> we need to locate social interest groupings, to specify their access to processes of educational negotiation and to analyze strategic power-play in these transactions. (Archer, 1984, p.x)

It is on this basis that she claims it is possible to begin to work towards an understanding of changes in educational policy and provision. However, Salter and Tapper (1981) and Dale (1982) argue that, by focusing on questions that relate to decision-making, political questions are bracketed out and politics is merely reduced to the study of administration. Accordingly, Salter and Tapper (1981) maintain that we need to address such questions as: Where is educational power located? What social forces determine educational power? As we have seen in many other areas of study that have been reviewed in this volume, there is some dispute about the kinds of questions that need to be addressed. However, it is agreed that sociologists need to place the study of educational politics firmly on the research agenda. One area where this has been done is in the analysis of the curriculum, as Lawton (1980, 1983, 1984) has discussed the politics of the school curriculum – a subject to which we briefly turn.

Studying the politics of education: the school curriculum

Traditionally, within the English school system it has been considered that central government and local education authorities exercised relatively weak control over what occurred in schools and classrooms, so much so that it has been relatively common for commentators to talk of a 'partnership' between central government, the local education authorities and teachers concerning curriculum matters. Indeed, even in 1980 the Department of Education and Science described the position in the following terms:

> Legally, the curriculum is the responsibility of the local authorities; in practice, decisions about its content and about teaching methods, timetabling and the selection of textbooks are usually left to head teachers and their staff. (DES, 1980a, pp.18–19)

However, it is this position that has become the subject of debate among social scientists concerned with education (cf. Kogan, 1978; Lawton, 1980, 1983, 1984) who claim that teacher autonomy has been questioned by the role that has been played by the Department of Education and Science. In particular, they point to the destruction of the teacher controlled curriculum development agency (the Schools Council) despite the support that it was given by the Trenaman Committee (DES, 1981d); the establishment of the Assessment of Performance Unit for national curriculum evaluation; and the appearance of a number of documents relating to the school curriculum and the education of teachers that suggest an increased form of central political control (cf. DES, 1980a, 1980b, 1981b, 1981c, 1983b, 1984).

The main DES watcher and commentator in recent years has been Denis Lawton. In his early discussion of the politics of the curriculum (Lawton, 1980), he identified three major themes. First, that the DES was moving away from its traditional non-interventionist stance on curriculum matters to a more positive *dirigiste* and centralist role. In particular, he charted the shift from 'partnership' to 'accountability' whereby local education authorities were *required* to provide information about curriculum matters (as reflected in Circular 14/77 (DES, 1977b) which asked LEAs for information on their curriculum provision). Secondly, he pointed to the kind of control involved which he argued was centralist and directive over curriculum matters in a bureaucratic, technicist and non-professional way – a situation that he maintained was reflected in the Assessment of Performance Unit. Thirdly, he argued that there was a disturbing degree of manipulation and secrecy associated with curriculum matters – a point that he sustained by making reference to the use of the Assessment of Performance Unit and the leaking of the DES Yellow Book in 1976 (for detailed discussion see Lawton, 1980). On the basis of a subsequent review of curriculum developments between 1979 and 1984, Lawton (1984) examines each of these judgements and argues that he did not exaggerate the drift towards a more centralist and *dirigiste* stance in the Department of Education and Science. Secondly, he feels he was right to be concerned about the bureaucratic, technicist

Figure 1: Curriculum Autonomy in Educational Systems

	Curriculum Autonomy		
	content	*pedagogy*	*evaluation*
Level			
National			
Regional			
Institutional			
Departmental			
Individual			

SOURCE: Lawton (1984) p. 14

trend in curriculum matters which has been underscored by the emphasis on objectives, tests and measurement in the name of accountability. Finally, he does concede that his charge of secrecy and manipulation by the DES over curriculum matters is not so evident in recent years.

However, as Lawton (1983, 1984) indicates, the key issue that confronts the researcher can be summed up in the question: *Who controls the curriculum?* To address this question, Lawton (1984) develops a model of curriculum autonomy in educational systems which he discusses in relation to England and which is shown in figure 1. Here, Lawton outlines five levels of curriculum responsibility:

1 National (the DES, although he does indicate this is disputed territory).
2 Regional (the Local Education Authorities).
3 Institutional (the school).
4 Departmental (probably only in secondary or large primary schools).
5 Individual (the teacher in the classroom).

However, Lawton also makes the point that it is not only important to be able to specify the level at which curriculum control occurs but also essential to be able to specify the dimension of the curriculum that is under discussion. Following Bernstein (1975), he identifies three areas of the curriculum.

1 Curriculum content.
2 Pedagogy (including teacher/pupil relations as well as teaching method).

3 Evaluation (including examinations, testing and assessment).

On the basis of these five levels of curriculum control and three dimensions of the curriculum, Lawton is able to construct a matrix with 15 cells (see figure 1) which he argues can be used to compare curriculum control in different societies at a paricular point in time or to examine changes within a particular society. Lawton argues that in England at secondary school level there has been a tendency for curriculum content to be controlled at the institutional level, and pedagogy has been the domain of the individual teacher, while evaluation has taken place outside the institution using regional and national guidelines. However, he makes the point that control is not static, with the result that in recent years there has been a shift towards control at national level over content and evaluation (cf. DES, 1981b, 1981c, 1983b).

Similarly, when Campbell (1985) attempts to apply Lawton's model to the primary school he finds similar trends. In examining the primary school curriculum, he takes the example of a mathematics curriculum whose content may be defined by a local authority working party (at the regional level) but where teaching methods (pedagogy) remain for the individual teacher to decide and where evaluation may occur on the basis of tests and techniques devised by a school staff (at the institutional level). While Campbell (1985) argues that this model has some value, he also maintains that it understates the complexity of the curriculum in two ways. First, he argues that all curriculum subjects cannot be treated equally as some subject syllabuses may be adopted by the local authority, while others may allow for the autonomy of the individual teacher. Secondly, he maintains that there is the question of the extent to which teachers may translate policy directives at the national and regional levels into practice at the institutional levels. Nevertheless, Campbell concludes that there is a strong central directive (often mediated through local authorities) about the priorities to be adopted in curriculum development in the primary school.

However, Lawton (1984) has indicated that his model can be modified, especially at the national level. In particular, he argues that there is a necessity to subdivide the central authority at national level into three groups:

1 The politicos (ministers, political advisers and so on).
2 Bureaucrats (DES officials).
3 The professionals (HMI).

He also argues that *what* a group wants to control can be seen in terms of different ideologies – that is different beliefs, values and tastes. As a consequence he suggests that the different ideologies held by the three groups are as shown in figure 2.

While Lawton acknowledges that reality is much more complex than

Figure 2: Ideologies in Education (Lawton's Model)

	Three Ideologies in Education		
	Beliefs	*Values*	*Tastes*
Politicos	market	freedom of choice	independent schools fees
Bureaucrats (DES)	good administration	efficiency	central control exams standard tests
Professionals (HMI)	professionalism	quality	impressionistic evaluation

SOURCE: Lawton (1984) p. 17

this model suggests, he does maintain that it can help us to specify the different views that exist in relation to educational policies. In particular, he suggests that researchers need to examine the tensions in the system and the ways in which these tensions are resolved. However, this analysis is at the national level. Clearly, similar kinds of analysis of educational politics also need to be conducted through intensive studies at regional and institutional levels. Such studies would demand the collection of basic data rather than the concern with concept spinning that appears in much sociology as well as in the sociology of education (cf. Davies, 1983). But we might ask: in what ways might the collection and analysis of basic data be developed in the sociology of education?

A way forward?

In this final section we examine some ways in which sociological studies in education might develop. In particular, attention is given to different styles of work within the sub-discipline. The sociological study of education could be developed as follows:

RESEARCHING EDUCATIONAL SYSTEMS AS WELL AS SCHOOLS AND CLASSROOMS

We have already pointed to Archer's work (Archer, 1979, 1981, 1983) that highlights the importance of studying educational systems as a way of examining the politics of education. Nevertheless, as Banks (1982b) has noted, this has been very much a minority interest in the sociology of education, as it is based on theoretical and comparative study. Yet a study of educational systems *as well as* schools and classrooms would provide an opportunity not only to study educational politics but also to examine educational decision-making and processes of educational change. It would give the sociology of education greater coverage, range and scope. The importance of this kind of analysis has been summed up by Archer in the following terms:

> Some of the elements needed to explain national phenomena, such as legislation, resource allocation, are not found in the classroom at all, while the presence of other elements in the classroom, e.g. the legal authority of teachers and heads, begs for explanation at a different level because these did not originate there but rather higher up in the educational system and further out in the wider society. (Archer, 1981, p.264)

Such an approach has implications for the methodology used by sociologists and for theoretical debates such as the relationship between macroscopic and microscopic analysis (for further discussion see Hammersley, 1984a, 1984b, 1985; A. Hargreaves, 1984, 1985). In turn, it also holds implications about the subject matter of the sociology of education.

A brief glance at the studies that have been discussed in this book reveals that education is often interpreted by researchers to mean education in schools and classrooms. Yet there are numerous other settings where educational activities occur in the wider society. For example, the educational activities that occur in churches, trade unions and work places are all ripe for study. Nevertheless, as Burgess (1984b) and Delamont (1981) have shown, there has been a tendency for 'education' to be narrowly defined among sociologists. In addition, Atkinson (1984) has indicated that there is much conservatism among many sociologists of education who have been unwilling to recognize the significance of studies of medical education, medical schools and medical settings for education. Indeed, the studies by Atkinson (1981) of a medical school and by Dingwall (1977) of health visitor training point to ways in which educational activities can be examined beyond the traditionally narrow confines of schools and classrooms. In addition, such studies can help to develop the analysis of education in school settings (cf. Delamont, 1981).

However, even within schools and classrooms, Delamont (1983) has shown how much of the work is restricted to state schools with children aged 8–16 who are doing subjects such as mathematics and English. Within the sociology of education, there is little work on private schools (Walford, 1984 being a recent exception) on pupils who are under five (Finch, 1984 being an exception), or on students engaged in teacher education (Stowell, 1985). As well as developing these areas of study it is also important to cover *a range* of subject areas in sociological investigation. Indeed, if this range of educational activities was examined, we would develop an understanding of what constituted 'education' in school and non-school settings which might have considerable comparative pay-off for sociological study.

MAKING EDUCATIONAL STUDIES TIME SPECIFIC

There are two important issues here. The first concerns historical time periods; the second, the ability to make comparisons over time. Sociologists have for some time drawn on historical evidence to examine educational activities in the nineteenth and early twentieth centuries (cf. Archer, 1979; Banks, 1955; Vaughan and Archer, 1971). Indeed, there is considerable evidence of historical study being used by sociologists to examine particular developments such as the education of women in the nineteenth and early twentieth centuries (cf. Delamont and Duffin, 1978; Purvis, 1981a, 1981b). In these situations, careful note has to be taken of the historical time period, as the meaning of 'education' and 'educational activity' may change over time. This is clearly shown by Alison Andrew in a commentary on her study of working class educational activity in nineteenth-century Preston, when she writes:

> 'Education' need not mean schools and classrooms as we now know them and much evidence has been produced which indicates that working class educational activity in the nineteenth century often explicitly challenged the dominant model. (Andrew, 1985, p.164)

The point that is being made here also has relevance for sociological studies of education in the twentieth century, where the time period involved has implications for the questions that are posed and the data that are collected. For example, English secondary education has undergone considerable change since the 1960s with the development of comprehensive education, the raising of the school leaving age to 16 and the increased opportunities to take public examinations. Yet there is a danger that sociologists who omit to consider the time period in relation to their studies will make gross assumptions about changes in educational activity over time (cf. Burgess, 1986b; Reid, 1981). Accordingly, the time dimension becomes important, especially when comparative work is done, on, for example, education in the pre and post 1944 periods or when research is conducted with a view to developing a particular line of enquiry over time. It is in these circumstances that careful specification needs to be made as to what constitutes 'education' at different points in time.

COLLECTING BASIC DATA

Throughout this book we have noted particular areas where we lack basic data. Accordingly, the following recommendations are made as far as data collection is concerned:

(a) On academic education the minimum data that are required include: terminal education age, number of years stayed beyond the school leaving age, last school attended, the duration of further or higher education, full time or part time, and details of educational qualifications (for a detailed discussion see Burgess, 1986b; Weinberg, 1969).

(b) It is important that we should not focus merely on those pupils who are academically successful. Accordingly, it is essential that we collect data on the educational activities of pupils who do not succeed in the conventional school system and are regarded as 'low achievers' (cf. Raybould, Roberts and Wedell, 1980) or as non-academic (cf. Burgess, 1983, 1984f). In turn we need to understand the way in which education takes place outside primary and secondary schools in special schools (cf. Tomlinson, 1981) and to examine the criteria that are used to allocate pupils to particular groups.

(c) Data relating to the educational experiences of academic and non-academic pupils need to be collected for girls and women as well as men and boys. We have already noted the criticisms that Blackstone (1980) and MacDonald (1981) have made concerning the Oxford Mobility Study that only collected data on boys and men. This kind of work also holds implications for the extent to which sociologists are able to generalize from a sample. For example, Halsey, Heath and Ridge (1980) continually generalize from a study of boys and men to the whole population – an activity for which they have been quite rightly criticized by Acker (1981a). In turn, Acker (1981b) has also pointed to the way in which difficulties arise when researchers overlook the study of girls. In particular she points to the problem that occurs when researchers such as Halsey, Heath and Ridge start to compare their work with other studies such as Jackson and Marsden's (1962) study of 88 working class children, which they incorrectly assume were all boys. As Acker perceptively remarks:

> Halsey *et al* ponder reasons why the results from the J. & M. [Jackson and Marsden] study were so different from their own and conclude that the different scale and scope of the two studies is probably responsible. This is no doubt true but it would seem that the 39 invisible girls might have played some part here too . . . (Acker, 1981b, p.13)

Such critical comments point to the importance of collecting data on boys *and* girls and to making *careful* comparisons with other samples. Indeed, sociologists might engage in secondary analysis of existing data sets in order to reinterpret some of the assumptions made about the education of boys and girls in earlier studies, while new studies need to question divisions based not only on class but also on gender (cf. Wilkin, 1982). In turn, wherever possible, sociologists might also use samples that are based on class, gender and race as this would help them to assess the complex interaction that occurs between these variables.

(d) Data that are collected on schools and classrooms invariably focus on the interactions that occur between teachers and pupils. As a consequence we have relatively little knowledge about the *content* of what occurs within the classrooms and the subject areas within which pupils work. In turn, we know relatively little about curriculum development and curriculum projects, as much of this work has been conducted beyond the frontiers of sociology (cf. Stenhouse, 1975, 1980, 1983a). Here, there is some potential for the kind of interdisciplinary enquiry that has been identified by Delamont (1983). Already we have some work in this area that brings together sociological and historical studies (cf. Goodson, 1982; Goodson and Ball, 1984; Goodson, 1985). It is this kind of work that would seem to hold much potential not only for the study of the curriculum but as a basis upon which to develop interdisciplinary enquiries in the study of education, and where sociology can play a significant role.

DEVELOPING METHODOLOGY

Many enquiries appear to focus either exclusively on the collection and analysis of quantitative data or upon the collection and analysis of qualitative data. Indeed, some commentators (cf. Bogdan and Biklen, 1982; Filstead, 1970) suggest that it is important to stress the superiority of one set of methods over another. Yet there seems to be considerable advantage to researchers if their projects are developed using a wide array of methodological tools that are relevant to the problem under study (cf. Burgess, 1984a, 1984d, 1985a, 1985b, 1985d). In addition, it is important for researchers to develop approaches that are capable of dealing specifically with 'education' and 'educational activities'. In recent years, educational researchers have focused on a series of methodological issues that have particular relevance in the study of educational settings, and which include:

1 the state and status of theory and theorizing in relation to empirical studies;
2 the way in which the researcher's value position can influence the conduct of enquiry;
3 the political dimensions of the research process and the implications that it has for the collection, analysis and reporting of research data;
4 the importance of ethical issues and the ways in which they can be handled by the researcher;
5 the development of strategies and styles of investigation – the ways in which qualitative and quantitative methods of investigation can be used alongside each other;
6 the relationship between research strategies and educational policy and practice.

In particular, it has been argued that, if researchers are going to understand the process of research in conducting educational enquiries, it is essential to work reflexively (Burgess, 1984e; Hammersley and

Atkinson, 1983; Hammersley, 1983). For example, Burgess (1984e) has argued that it is essential that researchers keep detailed accounts not only of data collection but also of their own research practices, as this, he believes, would provide the materials through which we could more carefully examine the research process and learn more about the problems and possibilities of conducting research in educational settings, especially as far as relationships between problems, theories and methods are concerned.

GENERALIZING AND TESTING THEORIES

As we indicated at the beginning of this book, research in the sociology of education is conducted from a variety of theoretical perspectives. In some cases, these approaches are incompatible, while in others they give rise to different questions and different fields of study. Among those working from different perspectives, a macro-micro problem has been identified where Marxists have come to be broadly associated with a macroscopic perspective, while interactionists have been broadly associated with microscopic work. As Hammersley (1984b) maintains, this has resulted in several problems. First, arguments surrounding the macro-micro debate have often resulted in the dismissal of one perspective by those working from a different point of view. Secondly, the debate has often conflated distinct methodological issues such as whether educational events can best be explained as the product of large-scale or small-scale structures. Some work in the sociology of education has attempted to bridge the gap between these two traditions, such as Sharp and Green's study of a progressive primary school (Sharp and Green, 1975) and Paul Willis's study of twelve lads in their transition from school to work (Willis, 1977). In both instances an attempt was made by the authors to develop links between the small-scale interaction of the people they studied and the structure of capitalist society. A further attempt at synthesis has been made by Andy Hargreaves (1978, 1980a), who argues that there is a need to fuse together Marxist analyses of contemporary society with interactionist studies of classrooms. In turn, he points to ways in which such a synthesis might be achieved through the use of such concepts as 'coping strategy' and 'structural limitation'. However, Hammersley (1984a) does not agree with Hargreaves. In particular, he suggests that, while different perspectives should not be treated as if they competed with each other, neither should they be integrated into one over-arching model. Hammersley (1984a, 1984b) argues that the future research efforts of sociologists should be directed towards developing and testing the theories that are currently available as well as developing new theories – a point that he has illustrated through a study of examinations (cf. Hammersley, Scarth and Webb, 1985). As a consequence, he maintains this would give rise to valid theories that could be used to provide explanations in the sociology of education as well as helping to formulate educational policies.

Clearly, there is much work to be done in developing the sociology of education theoretically, methodologically and substantively, for, although it is an area that is heavily researched, we have barely begun to understand what counts as 'education' in contemporary society. It is, therefore, important for us to extend the boundaries of the sub-discipline and to colonise the territory if we are to acquire a sociological understanding of education and educational activities.

Suggestions for further reading

The following suggestions predominantly focus upon the development of a sociology of educational politics which has been briefly discussed in this chapter.

Archer, M. S. (1981) 'Fields of specialization: educational systems', *International Social Science Journal*, vol. 33, no. 2, pp.261–284 includes a discussion of the way in which educational politics might be developed as an area of study. See also Archer (1979, 1983).

Burgess, R. G. (1984) 'Exploring frontiers and settling territory: shaping the sociology of education', *British Journal of Sociology*, vol. 35, no. 1, pp.122–137 provides a review of the directions in which the sociology of education has developed in the early 1980s.

Burgess, R. G. (1986) 'Education' in R. G. Burgess (ed) *Key Variables in Social Investigation*, London, Routledge and Kegan Paul, pp.100–122 includes a discussion of the way in which 'education' has been conceptualized in a variety of empirical studies and provides recommendations concerning the future conduct of empirical studies.

Campbell, R. J. (1985) *Developing the Primary School Curriculum*, London, Holt, Rinehart and Winston examines school-based curriculum development in the primary sector. The first chapter provides a discussion of the political context of the primary curriculum.

Hammersley, M. (1984) 'Some reflections upon the macro-micro problem in the sociology of education', *Sociological Review*, Vol. 32, no. 2, pp.316–24 provides a review of the macro-micro debate in the sociology of education. For further discussion see Hammersley (1984b) and Hargreaves (1980a).

Kogan, M. (1978) *The Politics of Educational Change*, London, Fontana is a review by a political scientist. The chapter on the curriculum is well worth consulting.

Lawton, D. (1980) *The Politics of the Curriculum*, London, Routledge and Kegan Paul.

Lawton, D. (1983) *Curriculum Studies and Educational Planning*, Sevenoaks, Hodder and Stoughton.

Lawton, D. (1984) *The Tightening Grip: Growth of Central Control of the School Curriculum*, Bedford Way Papers, No. 21, London, University of London Institute of Education contains three statements by Denis Lawton in which he develops a critique and a model of the politics of the school curriculum.

Salter, B. and Tapper, T. (1981) *Education, Politics and the State*, London, Grant

McIntyre provides an alternative formulation of educational politics. In particular the authors take issue with Archer (1979).

EMPIRICAL STUDIES

This book has discussed a range of empirical studies which are reviewed in journals of sociology *and* education. One way in which readers may keep up to date with the literature is through the books that are regularly reviewed in the following British journals:

British Educational Research Journal
British Journal of Educational Studies
British Journal of Sociology
British Journal of Sociology of Education
Durham & Newcastle Research Review
Educational Research
Educational Review
Journal of Curriculum Studies
Journal of Education Policy
Journal of Education for Teaching
Research in Education
School Organization
Secondary Education Journal
Sociological Review
Sociology: the Journal of the British Sociological Association

In addition, the following abstracting service provides an essential guide to recent work in the sociology of education through regular summaries of research and writing, especially from Britain and the USA, covering articles, books and edited collections: *Sociology of Education Abstracts*.

References

ACKER, S. (1981a) 'No-woman's land: British sociology of education 1960–1979', *Sociological Review*, vol. 29, no. 1, pp.77–104 reprinted in COSIN, B and HALES, M, (1983) (eds) *Education, Policy and Society: Theoretical Perspectives*, London, Routledge and Kegan Paul, pp.106–128

ACKER, S, (1981b) 'Letter to the editor of *Network*', *Network, the newsletter of the British Sociological Association*, May, p.13

ACKER, S. (1983) 'Women and teaching: a semi-detached sociology of a semi-profession' in WALKER, S. and BARTON, L. (eds) *Gender, Class and Education*, Lewes, Falmer Press, pp. 123–139

ACKER, S., MEGARRY, J., NISBET, S. and HOYLE, E. (1984) (eds) *World Yearbook of Education 1984: Women and Education*, London, Kogan Page; New York, Nichols Publishing

ACKER, S. and WARREN-PIPER, D. (1983) (eds) *Is Higher Education Fair to Women?* Guildford, Society for Research into Higher Education

ADAM, R. (1969) 'Project Headstart: LBJ's one success?', *New Society*, 30th October, pp.681–683

ALBROW, M. (1970) *Bureaucracy*, London, Pall Mall

ANDERSON, C.A. (1961) 'A skeptical note on education and mobility', in HALSEY, A. H., FLOUD, J. and ANDERSON, C.A. (eds) *Education, Economy and Society*, New York, Free Press, pp.164–179

ANDREW, A. (1985) 'In pursuit of the past: some problems in the collection, analysis and use of historical documentary evidence', in BURGESS, R. G. (ed) *Strategies of Educational Research: Qualitative Methods*, Lewes, Falmer Press, pp.153–178

ANTHIAS, F. and YUVAL-DAVIES, N. (1983) 'Contextualizing feminism – gender, ethnic and class divisions', *Feminist Review*, 15 (Winter), pp.62–75

ANYON, J. (1979) 'Ideology and United States history text books', *Harvard Educational Review*, vol. 49, no. 3, pp.361–386

APPLE, M. W. (1979a) *Ideology and Curriculum*, London, Routledge and Kegan Paul

APPLE, M. W. (1979b) 'The production of knowledge and the production of deviance in schools', in BARTON, L. and MEIGHAN, R. (eds) *Schools, Pupils and Deviance*, Driffield, Nafferton, pp.131–131

APPLE, M. W. (1982) (ed) *Cultural and·Economic Reproduction in Education*, London, Routledge and Kegan Paul

ARCHER, M. (1970) 'Egalitarianism in English and French educational sociology' in *European Journal of Sociology*, vol. XI, pp.116–129

ARCHER, M. S. (1979) *The Social Origins of Educational Systems*, Beverley Hills, Sage

ARCHER, M. S. (1981) 'Educational systems', *International Social Science Journal*, vol. 33, no. 2, pp.261–84

ARCHER, M. S. (1983) *The Social Origins of Educational Systems* University Edition, Beverley Hills, Sage

ARCHER, M. S. (1984) 'Foreword', in BARTON, L. and TOMLINSON, S. (eds) *Special Education and Social Interests*, London, Croom Helm, pp.ix–xi

ARNOT, M. (1983) *Educating Girls*, Open University Course U221 *The Changing Experience of Women*, (Unit 13), Milton Keynes, Open University Press

ASHTON, D. N. and FIELD, D. (1976) *Young Workers: from School to work*, London, Hutchinson

ATKINSON, P. (1981) *The Clinical Experience*, Aldershot, Gower

ATKINSON, P. (1984) 'Wards and deeds: Taking knowledge and control seriously', in BURGESS, R. G. (ed) *The Research Process in Educational Settings: Ten Case Studies*, Lewes, Falmer Press, pp.163–185

ATKINSON, P. (1985) *Language, Structure and Reproduction*, London, Tavistock

ATKINSON, P. and DELAMONT, S. (1980) 'The two traditions in educational ethnography: sociology and anthropology compared', *British Journal of Sociology of Education*, vol. 1, no. 2, pp.139–52

AULD, R. (1976) *Report on the Inquiry into William Tyndale School*, London, Inner London Education Authority

BALL, S. J. (1980) 'Initial encounters in the classroom and the process of establishment', in WOODS, P. (ed) *Pupil Strategies: Explorations in the Sociology of the School*, London, Croom Helm, pp.143–161

BALL, S. J. (1981) *Beachside Comprehensive: A Case Study of Secondary Schooling*, Cambridge, Cambridge University Press

BALL, S. J. (1983a) 'Case study research in education: some notes and problems', in HAMMERSLEY, M. (ed) *The Ethnography of Schooling*, Driffield, Nafferton, pp.79–104

BALL, S. J. (1983b) 'Competition and conflict in the teaching of English: a socio-historical analysis', *Journal of Curriculum Studies*, vol. 14, no. 1, pp.1–28

BALL, S. J. (1984a) 'Beachside reconsidered: Reflections on a methodological apprenticeship', in BURGESS, R. G. (ed) *The Research Process in Educational Settings: Ten Case Studies*, Lewes, Falmer Press, pp.69–96

BALL, S. J. (1984b) 'Becoming a comprehensive? Facing up to falling rolls', in BALL, S. J. (ed) *Comprehensive Schooling: A Reader*, Lewes, Falmer Press, pp.227–246

BALL, S. J. (1984c) *Comprehensive Education: Inside the School*, Open University Course E 205 *Conflict and Change in Education: A Sociological Perspective*, Milton Keynes, Open University Press

BALL, S. J. and GOODSON, I. F. (1985) (eds) *Teacher Careers and Life Histories* Lewes, Falmer Press

BALL, S. J. and LACEY, C. (1980) 'Subject disciplines as the opportunity for group action: a measured critique of subject sub-cultures', in WOODS, P. (ed) *Teacher Strategies: Explorations in the Sociology of the School*, London, Croom Helm, pp.149–177

BALLANTINE, J. H. (1983) *The Sociology of Education: A Systematic Analysis*, Englewood Cliffs, New Jersey, Prentice Hall

BAMFORD, T. W. (1967) *The Rise of the Public Schools*, London, Nelson

BANKS, O. (1955) *Parity and Prestige in English Secondary Education*, London, Routledge and Kegan Paul

BANKS, O. (1968) *The Sociology of Education*, London, Batsford

BANKS, O. (1976) *The Sociology of Education*, 3rd edn., London, Batsford

BANKS, O. (1978) 'School and society', in BARTON, L. and MEIGHAN, R. (eds) *Sociological Interpretations of Schooling and Classrooms: A Reappraisal*, Driffield, Nafferton, pp.37–46

BANKS, O. (1982a) 'The sociology of education' in COHEN, L., THOMAS, J. and MANION, L. (eds) *Educational Research and Development in Britain*, Windsor, NFER-Nelson, pp.43–54

BANKS, O. (1982b) 'The sociology of education 1952–1982', *British Journal of Educational Studies*, vol. XXX, no. 1, pp18–31

BARKER-LUNN, J. (1970) *Streaming in the Primary School*, Windsor, NFER

BARKER-LUNN, J. (1982) 'Junior schools and their organisational policies', *Educational Research*, vol. 24, no. 4, pp.250–261

BARON, G. (1955) 'The English notion of the school', unpublished paper, University of London Institute of Education, mimeo

BARTON, L. and TOMLINSON, S. (1981) (eds) *Special Education: Policy, Practices and Social Issues*, London, Harper and Row

BARTON, L. and TOMLINSON, S. (1984) (eds) *Special Education and Social Interests*, London, Croom Helm

BATES, I., CLARKE, J., COHEN, P., FINN, D., MOORE, R. and WILLIS, P. (1984) *Schooling for the Dole? The New Vocationalism*, London, Macmillan

BEALING, D (1972) 'The organization of junior school classrooms', *Educational Research* vol. 14, no. 4, pp. 231–233

BECKER, H. S. (1952) 'Social class variations in the teacher–pupil relationship', *Journal of Educational Sociology*, vol. 25, pp.451–465

BECKER, H. S. (1964), 'Personal change in adult life', *Sociometry*, vol. 27, no. 1, pp.40–53

BECKER, H. S. (1971) 'Comment' in WAX, M., DIAMOND, S. and GEARING, F. O. (eds) *Anthropological Perspectives on Education*, New York, Basic Books, p.10

BEDEMAN, T. and HARVEY, J. (1981) 'Young people on YOP: a national survey of entrants to the Youth Opportunities Programme', *MSC Research and Development Series No. 3*, Manpower Services Commission

BELL, L. (1980) 'The School as an organization: a reappraisal', *British Journal of Sociology of Education*, vol. 1, no. 2, pp.183–192

BELL, L. A., PENNINGTON, R. C. and BURRIDGE, J. B. A. (1979) 'Going mixed ability: some observations on one school's experience', *Forum for the Discussion of New Trends in Education*, vol. 21, no. 3, pp.109–122

BELLABY, P. (1979) 'Towards a political economy of decision-making in the classroom', in EGGLESTON, J. (ed) *Teacher Decision-Making in the Classroom*, London, Routledge and Kegan Paul, pp.93–117

BENN, C. and SIMON, B. (1972) *Half Way There: Report on the British Comprehensive School Reform*, 2nd edn., Harmondsworth, Penguin

BENNETT, N., ANDREAE, J., HEGARTY, P. and WADE, B. (1980) *Open Plan Schools*, Windsor, NFER

BENNETT, N., DESFORGES, C., COCKBURN, A. and WILKINSON, B. (1984) *The Quality of Pupil Learning Experiences*, London, Lawrence Erlbaum

BERG, I. (1973) *Education and Jobs: The Great Training Robbery*, Harmondsworth, Penguin

BERG, L. (1968) *Risinghill: The Death of a Comprehensive School*, Harmondsworth, Penguin

BERLAK, H. and BERLAK, A. (1981) *Dilemmas of Schooling*, London, Methuen

BERNBAUM, G. (1977) *Knowledge and Ideology in the Sociology of Education*, London, Macmillan

BERNSTEIN, B. (1970a) 'A critique of the concept of 'compensatory education', in RUBENSTEIN, D. and STONEMAN, C. (eds) *Education for Democracy*, Harmondsworth, Penguin, pp.110–121

BERNSTEIN, B. (1970b) 'Elaborated and restricted codes: their social origins and some consequences', in DANZIGER, K. (ed) *Readings in Child Socialization*, Oxford, Pergamon, pp.165–186

BERNSTEIN, B. (1971a) 'On the classification and framing of educational knowledge' in YOUNG, M.F.D. (ed) *Knowledge and Control: New Directions for the Sociology of Education*, London, Collier–Macmillan, pp. 47–69

BERNSTEIN, B. (1971b) *Class, Codes and Control, Volume 1*, London, Routledge and Kegan Paul

BERNSTEIN, B. (1971c) 'A socio-linguistic approach to socialization: with some reference to educability', in BERNSTEIN, B. *Class Codes and Control*, vol. 1, London, Routledge and Kegan Paul, pp.143–169

BERNSTEIN, B. (1974) 'Sociology and the sociology of education: a brief account', in REX, J. (ed) *Approaches to Sociology*, London, Routledge and Kegan Paul, pp.145–159

BERNSTEIN, B. (1975) *Class, Codes and Control, Volume 3*, London, Routledge and Kegan Paul

BERNSTEIN, B. and DAVIES, B. (1969) 'Some sociological comments on Plowden', in PETERS, R. S. (ed) *Perspectives on Plowden*, London, Routledge and Kegan Paul, pp.55–83

BEST, R., JARVIS, C. and RIBBENS, P. (1977) 'Pastoral care: concept and process', *British Journal of Educational Studies*, vol. XXV, no. 2, pp.124–135

BÉTEILLE, A. (1969) (ed) *Social Inequality*, Harmondsworth, Penguin

BEYNON, J. and ATKINSON, P. (1984) 'Pupils as data gatherers: mucking and sussing', in DELAMONT, S. (ed) *Readings on Interaction in the Classroom*, London, Methuen, pp.255–272

BIDWELL, C. E. (1965) 'The school as a formal organization', in MARCH, J. G. (ed) *Handbook of Organizations*, Chicago, Rand McNally, pp.972–1022

BLACKIE, P. (1977) 'Not quite proper', *The Times Educational Supplement*, 25 November

BLACKSTONE, T. (1970) *A Fair Start*, London, Allen Lane

BLACKSTONE, T. (1980) 'Falling short of meritocracy', *The Times Higher Education Supplement*, 18 January

BLACKSTONE, T. and CRISPIN, A. (1982) *How Many Teachers? Issues of Policy Planning and Demography, Bedford Way Paper No. 10*, London, University of London Institute of Education

BLAU, P. M. and DUNCAN, O.D. (1967) *The American Occupational Structure*, New York, Wiley

BLUESTONE, B. (1977) 'Economic theory and the fate of the poor', in KARABEL, J. and HALSEY, A. H. (eds) *Power and Ideology in Education*, New York, Oxford University Press, pp.335–340

BOARD OF EDUCATION (1938) *Secondary Education with special reference to Grammar Schools and Technical High Schools* (the Spens Report), London, HMSO

BOARD OF EDUCATION (1943) *Curriculum Examinations in Secondary Schools* (the Norwood Report), London, HMSO

BOGDAN, R. and BIKLEN, S. K. (1982) *Qualitative Research for Education: An Introduction to Theory and Method*, Boston, Allyn and Bacon

BOUDON, R. (1974) *Education, Opportunity, and Social Inequality*, New York, Wiley

BOUDON, R. (1977) 'Education and social mobility: a structural model', in KARABEL, J. and HALSEY, A. H. (eds) *Power and Ideology in Education*, New York, Oxford University Press, pp.186–196

BOURDIEU, P. (1971) 'Systems of education and systems of thought', in YOUNG, M.F.D. (ed) *Knowledge and Control: New Directions for the Sociology of Education*, London, Collier and Macmillan, pp.189–207

BOURDIEU, P. (1973) 'Cultural reproduction and social reproduction', in BROWN, R. K. (ed) *Knowledge, Education and Cultural Change*, London, Tavistock, pp.71–112

BOURDIEU, P. and BOLTANSKI, L. (1978) 'Changes in social structure and changes in the demand for education', in GINER, S. and ARCHER, M. S. (eds) *Contemporary Europe: Social Structures and Cultural Patterns*, London, Routledge and Kegan Paul

BOURDIEU, P. and PASSERON, J. C. (1977) *Reproduction in Education, Society and Culture*, Beverley Hills, Sage

BOWLES, S. and GINTIS, H. (1975) 'The problem with human capital theory – a Marxist critique', *American Economic Review*, vol. 65, pp.74–82

BOWLES, S. and GINTIS, H. (1976) *Schooling in Capitalist America*, London, Routledge and Kegan Paul

BOYDELL, D. (1981) 'Classroom organization', in SIMON, B. and WILLCOCKS, J. (eds) *Research and Practice in the Primary Classroom*, London, Routledge and Kegan Paul, pp.36–42

BOYSON, R. (1974) *Oversubscribed: The Story of Highbury Grove*, London, Ward Lock

BRITTAIN, A. and MAYNARD, M. (1984) *Sexism, Racism and Oppression*, Oxford, Basil Blackwell

BRITTAN, E. M. (1976) 'Multiracial education 2 – teacher opinion on aspects of school life: pupils and teachers', *Educational Research*, vol. 18, no. 3, pp.182–191

BRITTEN, N. and HEATH, A. (1983) 'Women, men and social class', in GAMARNIKOW, E., MORGAN, D., PURVIS, J. and TAYLORSON, D. (eds) *Gender, Class and Work*, London, Heinemann, pp.46–60

BROADFOOT, P. (1979) *Assessment, Schools and Society*, London, Methuen

BROADFOOT, P. (1983) 'Assessment constraints on curriculum practice: a comparative study', in HAMMERSLEY, M. and HARGREAVES, A. (eds) *Curriculum Practice: Some Sociological Case Studies*, Lewes, Falmer Press, pp.251–269

BROADFOOT, P. (1984) (ed) *Selection, Certification and Control: Social Issues in Educational Assessment*, Lewes, Falmer Press

BROOKS, D. (1983) 'Young blacks and Asians in the labour market – a critical overview', in TROYNA, B. and SMITH, D. I. (eds) *Racism, School and the Labour Market*, Leicester, National Youth Bureau, pp.78–94

BROOKS, D. and SINGH, K. (1979) 'Pivots and presents: Asian brokers in British foundries' in WALLMAN, S. (ed) *Ethnicity at Work*, London, Macmillan, pp.93–112

BROWN, R. K. (1973) (ed) *Knowledge, Education and Cultural Change*, London, Tavistock

BROWN, R. K. (1984a) 'Education for what work?', *British Journal of Sociology of Education*, vol. 5, no. 1, pp.97–101

BROWN R. K. (1984b) 'Work', in ABRAMS, P. and BROWN, R. K. (eds) *U.K. Society: Work, Urbanism and Inequality*, 2nd edn., London, Weidenfeld and Nicolson, pp.129–197

BULMER, M. (1984) (ed) *Sociological Research Methods: An Introduction*, 2nd edn., London, Macmillan

BULMER, M. (1986) 'Race and ethnicity', in BURGESS, R. G. (ed) *Key Variables in Social Investigation*, London Routledge and Kegan Paul, pp.54–75

BURGESS, H. (1983) *An Appraisal of Some Methods of Teaching Primary School Mathematics*, unpublished MA dissertation, University of London, Institute of Education

BURGESS, H. (1986) 'Doubting Thomas: The primary curriculum and classroom practice', *Journal of Education Policy*, vol. 1, no. 1

BURGESS, R. G. (1983) *Experiencing Comprehensive Education: A Study of Bishop McGregor School*, London, Methuen

BURGESS, R. G. (1984a) *In the Field: An Introduction to Field Research*, London, Allen and Unwin

BURGESS, R. G. (1984b) 'Exploring frontiers and settling territory:shaping the sociology of education', *British Journal of Sociology*, vol. 35, no. 1, pp.122–137

BURGESS, R. G. (1984c) 'Patterns and processes of education in the United Kingdom', in ABRAMS, P. and BROWN, R. K. (eds) *U.K. Society: Work, Urbanism and Inequality*, 2nd edn., London, Weidenfeld and Nicolson, pp.58–128

BURGESS, R. G. (1984d) (ed) *The Research Process in Educational Settings: Ten Case Studies*, Lewes, Falmer Press

BURGESS, R. G. (1984e) 'Autobiographical accounts and research experience', in BURGESS, R. G. (ed) *The Research Process in Educational Settings: Ten Case Studies*, Lewes, Falmer Press, pp.251–270

BURGESS, R. G. (1984f) 'It's Not a Proper Subject: it's just Newsom', in GOODSON, I. F. and BALL, S. J. (eds) *Defining the Curriculum: Histories and Ethnographies*, Lewes, Falmer Press, pp.181–200

BURGESS, R. G. (1984g) 'Headship: Freedom or Constraint?' in BALL, S. J. (ed) *Comprehensive Schooling: A Reader*, Lewes, Falmer Press, pp.201–226

BURGESS, R. G. (1985a) (ed) *Field Methods in the Study of Education*, Lewes, Falmer Press

BURGESS, R. G. (1985b) *Education, Schools and Schooling*, London, Macmillan

BURGESS, R. G. (1985c) (ed) *Strategies of Educational Research: Qualitative Methods*, Lewes, Falmer Press

BURGESS, R. G. (1985d) (ed) *Issues in Educational Research: Qualitative Methods*, Lewes, Falmer Press

BURGESS, R. G. (1986a) (ed) *Exploring Society*, London, Longman
BURGESS, R. G. (1986b) 'Education', in BURGESS, R. G. (ed) *Key Variables in Social Investigation*, London, Routledge and Kegan Paul, pp.100–122
BURGESS, R. G. (1986c) (ed) *Key Variables in Social Investigation*, London, Routledge and Kegan Paul
BURNS, T. (1967) 'Sociological explanation', *British Journal of Sociology*, vol. 18, no. 4, pp.353–369
BUSWELL, C. (1980) 'Pedagogic change and social change', *British Journal of Sociology of Education*, vol. 1, no. 3, pp.293–306
BUTLER, D. and STOKES, D. (1971) *Political Change in Britain*, Harmondsworth, Penguin
BYRNE, D. and WILLIAMSON, B. (1972), 'Some intra-regional variations in educational provision and their bearing upon educational attainment – the case of the North East', *Sociology*, vol. 6, no. 1, pp.71–87
BYRNE, D., WILLIAMSON, B. and FLETCHER, B. (1975) *The Poverty of Education: A Study in the Politics of Opportunity*, Oxford, Martin Robertson
BYRNE, E. (1978) *Women and Education*, London, Tavistock
CAMPBELL, R. J. (1984) 'In-school development: the role of the curriculum postholder', *School Organization*, vol. 4, no. 4, pp.345–357
CAMPBELL, R. J. (1985) *Developing the Primary School Curriculum*, Eastbourne, Holt, Rinehart and Winston
CARR-SAUDNERS, A. M. and WILSON, P. A. (1933) *The Professions*, Oxford, Oxford University Press
CENTRAL ADVISORY COUNCIL FOR EDUCATION (1967) *Children and their Primary Schools*, London, HMSO
CENTRAL STATISTICAL OFFICE (1982) *Social Trends 12*, London, HMSO
CENTRAL STATISTICAL OFFICE (1985) *Social Trends 15*, London, HMSO
CHANAN, G. and DELMONT, S. (1975) (eds) *Frontiers of Classroom Research*, Slough, NFER
CHODOROW, N. (1978) *The Reproduction of Mothering: Psychoanalysis and the Sociology of Gender*, Los Angeles, University of California Press
CICOUREL, A. V. and KITSUSE, J. I. (1963) *The Educational Decision-Makers*, New York, Bobbs–Merrill
CLARK, B. (1961) 'The "cooling out" function in higher education', in HALSEY, A. H., FLOUD, J. and ANDERSON, C. A. (eds) *Education, Economy and Society*, New York, Free Press pp.513–523
CLARRICOATES, K. (1978) 'Dinosaurs in the classroom: a re-examination of some aspects of the "hidden curriculum" in primary schools', *Women's Studies International Quarterly*, vol. 1, no. 4, pp.353–364
CLARRICOATES, K. (1980) 'The importance of being Ernest . . . Emma . . . Tom . . . Jane: the perception and categorization of gender conformity and gender deviation in primary schools', in DEEM, R. (ed) *Schooling for Women's Work*, London, Routledge and Kegan Paul, pp.26–41
COCKBURN, C. (1985) *Women and Technology*, London, Workers Educational Association
COHEN, L. and MANION, L. (1980) *Research Methods in Education*, London, Croom Helm
COHEN, L. and MANION, L. (1983) *Multicultural Classrooms: Perspectives for Teachers*, London, Croom Helm

COLE, M. (1983) 'Contradictions in the educational theory of Gintis and Bowles', *Sociological Review*, vol. 31, no. 3, pp.471–488

COLEMAN, J. (1968) 'The concept of equality of educational opportunity', *Harvard Educational Review*, vol. 38, pp.7–22

COLEMAN, J. (1969) *Equality of Educational Opportunity*, Cambridge, Mass. Harvard University Press

COLEMAN, J. (1975) 'What is meant by "an equal opportunity"?' *Oxford Review of Education*, vol. 1, no. 1, pp.27–29

COLEMAN, J. *et al* (1966) *Equality of Educational Opportunity*, Washington, U.S. Department of Health, Education and Welfare

COLLINS, R. (1975) *Conflict Sociology*, London, Academic Press

COOPER, B. (1984) 'On explaining change in school subjects', in GOODSON, I. F. and BALL, S. J. (eds) *Defining the Curriculum: Histories and Ethnographies*, Lewes, Falmer Press, pp. 45–63

CORBISHLEY, P., and EVANS, J. (1980) 'Teachers and pastoral care: an empirical comment', in BEST, R., JARVIS, C. and RIBBENS, P. (eds) *Perspectives on Pastoral Care*, London, Heinemann, pp.201–224

CORBISHLEY, P., EVANS, J., KENRICK, C. and DAVIES, B. (1981) 'Teacher strategies and pupil identities in mixed ability curricula: a note on concepts and some examples from Maths', in BARTON, L. and WALKER, S. (eds) *Schools, Teachers and Teaching*. Lewes, Falmer Press, pp.177–195

CORWIN, R. G. (1974) *Education in Crisis: A Sociological Analysis of Schools and Universities in Transition*, New York, Wiley

COULSON, A. A. (1976) 'The role of the primary head', in PETERS, R. S. (ed) *The Role of Head*, London, Routledge and Kegan Paul, pp.92–108

COULSON, M. A. (1972) 'Role: a redundant concept in sociology? some educational considerations', in JACKSON, J. A. (ed) *Role*, Cambridge University Press, pp.107–128

COVENTRY EDUCATION COMMITTEE (1983) *Comprehensive Education for Life: A Consultative Document*, Coventry, Coventry Education Committee

COX, C. B. and DYSON, A. E. (1969) *Fight for Education: A Black Paper*, London, The Critical Quarterly Society

COX, C. B. and DYSON, A. E. (1970a) *Black Paper Two*, London, The Critical Quarterly Society

COX, C. B. and DYSON, A. E. (1970b) *Goodbye Mr Short, Black Paper Three*, London, The Critical Quarterly Society

CRAFT, M. and CRAFT, A. (1983) 'The participation of ethnic minority pupils in further and higher education', *Educational Review*, vol. 25, no. 1, pp.10–19

CROLL, P. (1986) *Systematic Classroom Observation*, Lewes, Falmer Press

CROSLAND, A. (1956) *The Future of Socialism*, London, Jonathan Cape

CROSS, M. (1978) 'West Indians and the problem of the metropolitan majority', in DAY, M. and MARSLAND, D. (eds) *Black Kids, White Kids – What Hope?*, Leicester, National Youth Bureau, pp.19–29

CROSS, M. (1982) *Transformation Through Training?* CEDEFOP

DALE, R. (1982) 'Education and the capitalist State: contributions and contradictions', in APPLE, M. W. (1981) (eds) *Cultural and Economic Reproduction in Education*, London, Routledge and Kegan Paul, pp. 127–161

DALE, R., ESLAND, G., FERGUSSON, R. and MACDONALD, M. (1981) (eds) *Education and the State, Volume 1 Schooling and the National Interest*, Lewes, Falmer Press

DAVID, M. E. (1985) 'Motherhood and social policy – a matter of education?', *Critical Social Policy*, Issue 12, pp. 28–43

DAVIE, R., BUTLER, M. and GOLDSTEIN, H. (1972) *From Birth to Seven*, London, Longman

DAVIES, B. (1973) 'On the contribution of organizational analysis to the study of educational institutions', in BROWN, R. K. (ed) *Knowledge, Education and Cultural Change*, London, Tavistock, pp.249–295

DAVIES, B. (1976) *Social Control and Education*, London, Methuen

DAVIES, B. (1981a) (ed) *The State of Schooling*, special issue of *Educational Analysis*, vol. 3, no. 1, pp.1–149

DAVIES, B. (1981b) 'Schools as organizations and the organization of schooling', *Educational Analysis* vol. 3, no. 1, pp. 47–67

DAVIES, B. (1983) 'The sociology of education' in HIRST, P. H. (ed) *Educational Theory and its Foundation Disciplines*, London, Routledge and Kegan Paul, pp.100–145

DAVIES, B. and CAVE, R. G. (1977) (eds) *Mixed Ability Teaching in the Secondary School*, London, War Lock

DAVIES, I. (1971) 'The management of knowledge: a critique of the use of typologies in the sociology of education', in YOUNG, M. F. D. (ed) *Knowledge and Control: New Directions for the Sociology of Education*, London, Collier–Macmillan, pp.267–288

DAVIN, A. (1979) ' "Mind that you do as you are told": reading books for Board School Girls, 1870–1902', *Feminist Review*, 3, pp. 80–98

DAWSON, P. (1981) *Making a Comprehensive Work: The Road from Bomb Alley*, Oxford, Basil Blackwell

DEEM, R. (1976) 'Professionalism, unity and militant action: the case of teachers', *Sociological Review*, vol. 24, no. 1, pp.43–61

DEEM, R. (1978) *Women and Schooling*, London, Routledge and Kegan Paul

DEEM, R. (1980) (ed) *Schooling for Women's Work*, London, Routledge and Kegan Paul

DEEM, R. (1981) 'State policy and ideology in the education of women, 1944–1980', *British Journal of Sociology of Education*, vol. 2, no. 2, pp.131–144

DEEM, R. (1983) 'Gender, patriarchy and class in the popular education of women', in WALKER, S. and BARTON, L. (eds) *Gender, Class and Education*, Lewes, Falmer Press, pp.107–121

DEEM, R. (1984a) 'Introduction to Block Six' Open University Course E 205 *Gender and Change in Education: A Sociological Introduction*, Milton Keynes, Open University Press, pp.3–6

DEEM, R. (1984b) *Gender Differentiation in Schools*, Open University Course E 205 *Conflict and Change in Education: A Sociological Introduction*, Milton Keynes, Open University Press

DEEM, R. (1984c) (ed) *Co-Education Reconsidered*, Milton Keynes, Open University Press

DELAMONT, S. (1978a) 'The domestic ideology and women's education' in DELAMONT, S. and DUFFIN, L. (eds) *The Nineteenth Century Woman*, London, Croom Helm, pp.164–187

DELAMONT, S. (1978b) 'The contradictions in ladies' education' in DELAMONT, S. and DUFFIN, L. (eds) *The Nineteenth Century Woman*, London, Croom Helm, pp.134–163

DELAMONT, S. (1980) *Sex Roles and the School*, London, Methuen

DELAMONT, S. (1981) 'All too familiar? A decade of classroom research', *Educational Analysis*, vol. 3, no. 1, pp.69–83

DELAMONT, S. (1983) *Interaction in the Classroom*, 2nd edn., London, Methuen

DELAMONT, S. (1984a) (ed) *Readings on Interaction in the Classroom*, London, Methuen

DELAMONT, S. (1984b) 'The old girl network: recollections on the fieldwork at St. Luke's', in BURGESS, R. G. (ed) *The Research Process in Educational Settings: Ten Case Studies*, Lewes, Falmer Press, pp.15–38

DELAMONT, S. (1984c) 'Debs, dollies, swots and weeds: classroom styles at St. Luke's', in WALFORD, G. (ed) *British Public Schools: Policy and Practice*, Lewes, Falmer Press, pp.65–86

DELAMONT, S. and DUFFIN, L. (1978) (eds) *The Nineteenth Century Woman*, London, Croom Helm

DEMAINE, J. (1977) *Contemporary Theories in the Sociology of Education*, London, Macmillan

DENSCOMBE, M. (1980) 'Pupil strategies and the open classroom' in WOODS, P. (ed) *Pupil Strategies: Explorations in the Sociology of the School*, London, Croom Helm, pp.50–73

DEPARTMENT OF EDUCATION AND SCIENCE (1965) *The Organization of Secondary Education*, (Circular 10/65), London, HMSO

DEPARTMENT OF EDUCATION AND SCIENCE (1972) *Education: A Framework for Expansion*, Cmnd. 5174, London, HMSO

DEPARTMENT OF EDUCATION AND SCIENCE (1977a) *Education in Schools: A Consultative Document*, Cmnd. 6869, London, HMSO

DEPARTMENT OF EDUCATION AND SCIENCE (1977b) *Local Authority Arrangements for the School Curriculum* (Circular 14/77), London, HMSO

DEPARTMENT OF EDUCATION AND SCIENCE (1978a) *Primary Education in England: A Survey by HM Inspectors of Schools*, London, HMSO

DEPARTMENT OF EDUCATION AND SCIENCE (1978b) *Mixed Ability Work in Comprehensive Schools*, London, HMSO

DEPARTMENT OF EDUCATION AND SCIENCE (1979) *Aspects of Secondary Education in England: A Survey by HM Inspectors of Schools*, London, HMSO

DEPARTMENT OF EDUCATION AND SCIENCE (1980a) *A View of the Curriculum*, London, HMSO

DEPARTMENT OF EDUCATION AND SCIENCE (1980b) *A Framework for the School Curriculum*, London, HMSO

DEPARTMENT OF EDUCATION AND SCIENCE (1981a) *Statistics of Education 1979, Volume 2: School Leavers*, London, HMSO

DEPARTMENT OF EDUCATION AND SCIENCE (1981b) *Curriculum 11–16*, London, HMSO

DEPARTMENT OF EDUCATION AND SCIENCE (1981c) *Report by HMI on the effects of the education service of local authority expenditure policies*, London, HMSO

DEPARTMENT OF EDUCATION AND SCIENCE (1981d) *Review of the Schools Council* (The Trenaman Report), London, HMSO

DEPARTMENT OF EDUCATION AND SCIENCE (1983a) *Education Statistics for the United Kingdom 1983 Edition*, London, HMSO

DEPARTMENT OF EDUCATION AND SCIENCE (1983b) *Teaching Quality*, London, HMSO

DEPARTMENT OF EDUCATION AND SCIENCE (1983c) *Statistics of Teachers in Service in England and Wales*, London, HMSO

DEPARTMENT OF EDUCATION AND SCIENCE (1984) *The Organization and Content of the 5–16 Curriculum*,London, HMSO

DEPARTMENT OF EMPLOYMENT (1983) 'Statistical series', *Employment Gazette*, vol. 91, no. 2, pp.51–564

DINGWALL, R. (1977) *The Social Organization of Health Visitor Training*, London, Croom Helm

DODD, T. (1978) *Design and Technology in the School Curriculum*, London, Hodder and Stoughton

DORE, R. (1976) *The Diploma Disease*, London, Allen and Unwin

DOUGLAS, J. W. B. (1964) *The Home and the School*, London, Panther

DOUGLAS, J. W. B. (1976) 'The use and abuse of national cohorts', in SHIPMAN, M. (ed) *The Organization and Impact of Social Research*, London, Routledge and Kegan Paul, pp.3–21

DOUGLAS, J. W. B. and ROSS, J. M. (1964) 'Subsequent progress of nursery school children', *Educational Research*, vol. 7, pp. 83–94

DOUGLAS, J. W. B., ROSS, J. M. and SIMPSON, H. R. (1968) *All Our Future*, London, Panther

DRIVER, G. (1977) 'Cultural competence, social power and school achievement: West Indian pupils in the West Midlands', *New Community*, vol. 5, no. 4, pp.353–359

DRIVER, G. (1979) 'Classroom stress and school achievement', in KHAN, V. S. (ed) *Minority Families in Britain*, London, Macmillan, pp.131–144

DYHOUSE, C. (1977) 'Good wives and little mothers: social anxieties and the schoolgirls' curriculum', *Oxford Review of Education*, vol. 3, no. 1, pp.21–25

DYHOUSE, C. (1981) *Girls Growing Up in Late Victorian and Edwardian England*, London, Routledge and Kegan Paul

EDUCATION GROUP, CENTRE FOR CONTEMPORARY CULTURAL STUDIES (1981) *Unpopular Education: Schooling and Social Democracy in England since 1944*, London, Hutchinson

EDWARDS, A. D. (1976) *Language in Culture and Class*, London, Heinemann

EDWARDS, A. D. (1980) 'Perspectives on classroom language', *Educational Analysis*, vol. 2, no. 2, pp.31–46

EDWARDS, A. and FURLONG, V. J. (1978) *The Language of Teaching*, London, Heinemann

EDWARDS, V. (1976) *West Indian Language: Attitudes and the School*, London, National Association for Multiracial Education

EDWARDS, V. (1979) *The West Indian Language Issue in British Schools*, London, Routledge and Kegan Paul

EDWARDS, V. (1981) *Language in Multicultural Classrooms*, London, Batsford

EGGLESTON, J. (1967) 'Some environmental correlates of extended secondary education in England', *Comparative Education*, vol. 3, no. 2, pp.85–99

EGGLESTON, J. (1974) (ed) *Contemporary Research in the Sociology of Education*, London, Methuen

EGGLESTON, J. (1977a) *The Ecology of the School*, London, Methuen

EGGLESTON, J. (1977b) *The Sociology of the School Curriculum*, London, Routledge and Kegan Paul

EGGLESTON, J. (1982) (ed) *Work Experience in Secondary Schools*, London, Routledge and Kegan Paul

EMBLING, J. (1974) *A Fresh Look at Higher Education: European Implications of the Carnegie Commission Reports*, Amsterdam, Elsevier

EPSTEIN, C. F. (1973) 'Positive effects of the multiple negative: explaining the success of black professional women', *American Journal of Sociology*, vol. 78, no. 4, pp.912–935

EQUAL OPPORTUNITIES COMMISSION (1982) *Gender and the Secondary School Curriculum*, Manchester, Equal Opportunities Commission

EQUAL OPPORTUNITIES COMMISSION (1983a) *Women in Engineering*, Manchester, Equal Opportunities Commission

EQUAL OPPORTUNITIES COMMISSION (1983b) *Formal Investigation Report: Sidney Stringer School and Community College, Coventry*, Manchester, Equal Opportunities Commission

EQUAL OPPORTUNITIES COMMISSION (1985) *Equal Opportunities and the Woman Teacher*, Manchester, Equal Opportunities Commission

ESLAND, G. M. and CATHCART, H. (1981) *Education and the Corporate Economy*, Open University Course E 353, *Society, Education and the State*, Block 1, Unit 2, Milton Keynes, Open University Press

ESSEN, J., FOGELMAN, K. and HEAD, J. (1978) 'Childhood, housing experience and school attainment', *Child Care, Health and Development*, vol. 4, pp.41–58

ETZIONI, A. (1969) (ed) *The Semi-Professions and their Organization: Teachers, Nurses and Social Workers*, New York, Free Press

EVANS, J. (1985) *Teaching in Transition: the challenge of mixed-ability teaching*, Milton Keynes, Open University Press

EVETTS, J. (1973) *The Sociology of Educational Ideas*, London, Routledge and Kegan Paul

EYSENCK, H. J. (1971) *Race, Intelligence and Education*, London, Temple-Smith

FAIRBAIRN, A. (1971) *The Leicestershire Community Colleges*, London, National Institute of Adult Education

FAIRBAIRN, A. (1979) *The Leicestershire Community Colleges and Centres*, Nottingham, University of Nottingham, Department of Adult Education

FARRANT, J. H. (1981) 'Trends in admissions', in FULTON, O. (ed) *Access to Higher Education*, Guildford, Society for Research into Higher Education, pp.42–88

FIDDY, R. (1983) (ed) *In Place of Work: Policy and Provision for the Young Unemployed*, Lewes, Falmer Press

FILSTEAD, W. J. (1970) *Qualitative Methodology*, Chicago, Rand McNally

FINCH, J. (1983) 'Dividing the rough and the respectable: working class women and pre-school playgroups', in GARMARNIKOW, E., MORGAN, D., PURVIS, J. and TAYLORSON, D. (eds) *The Public and the Private*, London, Heinemann, pp.106–117

FINCH, J. (1984) 'Working-class playgroups as pre-school experience', *British Educational Research Journal*, vol. 10, no. 1, pp.3–17

FINN, D. (1982) 'Whose needs? Schooling and the "needs" of industry', in REES, T. L. and ATKINSON, P. (eds) *Youth Unemployment and State Intervention*, London, Routledge and Kegan Paul, pp. 41–55

FINN, D. (1984) 'Leaving school and growing up: work experience in the juvenile labour market', in BATES, I. *et al, Schooling for the Dole? The New Vocationalism*, London, Macmillan, pp.17–84

FINN, D. and FRITH, S. (1981) 'Education and the labour market' in Open University, *The State and the Politics of Education*, Course E 353, Block I, Part 2, Unit 4, Milton Keynes, Open University Press, pp.41–85

FINN, D., GRANT, N. and JOHNSON, R. (1978) 'Social democracy, education and the crisis' in Centre for Contemporary Cultural Studies, *On Ideology*, London, Hutchinson

FIRTH, G. C. (1963) *Comprehensive Schools in Coventry and Elsewhere*, Coventry, Coventry Education Committee

FIRTH, G. C. (1977) *Seventy Five Years of Service to Education*, Coventry, Coventry Education Committee

FLANDERS, N. (1970) *Analyzing Teacher Behaviour*, Reading, Mass., Addison Wesley

FLETCHER, R. (1984) *Education in Society*, Harmondsworth, Penguin

FLETCHER, C. and THOMPSON, N. (1980) (eds) *Issues in Community Education*, Lewes, Falmer Press

FLOUD, J. and HALSEY, A. H. (1961) 'Introduction', in HALSEY, A. H., FLOUD, J. and ANDERSON, C. A. (eds) *Education, Economy and Society*, New York, Free Press, pp.1–12

FLOUD, J. and SCOTT, W. (1961) 'Recruitment to teaching in England and Wales', in HALSEY, A. H., FLOUD, J. and ANDERSON, C. A. (eds) *Education, Economy and Society*, New York, Free Press, pp.527–544

FOGELMAN, K. (1975) 'Developmental correlates of family size', *British Journal of Social Work*, vol. 5, no. 1, pp. 43–57

FOGELMAN, K. (1976) (ed) *Britain's Sixteen Year Olds*, London, National Children's Bureau

FOGELMAN, K. (1983) (ed) *Growing Up in Great Britain: Papers from the National Child Development Study*, London, Macmillan.

FOGELMAN, K. and GOLDSTEIN, H. (1976) 'Social factors associated with changes in educational attainment between 7 and 11 years of age', *Educational Studies*, vol. 2, no. 2, pp.95–109

FREEMAN, R. B. (1971) *The Market for College-Trained Manpower*, Boston, Mass., Harvard University Press

FRITH, S. (1978) 'Education, training and the labour process', Paper presented to the Conference of Socialist Economists Education Group

FULLER, M. (1980) 'Black girls in a London Comprehensive school', in DEEM, R. (ed) *Schooling for Women's Work*, London, Routledge and Kegan Paul, pp.52–65

FULLER, M. (1983) 'Qualified criticism, critical qualifications', in BARTON, L. and WALKER, S. (eds) *Race, Class and Education*, London, Croom Helm, pp.166–190

FULLER, M. (1984a) *Inequality: Gender, Race and Class*, Open University Course E 205, *Conflict and Change in Education: A Sociological Introduction*, Milton Keynes, Open University Press

FULLER, M. (1984b) 'Dimensions of gender in a school: reinventing the wheel?' in BURGESS, R. G. (ed) *The Research Process in Educational Settings: Ten Case Studies*, Lewes, Falmer Press, pp.97–115

GALTON, M. and DELAMONT, S. (1980) 'The first weeks of middle school', in HARGREAVES, A. and TICKLE, L. (eds) *Middle Schools: Origins, Ideology and Practice*, London, Harper and Row, pp.207–227

GALTON, M., SIMON, B. and CROLL, P. (1980) *Inside the Primary Classroom*, London, Routledge and Kegan Paul

GALTON, M. and WILLCOCKS, J. (1983) *Moving from the Primary Classroom*, London, Routledge and Kegan Paul

GANNAWAY, H. (1976) 'Making sense of school', in STUBBS, M. and DELAMONT, S. (eds) *Explorations in Classroom Observation*, Chichester, Wiley, pp.45–82

GARLAND, P. (1979) 'Pat Garland' in MCCRINDLE, J. and ROWBOTHAM, S. (eds) *Dutiful Daughters: Women talk about their lives*, Harmondsworth, Penguin, pp.266–299

GEER, B. (1966) 'Occupational commitment and the teaching profession', *School Review*, vol. 74, no. 1, pp.31–47

GERTH, H. and MILLS, C. W. (1948) *From Max Weber*, London, Routledge and Kegan Paul

GINSBURG, M. B., MEYENN, R. J. and MILLER, H. D. R. (1980) 'Teachers' conceptions of professionalism and trades unionism: an ideological analysis', in WOODS, P. (ed) *Teacher Strategies Explorations in the Sociology of the School*, London, Croom Helm, pp.178–212

GINTIS, H. (1971) 'Education and the characteristics of worker productivity', *American Economic Review*, vol. 61, pp. 266–279

GINTIS, H. (1972) 'Towards a political economy of education: a radical critique of Ivan Illich's *Deschooling Society*', *Harvard Educational Review*, vol. 42, no. 1, pp.70–96

GITTUS, E. (1972) (ed) *Key Variables in Social Research*, London, Heinemann

GLASS, D. (1954) (ed) *Social Mobility in Britain*, London, Routledge and Kegan Paul

GLEESON, D. (1983) (ed) *Youth Training and the Search for Work*, London, Routledge and Kegan Paul

GOBLE, N. M. and PORTER, I. F. (1977) *The Changing Role of the Teacher*, Paris, UNESCO

GOFFMAN, E. (1961) *Asylums*, New York, Doubleday

GOLDSTEIN, H. (1980) 'Fifteen Thousand Hours: a review of the statistical procedures', *Journal of Child Psychology and Psychiatry*

GOLDTHORPE, J. H. and LLEWELLYN, C. (1977a) 'Class mobility in Britain: Three theses examined', *Sociology*, vol. 11, no. 2, pp.257–287

GOLDTHORPE, J. and LLEWELLYN, C. (1977b) 'Class mobility: integrational and worklife patterns', *British Journal of Sociology*, vol. 28, no. 3, pp.269–302

GOLDTHORPE, J. (with LLEWELLYN, C. and PAYNE, C.) (1980) *Social Mobility and Class Structure in Modern Britain*, Oxford, Clarendon Press

GOLDTHORPE, J. (1983) 'Women and class analysis: In defence of the conventional view', *Sociology*, vol. 17, no. 4, pp.465–488

GOLDTHORPE, J. (1984) 'Women and class analysis: a reply to the replies', *Sociology*, vol. 18, no. 4, pp.491–499

GOODSON, I. (1982) *School Subjects and Curriculum Change*, London, Croom Helm

GOODSON, I. (1985) *Social Histories of the Secondary Curriculum: Subjects for Study*, Lewes, Falmer Press

GOODSON, I. F. and BALL, S. J. (1984) (eds) *Defining the Curriculum: Histories and Ethnographies*, Lewes, Falmer Press

GORBUTT, D. (1972) 'The new sociology of education', *Education for Teaching*, Autumn, no. 89, pp.3–11

GORDON, J. C. B. (1981) *Verbal Deficit: A Critique*, London, Croom Helm

GORDON, P. and LAWTON, D. (1978) *Curriculum Change in the Nineteenth and Twentieth Centuries*, London, Hodder and Stoughton

GOSLIN, D. A. (1965) *The School in Contemporary Society*, Illinois, Scott, Foreman

GRACE, G. (1972) *Role Conflict and the Teacher*, London, Routledge and Kegan Paul

GRACE, G. (1978) *Teachers, Ideology and Control*, London, Routledge and Kegan Paul

GRAY, J., MCPHERSON, A. and RAFFE, D. (1983) *Reconstruction of Secondary Education: Theory, Myth and Practice Since the War*, London, Routledge and Kegan Paul

GRAY, J. L. and MOSHINSKY, P. (1938) 'Ability and opportunity in English education', in HOGBEN, L. (ed) *Political Arithmetic*, London, Allen and Unwin

GRETTON, J. and JACKSON, M. (1976) *William Tyndale: Collapse of a School or a System?* London, Allen and Unwin

GRIFFIN, C. (1985a) 'Qualitative methods and cultural analysis: young women and the transition from school to un/employment', in BURGESS, R. G. (ed) *Field Methods in the Study of Education*, Lewes, Falmer Press, pp.97–114

GRIFFIN, C. (1985b) *Typical Girls? The Transition from School to Un/employment for Young Working Class Women*, London, Routledge and Kegan Paul

HAKIM, C. (1982) *Secondary Analysis in Social Research: A Guide to Data Sources and Methods with Examples*, London, Allen and Unwin

HALLIDAY, M. (1973) *Explorations in the Functions of Language*, London, Edward Arnold

HALSEY, A. H. (1972) *Educational Priority, Volume 1*, London, HMSO

HALSEY, A. H. (1975) 'Sociology and the equality debate', *Oxford Review of Education*, vol. 1, no.1 pp.9–23

HALSEY, A. H. (1977a) 'Towards meritocracy? The case of Britain' in KARABEL, J. and HALSEY, A. H. (eds) *Power and Ideology in Education*, New York, Oxford University Press, pp.173–186

HALSEY, A. H. (1977b) *Change in British Society*, Oxford, Oxford University Press

HALSEY, A. H. (1982) 'Provincials and professionals: the British post-war sociologists', *Archives Européennes de Sociologie*, vol. 23, pp.150–175

HALSEY, A. H. and FLOUD, J. (1958) 'The sociology of education: a trend report and bibliography', *Current Sociology*, vol. 7, pp.165–235

HALSEY, A. H., FLOUD, J. and ANDERSON, C. A. (1961) (eds) *Education, Economy and Society: A Reader in the Sociology of Education*, New York, Free Press

HALSEY, A. H., HEATH, A. F. and RIDGE, J. M. (1980) *Origins and Destinations: Family, Class and Education in Modern Britain*, Oxford, Clarendon Press

HAMILTON, D. (1975) 'Handling innovation in the classroom: two Scottish examples', in REID, W. A. and WALKER, D. F. (eds) *Case Studies in Curriculum Change*, London, Routledge and Kegan Paul, pp.179–207

HAMILTON, D. (1977) *In Search of Structure*, London, Hodder and Stoughton

HAMILTON, D. and DELAMONT, S. (1976) 'Classroom research: a critique and a new approach', in STUBBS, M. and DELAMONT, S. (eds) *Explorations in Classroom Observation*, Chichester, Wiley, pp.3–20

HAMILTON, D. and DELAMONT, S. (1984) 'Revisiting classroom research: a continuing cautionary tale', in DELAMONT, S. (ed) *Readings on Interaction in the Classroom*, London, Methuen, pp. 3–37

HAMMERSLEY, M. (1977) *Teacher Perspectives*, Open University Course E 202, *Schooling and Society*, Milton Keynes, Open University Press

HAMMERSLEY, M. (1980) 'Classroom ethnography', *Educational Analysis*, vol. 2, no. 2, pp.47–74

HAMMERSLEY, M. (1983) (ed) *The Ethnography of Schooling*, Driffield, Nafferton

HAMMERSLEY, M. (1984a) *Interpretive Sociology and the Macro-Micro Problem*, Open University Course E 205, *Conflict and Change in Education: A Sociological Introduction*, Milton Keynes, Open University Press

HAMMERSLEY, M. (1984b) 'Some reflections upon the macro-micro problem in the sociology of education', *Sociological Review*, vol. 32, no. 2, pp.316–324

HAMMERSLEY, M. (1984c) 'The researcher exposed: a natural history', in BURGESS, R. G. (ed) *The Research Process in Educational Settings: Ten Case Studies*, Lewes, Falmer Press, pp.39–67

HAMMERSLEY, M. (1985) 'From ethnography to theory: a programme and paradigm in the sociology of education', *Sociology*, vol. 19, no. 2, pp.244–259

HAMMERSLEY, M. and ATKINSON, P. (1983) *Ethnography: Principles in Practice*, London, Tavistock

HAMMERSLEY, M. and HARGREAVES, A. (1983) (eds) *Curriculum Practice: Some Sociological Case Studies*, Lewes, Falmer Press

HAMMERSLEY, M., SCARTH, J. and WEBB, S. (1985) 'Developing and testing theory: the case of research on pupil learning and examinations', in BURGESS, R. G. (ed) *Issues in Educational Research: Qualitative Methods*, Lewes, Falmer Press, pp.48–66

HAMMERSLEY, M. and WOODS, P. (1984) (eds) *Life in School: The Sociology of Pupil Culture*, Milton Keynes, Open University Press

HANNAM, C., SMYTH, P. and STEPHENSON, N. (1976) *The First Year of Teaching*, Harmondsworth, Penguin

HANSON, D. (1971) 'The development of a professional association of art teachers', *Studies in Design Education*, vol. 3, no. 2, pp. 30–40

HARGREAVES, A. (1978) 'The significance of classroom coping strategies' in BARTON, L. and MEIGHAN, R. (eds) *Sociological Interpretations of Schooling and Classrooms: A Reappraisal*, Driffield, Nafferton, pp.73–100

HARGREAVES, A. (1980a) 'Synthesis and the study of strategies: a project for the sociological imagination', in WOODS, P. (ed) *Pupil Strategies: Explorations in the Sociology of the School*, London, Croom Helm, pp.162–197

HARGREAVES, A. (1980b) 'Review article on Fifteen Thousand Hours', *British Journal of Sociology of Education*, vol. 1, no.2, pp.211–216

HARGREAVES, A. (1984) *Marxism and Relative Autonomy*, Open University Course E 205, *Conflict and Change in Education: A Sociological Introduction*, Milton Keynes, Open University Press

HARGREAVES, A. (1985) 'The micro-macro problem in the sociology of education', in BURGESS, R. G. (ed) *Issues in Educational Research: Qualitative Methods*, Lewes, Falmer Press, pp.21–47

HARGREAVES, A. and WOODS, P. (1984) (eds) *Classrooms and Staffrooms: The Sociology of Teachers and Teaching*, Milton Keynes, Open University Press

HARGREAVES, D. H. (1967) *Social Relations in a Secondary School*, London, Routledge and Kegan Paul

HARGREAVES, D. H. (1977) 'The process of typification in classroom interaction models and methods', *British Journal of Educational Psychology*, vol. 47, pp.274–284

HARGREAVES, D. H. (1978a) 'Whatever happened to symbolic interactionism?' in BARTON, L. and MEIGHAN, R. (eds) *Sociological Interpretations of Schooling and Classrooms: A Reappraisal*, Driffield, Nafferton, pp.7–22

HARGREAVES, D. H. (1978b) 'Power and the paracurriculum', in RICHARDS, C. (ed) *Power and the Curriculum: Issues in Curriculum Studies*, Driffield, Nafferton, pp.97–108

HARGREAVES, D. H. (1980a) (ed) *Classroom Studies, Educational Analysis*, vol. 2, no. 2, pp.1–95

HARGREAVES, D. H. (1980b) 'The occupational culture of teachers', in WOODS, P. (ed) *Teacher Strategies: Explorations in the Sociology of the School*, London, Croom Helm, pp.125–148

HARGREAVES, D. H. (1982) *The Challenge for the Comprehensive School*, London, Routledge and Kegan Paul

HARGREAVES, D. H. (1984) 'School and community', *Community Education Network*, vol. 4, no. 6, p.3 and vol. 4, no. 7, p.3 (also in RANSON, S. and TOMLINSON, J. (eds) *The Changing Government of Education*, London, Allen and Unwin).

HARGREAVES, D. H., HESTER, S. and MELLOR, F. (1975) *Deviance in Classrooms*, London, Routledge and Kegan Paul

HARRIS, K. (1982) *Teachers and Classes: A Marxist Analysis*, London, Routledge and Kegan Paul

HARTNETT, A. (1982) (ed) *The Social Sciences in Educational Studies*, London, Heinemann

HEATH, A. F. (1980) 'Class and meritocracy in British education', in FINCH, A. and SCRIMSHAW, P. (eds) *Standards, Schooling and Education*, London, Hodder and Stoughton, pp.270–297

HEATH, A. F. (1981) *Social Mobility*, London, Fontana

HENRY, J. (1963) *Culture Against Man*, London, Tavistock

HMSO (1972) *Education: A Framework for Expansion*, London, HMSO

HERRNSTEIN, R. (1973) *IQ in the Meritocracy*, Boston, Atlantic-Little Brown

HEWARD, C. M. (1984) 'Parents, sons and their careers: a case study of a public school, 1930–50', in WALFORD, G. (ed) *British Public Schools: Policy and Practice*, Lewes, Falmer Press, pp.137–162

HOLLAND REPORT (1977) *Young People and Work: Report on the Feasibility of a New Programme of Opportunities for Unemployed Young People*, London, Manpower Services Commission

HOME AFFAIRS COMMITTEE (1981) *Commission for Racial Equality 1981–1982*, London, HMSO

HOPE, K. (1984) *As Others See Us: Schooling and Social Mobility in Scotland and the United States*, Cambridge, Cambridge University Press

HOPPER, E. (1971a) (ed) *Readings in the Theory of Educational System*, London, Hutchinson

HOPPER, E. (1971b) 'Educational systems and selected consequences of patterns of mobility and non-mobility in industrial societies: a theoretical discussion' in HOPPER, E. (ed) *Readings in the Theory of Educational Systems*, London, Hutchinson, pp.292–336

HOPPER, E. (1977) 'A typology for the classification of educational systems', in KARABEL, J. and HALSEY, A. H. (eds) *Power and Ideology in Education*, Oxford, Oxford University Press, pp.153–166

HOPPER, E. and OSBORN, M. (1975) *Adult Students: Education Selection and Social Control*, London, Frances Pinter

HOUGHTON REPORT (1974) *Report of the Committee of Inquiry into the Pay of Non-University Teachers*, Cmnd. 5848, London, HMSO

HOYLE, E. (1965) 'Organisational analysis in the field of education', *Educational Research*, vol. 7, no. 2, pp.97–114

HOYLE, E. (1969) *The Role of the Teacher*, London, Routledge and Kegan Paul

HUSÉN, T. (1979) *The School in Question*, Oxford, Oxford University Press

HUSSAIN, A. (1976) 'The economy and the education system in capitalist societies', *Economy and Society*, vol. 5, no. 4, pp.413–434

HYNDMAN, M. (1978) *Schools and Schooling in England and Wales: A Documentary History*, London, Harper and Row

HUGHES, P. (1980) 'Pastoral care – the historical context' in R. BEST et al, (eds) *Perspective on Pastoral Care*, London, Heinemann, p.24–31

JACKSON, B. (1964) *Streaming: An Education System in Miniature*, London, Routledge and Kegan Paul

JACKSON, B. and MARSDEN, D. (1962) *Education and the Working Class*, Harmondsworth, Penguin

JACKSON, P. (1968) *Life in Classrooms*, New York, Holt, Rinehart and Winston

JEFFCOATE, R. (1982) *The Education of Ethnic Minority Children in Britain 1960–1980*, Open University Course E 354, Milton Keynes, Open University Press

JEFFCOATE, R. (1984) *Ethnic Minorities and Education*, London, Harper and Row

JENCKS, C. *et al* (1972) *Inequality: A reassessment of the effect of family and schooling in America*, New York, Basic Books

JENKINS, R. (1983) *Lads, Citizens and Ordinary Kids: Working Class Youth Life-styles in Belfast*, London, Routledge and Kegan Paul

JENKINS, R. and TROYNA, B. (1983) 'Educational myth, labour market reality', in TROYNA, B. and SMITH, D. I. (eds) *Racism, School and the Labour Market*, Leicester, National Youth Bureau, pp.5–17

JENSEN, A. (1969) 'How much can we boost IQ and scholastic achievement?' *Harvard Educational Review*, vol. 39, no. 1, pp.1–123

JOHNSON, D. and RANSOM, E. (1983) *Family and School*, London, Croom Helm

JOHNSON, R. (1970) 'Educational policy and social control in early Victorian England', *Past and Present*, no. 49, pp.96–119

JOHNSON, R. (1976) 'Notes on the schooling of the English working class 1780–1850', in DALE, R. *et al* (eds) *Schooling and Capitalism*, London, Routledge and Kegan Paul, pp.44–54

JOHNSON, T. (1972) *Professions and Power*, London, Macmillan.

KARABEL, J. and HALSEY, A. H. (1977a) 'Educational research: A review and an interpretation' in KARABEL, J. and HALSEY, A. H. (eds) *Power and Ideology in Education*, Oxford, Oxford University Press, pp.1–85

KARABEL, J. and HALSEY, A. H. (1977b) (eds) *Power and Ideology in Education*, Oxford Oxford University Press

KEDDIE, N. (1971) 'Classroom Knowledge', in YOUNG, M. F. D. (ed) *Knowledge and Control: New Directions for the Sociology of Education*, London, Collier Macmillan, pp.133–160

KELLY, A. (1981a) (ed) *The Missing Half: Girls and Science Education*, Manchester, Manchester University Press

KELLY, A. (1981b) 'Science achievement as an aspect of sex roles', in KELLY, A. (ed) *The Missing Half: Girls and Science Education*, Manchester, Manchester University Press, pp.73–84

KELSALL, R. K. (1957) *Report of an Inquiry into Applications for Admissions to Universities*, London, AUBC

KELSALL, R. K., POOLE, A. and KUHN, A. (1972) *Graduates: The Sociology of an Elite*, London, Tavistock

KING, R. (1971) 'Unequal access in education – sex and social class', *Social and Economic Administration*, vol. 5, no. 3, pp.167–174

KING, R. (1978) *All Things Bright and Beautiful? A Sociological Study of Infants' Classrooms*, Chichester, Wiley

KING, R. (1983) *The Sociology of School Organization*, London, Methuen

KOGAN, M. (1975) *Educational Policy Making*, London, Allen and Unwin

KOGAN, M. (1978) *The Politics of Educational Change*, London, Fontana

LABOV, W. (1972) 'The logic of non-standard English', in GIGLIOLI, P. P. (ed) *Language and Social Context*, Harmondsworth, Penguin, pp.179–215

LACEY, C. (1966) 'Some sociological concomitants of academic streaming in a grammar school', *British Journal of Sociology*, vol. 17, no. 3, pp.245–262

LACEY, C. (1970) *Hightown Grammar: The School as a Social System*, Manchester, Manchester University Press

LACEY, C. (1977) *The Socialization of Teachers*, London, Mehuen

LAMBART, A. (1976) 'The Sisterhood', in HAMMERLSEY, M. and WOODS, P. (eds) *The Process of Schooling*, London, Routledge and Kegan Paul, pp.152–159

LAMBART, A. (1982) 'Expulsion in context: a school as a system in action', in FRANKENBERG, R. (ed) *Custom and Conflict in British Society*, Manchester, Manchester University Press, pp.188–208

LAMBERT, R. *et al* (1975) *The Hothouse Society*, Harmondsworth, Penguin

LANG, P. and MARLAND, M. (1985) (eds) *New Directions in Pastoral Care*, Oxford, Basil Blackwell

LASHLEY, H. (1981) 'Culture, education and children of West Indian background', in LYNCH, J. (ed) *Teaching in the Multicultural School*, London, Ward Lock, pp.227–248

LAWTON, D. (1973) *Social Change, Educational Theory and Curriculum Planning*, London, University of London Press

LAWTON, D. (1975) *Class, Culture and the Curriculum*, London, Routledge and Kegan Paul

LAWTON, D. (1980) *The Politics of the School Curriculum*, London, Routledge and Kegan Paul

LAWTON, D. (1983) *Curriculum Studies and Educational Planning*, London, Hodder and Stoughton

LAWTON, D. (1984) *The Tightening Grip: Growth of Central Control of the School Curriculum, Bedford Way Paper No. 21*, London, University of London Institute of Education

LAYARD, R. and PSACHAROPOULOS, G. (1974) 'The screening hypothesis and the resturns to education', *Journal of Political Economy*, vol. 82, pp.985–998

LAYTON, D. (1973) *Science for the People*, London, Allen and Unwin

LEE, D. and NEWBY, H. (1983) *The Problem of Sociology*, London, Hutchinson

LEE, G. and WRENCH, J. (1981) 'Where are the black apprentices?' *New Society*, 24 September, vol. 57, no. 984, pp.517–518

LEE, G. and WRENCH, J. (1983) *Skill Seekers: black youth, apprenticeships and disadvantage*, Leicester, National Youth Bureau

LEGGATT, T. (1970) 'Teaching as a profession', in JACKSON, J. A. (ed) *Professions and Professionalization*, Cambridge, Cambridge University Press, pp.153–177

LIPPITT, R. and WHITE, R. K. (1943) 'The "social climate" of children's groups', in

BARKER, R. G., KOUNIN, J. S. and WRIGHT, H. F. (eds) *Child Behaviour and Development*, New York, McGraw Hill, pp.485–508

LITTLE, A. (1975) 'Performance of children from ethnic minority backgrounds in primary schools', *Oxford Review of Education*, vol. 1, no. 2, pp.117–135

LITTLE, A. (1978) *Five Views of Multiracial Britain*, London, Commission for Racial Equality

LITTLE, A. (1981) 'Education and race relations in the United Kingdom', in MEGARRY, J., NISBET, S. and HOYLE, E. (eds) *World Yearbook of Education*, London, Kogan Page; New York, Nichols Publishing, pp.129–143

LITTLE, A. and MABEY, C. (1972) 'An index for designation of Educational Priority Areas', in SHONFIELD, S. and SHAW, S. (eds) *Social Indicators and Social Policy*, London, Heinemann, pp.67–93

LITTLE, A. and ROBBINS, D. (1981) 'Race bias', in WARREN-PIPER, D. (ed) *Is Higher Education Fair?* Guildford, Society for Research into Higher Education, pp. 57–79

LITTLE, A. and WESTERGAARD, J. (1964) 'The trend of class differentials in educational opportunity in England and Wales', *British Journal of Sociology*, vol. 15, no. 4, pp.301–316

LLEWELLYN, M. (1980) 'Studying girls at school: the implications of confusion', in DEEM, R. (ed) *Schooling for Women's Work*, London, Routledge and Kegan Paul, pp.42–51

LOBBAN, G. (1975) 'Sex roles in reading schemes', *Educational Review*, vol. 27, no. 3, pp.202–210

LODGE, P. and BLACKSTONE, T. (1982) *Educational Policy and Educational Inequality*, Oxford, Martin Robertson

LORTIE, D. (1975) *School-teacher: a Sociological Study*, Chicago, University of Chicago Press

LYNCH, J. (1981) *The Multicultural Curriculum*, London, Batsford

LYONS, G. (1981) *Teacher Careers and Career Peceptions*, Slough, NFER

MABEY, C. (1981) 'Black British literacy', *Educational Research*, vol. 23, no. 2, pp.83–95

MACDONALD, K. and RIDGE, J. M. (1972) 'Social mobility', in HALSEY, A. H. (ed) *Trends in British Society Since 1900*, London, Macmillan, pp.129–145

MACDONALD, M. (1980a) 'Cultural reproduction: the pedagogy of sexuality', *Screen Education*, 32/33, pp.141–153

MACDONALD, M. (1980b) 'Socio-cultural reproduction and women's education', in DEEM, R. (ed) *Schooling for Women's Work*, London, Routledge and Kegan Paul, pp.13–25

MACDONALD, M. (1981) *Class Gender and Education*, Open University Course E353, *Society, Education and the State*, Milton Keynes, Open University Press

MACKENZIE, R. F. (1977) *The Unbowed Head*, Edinburgh, Edinburgh University Press

MACKINTOSH, N. J. and MASCIE-TAYLOR, C. G. N. (1985) 'The IQ question', in SWANN, M., *Education for All: The Report of the Committee of Inquiry into the Education of Children from Ethnic Minority Groups*, London, HMSO, pp.126–163

MAGUIRE, M. J. and ASHTON, D. N. (1981) 'Employers' perceptions and use of educational qualifications', *Educational Analysis*, vol. 3, no.2, pp.25–36

MARJORIBANKS, K. (1975) 'Equal educational opportunity: a definition', *Oxford Review of Education*, vol. 1, no.1, pp.25–6

MARSH, C. (1986) 'Social class and occupation', in BURGESS, R. G. (ed) *Key Variables in Social Investigation*, London, Routledge and Kegan Paul, pp.123–152

MASON, S. (1957) *The Leicestershire Experiment*, London, Councils and Education Press

MAXWELL, J. (1969) *Sixteen Years On*, London, University of London Press

MCALEESE, R. and HAMILTON, D. (1978) (eds) *Understanding Classroom Life*, Slough, NFER

MCCANN, P. (1977) (ed) *Popular Education and Socialization in the Nineteenth Century*, London, Methuen

MCINTOSH, N., CALDER, J. and SWIFT, D. (1976) *A Degree of Difference: A Study of the First Year's Intake to the Open University of the United Kingdom*, Guildford, Society for Research in Higher Education

MCINTYRE, D. I. (1980) 'Systematic observation of classroom activities', *Educational Analysis*, vol. 2, no. 2, pp.3–30

MCROBBIE, A. (1978) 'Working class girls and the culture of femininity', in Women's Studies Group, Centre for Contemporary Cultural Studies, *Women Take Issue: Aspects of Women's Subordination*, London, Hutchinson

MEASOR, L. (1984) 'Pupil perceptions of subject status', in GOODSON, I. F. and BALL, S. J. (eds) *Defining the Curriculum: Histories and Ethnographies*, Lewes, Falmer Press, pp.201–217

MEASOR, L. and WOODS, P. (1984) *Changing Schools: Pupil Perspectives on Transfer to a Comprehensive*, Milton Keynes, Open University Press

MEGARRY, J., NISBET, S. and HOYLE, E. (1981) (eds) *World Yearbook of Education 1981: Education of Minorities*, London, Kogan Page; New York, Nichols Publishing

MILLER, S. M. (1960) 'Comparative social mobility', *Current Sociology*, vol. 9, no. 1, pp.1–89

MILLERSON, G. (1964) *The Qualifying Associations: A Study in Professionalization*, London, Routledge and Kegan Paul

MINISTRY OF EDUCATION (1959) *15 to 18* (the Crowther Report), London, HMSO

MINISTRY OF EDUCATION (1963) *Half Our Future* (the Newsom Report), London, HMSO

MONKS, T. G. (1968) *Comprehensive Education in England and Wales*, Windsor, NFER

MOODY, E. (1968) 'Right in front of everyone', *New Society*, vol. 12, no. 326, pp.952–3

MOORE, R. (1984) 'Schooling and the world of work', in BATES, I. *et al*, *Schooling for the Dole?: The New Vocationalism*, London, Macmillan, pp.65–103

MOORE, R. (1986) 'Immigration and racism', in BURGESS, R. G. (ed) *Exploring Society*, London, Longman

MORGAN, C., HALL, V. and MACKAY, H. (1983) *The Selection of Secondary School Headteachers*, Milton Keynes, Open University Press

MORGAN, D. H. J. (1986) 'Gender', in BURGESS, R. G. (ed) *Key Variables in Social Investigation*, London, Routledge and Kegan Paul, pp.31–53

MORTIMORE, J. and BLACKSTONE, T. (1981) *Disadvantage and Education*, London, Heinemann

MURRAY, R. (1974) 'Overcrowding and aggression in primary school children', in MORRISON, C. M. (ed) *Educational Priority*, volume 5, London, HMSO, pp.116–123

MUSGRAVE, P. W. (1965) *The Sociology of Education*, London, Methuen
MUSGRAVE, P. W. (1979) *The Sociology of Education*, 3rd edn., London, Methuen
MUSGROVE, F. (1968) 'The contribution of sociology to the study of the curriculum', in KERR, J. F. (ed) *Changing the Curriculum*, London, University of London Press, pp.96–109
MUSGROVE, F. (1979) *School and the Social Order*, Chichester, Wiley
NASH, R. (1971) 'Camouflage in the classroom', *New Society*, no. 447, 22 April, pp.667–9
NASH, R. (1973) *Classrooms Observed*, London, Routledge and Kegan Paul
NASH, R. (1980) *Schooling in Rural Societies*, London, Methuen
NEWBOLD, D. (1977) *Ability Grouping – the Banbury Enquiry*, Slough, NFER
NEWSON, J. and NEWSON, E. (1965) *Patterns of Infant Care*, Harmondsworth, Penguin
NEWSON, J. and NEWSON, E. (1970) *Four Years Old in an Urban Community*, Harmondsworth, Penguin
NEWSON, J. and NEWSON, E. (1976) 'Parental roles and social contexts', in SHIPMAN, M. (ed) *The Organisation and Impact of Social Research*, London, Routledge and Kegan Paul, pp.22–48
NEWSON, J. and NEWSON, E. (1977) *Perspectives on School at Seven Years Old*, London, Allen and Unwin
NIGHTINGALE, C. (1977) 'Boys will be boys but what will girls be', in HOYLES, M. (ed) *The Politics of Literacy*, London, Writers and Readers Publishing Cooperative, pp.95–98
NOEL, E. W. (1962) 'Sponsored and contest mobility in America and England: a rejoinder to Ralph H. Turner', *Comparative Education Review*, vol. 6, no. 2, pp.148–151
OAKLEY, A. (1981) *Subject Women*, Oxford, Martin Robertson
O'BRIEN, M. (1981) *The Politics of Reproduction*, London, Routledge and Kegan Paul
OFFICE OF POPULATION, CENSUSES AND SURVEYS (1973) *The General Household Survey: Introductory Report*, London, HMSO
OFFICE OF POPULATION, CENSUSES AND SURVEYS (1981) *The General Household Survey 1979*, London, HMSO
OFFICE OF POPULATION, CENSUSES AND SURVEYS (1984) *The General Household Survey 1982*, London, HMSO
OKELY, J. (1978) 'Privileged, schooled and finished: boarding education for girls', in ARDENER, S. (ed) *Defining Females: The Nature of Women in Society*, London, Croom Helm, pp.109–139
OZGA, J. (1981) *The Politics of the Teaching Profession*, Open University Course E353, *Society Education and the State*, Milton Keynes, Open University Press
OZGA, J. and LAWN, M. (1981) *Teachers Professionalism and Class*, Lewes, Falmer Press
OZOLINS, U. (1979) 'Lawton's "refutation" of a working class curriculum', in JOHNSON, L. and OZOLINS, U. (eds) *Melbourne Working Papers*, Melbourne, University of Melbourne. Reprinted in HORTON, T. and RAGGATT, P. (1982) (eds) *Challenge and Change in the Curriculum*, London, Hodder and Stoughton, pp.37–52
PARRY, N. and PARRY, J. (1974) 'The teachers and professionalism: the failure of an occupational strategy', in FLUDE, M. and AHIER, J. (eds) *Educability, Schools and Ideology*, London, Croom Helm, pp.160–185

PARSONS, T. (1959) 'The school class as a social system', *Harvard Educational Review*, vol. 29, pp.297–318. Reprinted in HALSEY, A. H., FLOUD, J. and ANDERSON, C. A. (eds) *Education, Economy and Society*, New York, Free Press, pp.434–455

PARSONS, T. (1968) 'Social systems', in SILLS, D. L. (ed) *International Encyclopedia of the Social Sciences*, vol. 15, New York, Macmillan and Free Press, pp.458–473

PARTINGTON, G. (1976) *Women Teachers in England and Wales*, Slough, NFER

PAYNE, G., FORD, G. and ROBERTSON, C. (1976) 'Changes in occupational mobility in Scotland', *Scottish Journal of Sociology*, vol. 1, no. 1, pp.57–79

PAYNE, G., FORD, G. and ROBERTSON, C. (1977) 'A reappraisal of social mobility in Britain', *Sociology*, vol. 11, no. 2, pp.289–310

PAYNE, I. (1980) 'A working class girl in a grammar school', in SPENDER, D. and SARAH, E. (eds) *Learning to Lose: Sexism and Education*, London, The Women's Press, pp.12–19

PETERS, R. S. (1976) (ed) *The Role of the Head*, London, Routledge and Kegan Paul

PILKINGTON, A. (1984) *Race Relations in Britain*, Slough, University Tutorial Press

PILLING, D. (1980) 'The attainment of immigrant children: a review of research', *Highlights no. 40*, London, National Children's Bureau

PLASKOW, M. (1985) (ed) *Life and Death of the Schools Council*, Lewes, Falmer Press

POLLARD, A. (1982) 'A model of coping strategies', *British Journal of Sociology of Education*, vol. 3, no. 1, pp.19–37

POLLARD, A. (1984) 'Coping strategies and the multiplication of differentiation in infant classrooms', *British Educational Research Journal*, vol. 10, no. 1, pp.33–48

POLLARD, A. (1985) *The Social World of the Primary School*, Eastbourne, Holt, Rinehart and Winston

POSTER, C. (1982) *Community Education: its Development and Management*, London, Heinemann

PSACHAROPOULOS, G. (1977) 'Family background, education and achievement: a path model of earnings determinants in the U.K. and some alternatives', *British Journal of Sociology*, vol. 28, no. 3, pp.321–335

PSACHAROPOULOS, G. and WILES, P. (1980), 'Early education, ability and earning capacity', *International Journal of Social Economics*, vol. 7, no. 3

PURVIS, J. (1973) 'School teaching as a professional career', *British Journal of Sociology*, vol. 24, no. 1, pp.43–57

PURVIS, J. (1981a) 'The double burden of class and gender in the schooling of working class girls in nineteenth century England, 1800–1870', in BARTON, L. and WALKER, S. (eds) *Schools, Teachers and Teaching*, Lewes, Falmer Press, pp.97–116

PURVIS, J. (1981b) 'Women and teaching in the nineteenth century', in DALE, R. *et al* (eds) *Education and the State: Politics, Patriarchy and Practice*, Lewes, Falmer Press, pp.359–375

PURVIS, J. (1984) *Women and Education*, Open University Course E 205, *Conflict and Change in Education: A Sociological Introduction*, Milton Keynes, Open University Press

PURVIS, J. and HALES, M. (1983) (eds) *Achievement and Inequality in Education*, London, Routledge and Kegan Paul

RADICAL STATISTICS EDUCATION GROUP (1982) *Reading Between the Numbers: A Critical Guide to Educational Research*, London, BSSRS Publications Ltd

RAFFE, D. (1979) 'The "alternative route" reconsidered: part time further education and social mobility in England and Wales', *Sociology*, vol. 13, no. 1, pp.47–73

RAFFE, D. (1981) 'Special programmes in Scotland: the first year of YOP', *Policy and Politics*, vol. 9, no. 4, pp.471–487

RAFFE, D. (1983) 'Education and unemployment: does YOP make a difference (and will the Youth Training Scheme)?', in GLEESON, D. (ed) *Youth Training and the Search for Work*, London, Routledge and Kegan Paul, pp.291–308

RAFFE, D. (1984) 'The transition from school to work and the recession: evidence from the Scottish school leavers surveys, 1977–1983', *British Journal of Sociology of Education*, vol. 5, no. 3, pp.247–265

RAMPTON, A. (1981) *West Indian Children in Our Schools*, Cmnd. 8273, London, HMSO

RATCLIFFE, P. (1981) *Racism and Reaction*, London, Routledge and Kegan Paul

RAYBOULD, E. C., ROBERTS, B. and WEDELL, K. (1980) (eds) *Helping the Low Achiever in the Secondary School*, Educational Review Occasional Publications no. 7

REEDER, D. (1979) 'A recurring debate: education and industry', in BERNBAUM, G. (ed) *Schooling in Decline*, London, Macmillan, pp.115–148

REES, T. (1983) 'Boys off the street and girls in the home: youth unemployment and state intervention in Northern Ireland', in FIDDY, R. (ed) *In Place of Work: Policy and Provision for the Young Unemployed*, Lewes, Falmer Press, pp.167–182

REES, T. and ATKINSON P. (1982) (eds) *Youth Unemployment and State Intervention*, London, Routledge and Kegan Paul

REES, T. and GREGORY, D. (1981) 'Youth employment and unemployment: a decade of decline', *Educational Analysis*, vol. 3, no. 2, pp.7–24

REEVES, F. and CHEVANNES, M. (1981) 'The underachievement of Rampton', *Multiracial Education*, vol. 10, no. 1, pp.35–42

REID, E. (1980) 'Employers' use of educational qualifications', *Education Policy Bulletin*, vol. 8, no. 1, pp.49–64

REID, I. (1978) *Sociological Perspectives on School and Education*, London, Open Books

REID, I. (1981) *Social Class Differences in Britain*, 2nd edn., London, Grant McIntyre

REID, W. A. (1972) *The University and the Sixth Form Curriculum*, London, Macmillan

RENDEL, M. (1980) 'How many women academics 1912–76?', in DEEM, R. (ed) *Schooling for Women's Work*, London, Routledge and Kegan Paul, pp.142–161

REX, J. and MOORE, R. (1967) *Race, Community and Conflict*, Oxford, Oxford University Press for the Institute of Race Relations

REX, J. and TOMLINSON, S. (1979) *Colonial Immigrants in a British City – A Class Analysis*, London, Routledge and Kegan Paul

REYNOLDS, D. (1975) 'When teachers and pupils refuse a truce', in MUNGHAM, G. and PEARSON, G. (eds) *Working Class Youth Culture*, London, Routledge and Kegan Paul, pp.124–137

REYNOLDS, D. (1976) 'The delinquent school', in HAMMERSLEY, M. and WOODS, P. (eds) *The Process of Schooling*, London, Routledge and Kegan Paul, pp.217–229

REYNOLDS, D. (1982) 'The search for effective schools', *School Organization*, vol. 2, no. 3, pp.215–237

REYNOLDS, D. *et al* (1976) 'Schools do make a difference', *New Society*, 29 July, vol. 37, no. 72, pp.223–225

RICHARDSON, E. (1973) *The Teacher, the School and the Task of Management*, London, Heinemann

RICHARDSON, E. (1975) *Authority and Organization in the Secondary School*, London, Macmillan

RIDGE, J. M. (1974) (ed) *Mobility in Britain Reconsidered*, Oxford, Oxford University Press

RIESMAN, F. (1962) *The Culturally Deprived Child*, New York, Harper and Row

RISEBOROUGH, G. F. (1981) 'Teacher careers and comprehensive schooling: an empirical study', *Sociology*, vol. 15, no. 3, pp.352–380

ROBBINS, L. (1963a) *Higher Education – Report*, London, HMSO

ROBBINS, L. (1963b) *Higher Education: Appendix One*, London, HMSO

ROBBINS, L. (1963c) *Higher Education: Appendix 2B*, London, HMSO

ROBERTS, H. (1986) 'After sixteen: what choice?', in BURGESS, R. G. (ed) *Exploring Society*, London, Longman

ROBERTS, K. (1984) *School Leavers and their Prospects: Youth and the Labour Market in the 1980s*, Milton Keynes, Open University Press

ROBERTS, K., DUGGAN, J. and NOBLE, M. (1981) *Unregistered Youth Unemployment and Outreach Careers Work, Part One, Non Registration*, Department of Employment Research Paper 31

ROBINS, D. and COHEN, P. (1978) *Knuckle Sandwich*, Harmondsworth, Penguin

ROBINSON, P. (1981a) *Perspectives on the Sociology of Education*, London, Routledge and Kegan Paul

ROBINSON, P. (1981b) 'Whatever happened to educability?', *Educational Analysis*, vol. 3, no. 1, pp.37–46

ROSEN, H. (1972) *Language and Class: A Critical Look at the Theories of Basil Bernstein*, Bristol, Falling Wall Press

ROY, W. (1983) *Teaching Under Attack*, London, Croom Helm

RUDDUCK, J., HOPKINS, D., GROUNDWATER-SMITH, S. and LABBETT, B. (1983) *Library Access and Sixth Form Study*, report to the British Library Research and Development Department

RUTTER, M. *et al* (1970) *Education, Health and Behaviour*, London, Longman

RUTTER, M. and MADGE, N. (1976) *Cycles of Disadvantage*, London, Heinemann

RUTTER, M., MAUGHAN, B., MORTIMORE, P. and OUSTON, J. (1979) *Fifteen Thousand Hours: Secondary Schools and their Effects on Children*, London, Open Books

SALTER, B. and TAPPER, T. (1981) *Education, Politics and the State: The Theory and Practice of Educational Change*,, London, Grant McIntyre

SAMUEL, J. (1981) 'The teachers' viewpoint: Feminism and science teaching: some classroom observations', in KELLY, A. (ed) *The Missing Half: Girls and Science Education*, Manchester, Manchester University Press, pp.246–256

SANDERSON, M. (1972a) *The Universities and British Industry 1850–1970*, London, Routledge and Kegan Paul

SANDERSON, M. (1972b) 'Literacy and social mobility in the industrial revolution', *Past and Present*, no. 56, pp.75–104

SCHULTZ, T. (1961) 'Investment in human capital', *American Economic Review*, vol. 51, pp.1–17. Reprinted in KARABEL, J. and HALSEY, A. H. (1977) (eds) *Power and Ideology in Education*, New York, Oxford University Press, pp.313–324

SECONDARY HEADS ASSOCIATION (1983) 'The selection of secondary heads: suggestions for good practice', Occasional Paper, 2

SEELEY, J. (1966) 'The "making" and "taking" of problems', *Social Problems*, vol. 14, no. 4, pp. 382–389

SHARP, R. and GREEN, A. (1975) *Education and Social Control*, London, Routledge and Kegan Paul

SHARPE, S. (1976) *Just Like a Girl*, Harmondsworth, Penguin

SHAW, J. (1980) 'Education and the individual: schooling for girls or mixed schooling – a mixed blessing?', in DEEM, R. (ed) *Schooling for Women's Work*, London, Routledge and Kegan Paul, pp.66–75

SHAW, K. E. (1969) 'Why no sociology of schools?', *Education for Teaching*, no. 69, pp.61–7

SHINMAN, S. (1981) *A Chance for Every Child? Access and Response to Pre-School Provision*, London, Tavistock

SHIPMAN, M. D. (1968) *Sociology of the School*, London, Longman

SHIPMAN, M. (1971) 'Curriculum for inequality?', in HOOPER, R. (ed) *The Curriculum: Context, Design and Development*, Edinburgh, Oliver and Boyd, pp.101–106

SHIPMAN, M. (1974) *Inside a Curriculum Project*, London, Methuen

SHIPMAN, M. (1978) *In-School Evaluation*, London, Heinemann

SIKES, P. J. (1984) 'Teacher careers in the comprehensive school', in BALL, S. J. (ed) *Comprehensive Schooling: A Reader*, Lewes, Falmer Press, pp.247–271

SILVER, H. (1973) (ed) *Equal Opportunity in Education*, London, Methuen

SILVERMAN, D. and JONES, J. (1973) 'Getting in: the managed accomplishment of "correct" selection outcomes', in CHILD, J. (ed) *Man and Organization*, London, Allen and Unwin, pp.63–106

SIMPSON, R. L. and SIMPSON, I. H. (1969) 'Women and bureaucracy in the semi-professions', in ETZIONI, A. (ed) *The Semi-Professions and their Organization*, New York, Free Press, pp.196–265

SKILBECK, M. (1982) *A Core Curriculum for the Common School*, London, University of London Institute of Education

SMITH, D. (1976) 'Codes, paradigms and folk norms: an approach to educational change with particular reference to the work of Basil Berstein', *Sociology*, vol. 10, no.1, pp.1–19

SMITH, D. (1977) *Racial Disadvantage in Britain*, Harmondsworth, Penguin

SMITH, M. and BISSELL, J. (1970) 'The Impact of Headstart: the Westinghouse Ohio Headstart evaluation', *Harvard Educational Review*, March, vol. 40, pp.51–104

SNYDER, B. (1971) *The Hidden Curriculum*, Cambridge, Mass., MIT Press

SPENDER, D. (1981) 'Sex bias' in WARREN-PIPER, D. (ed) *Is Higher Education Fair?* Guildford, Society for Research in Higher Education, pp.104–127

SPENDER, D. (1982) *Invisible Women: the Schooling Scandal*, London, Writers and Readers Publishing Cooperative

SPENDER, D. and SARAH, E. (1980) (eds) *Learning to Lose: Sexism and Education*, London, The Women's Press

SPINDLER, G. (1982) (ed) *Doing the Ethnography of Schooling: Educational Anthropology in Action*, New York, Holt, Rinehart and Winston

SPINDLER, G. and SPINDLER, L. (1982) 'Roger Harker and Schönhausen: From the familiar to the strange and back again', in SPINDLER, G. (ed) *Doing the Ethnography of Schooling: Educational Anthropology in Action*, New York, Holt, Rinehart and Winston, pp.20–46

SQUIBB, P. (1973) 'The concept of intelligence', *Sociological Review*, vol. 21, no. 1, pp.57–75

STACEY, M. (1969) (ed) *Comparability in Social Research*, London, Heinemann

STACEY, M. (1981) 'The division of labour revisited or overcoming the two adams', in ABRAMS, P., DEEM, R., FINCH, J., ROCK, P. (eds) *Practice and Progress: British Sociology 1950–1980*, London, Allen and Unwin pp.172–190

STACEY, M. (1982) 'Social sciences and the state: fighting like a woman', *Sociology*, vol. 16, no. 3, pp.406–421

STANLEY, A. P. (1903) *Life of Dr. Arnold* (ed. A. Reynolds) London, Hutchinson

STANWORTH, M. (1981) *Gender and Schooling: A Study of Sexual Division in the Classroom*, London, Women's Research and Resources Centre (reprinted by Hutchinson in 1983)

STANWORTH, M. (1984) 'Women and class analysis: a reply to Goldthorpe', *Sociology*, vol. 18, no. 2, pp.159–170

STANWORTH, P. (1984) 'Elites and privilege', in ABRAMS, P. and BROWN, R. K. (eds) *U.K. Society: Work, Urbanism and Inequality*, 2nd edn., London, Weidenfeld and Nicolson, pp.246–293

STARES, R., IMBERG, D. and MCROBBIE, J. (1982) 'Ethnic minorities: their involvement in MSC special programmes', *MSC Research and Development Series*, No. 6, London, Manpower Services Commission

STARTUP, R. (1976) *The University Teacher and his World: A Sociological and Educational Study*, Aldershot, Gower

STARTUP, R. (1985) 'The changing perspective of academic researchers, 1973–1983', *Studies in Higher Education*, vol. 10, no. 1, pp.69–78

STEBBINS, R. A. (1976) 'Physical context influences on behaviour: the case of classroom disorderliness', in HAMMERSLEY, M. and WOODS, P. (eds) *The Process of Schooling*, London, Routledge and Kegan Paul, pp.208–216

STENHOUSE, L. (1963) 'A cultural approach to the study of the curriculum', *Pedagogisk Forskning*, vol. 3, pp.120–134 and reprinted in STENHOUSE, L. (1983) *Authority, Education and Emancipation*, London, Heinemann, pp.20–34

STENHOUSE, L. (1973) 'The Humanities Curriculum Project', in BUTCHER, H. J. and PONT, H. B. (eds) *Educational Research in Britain 3*, London, University of London Press, pp.149–167

STENHOUSE, L. (1975) *An Introduction to Curriculum Research and Development*, London, Heinemann

STENHOUSE, L. (1980) (ed) *Curriculum Research and Development in Action*, London, Heinemann

STENHOUSE, L. (1983a) *Authority, Education and Emancipation*, London, Heinemann

STENHOUSE, L. (1983b) 'The legacy of the curriculum movement', in GALTON, M. and MOON, B. (eds) *Changing Schools . . . Changing Curriculum*, London, Harper and Row, pp.346–355

STEVENS, F. (1960) *The Living Tradition*, London, Hutchinson

STONE, L. (1969) 'Literacy and education in England 1640–1900', *Past and Present*, no. 42, pp.69–139

STOWELL, M. (1985) *Negotiating Professional Socialization: the case of student teachers, Warwick Working Papers in Sociology*, No. 9

STUBBS, M. (1983) *Language, Schools and Classrooms* 2nd edn., London, Methuen

SWANN, M. (1985a) *Education for All: the Report of the Committee of Inquiry into the Education of Children from Ethnic Minority Groups*, London, HMSO

SWANN, M. (1985b) *Education for All: A brief guide to the main issues of the report*, London, HMSO

SWINDLER, A. (1979) *Organization without Authority: Dilemmas of Social Control in Free Schools*, Cambridge, Mass., Harvard University Press

SZRETER, R. (1983) 'Opportunities for women as university teachers in England since the Robbins Report of 1963', *Studies in Higher Education* vol. 8, no. 2, pp.139–150

SZRETER, R. (1984) 'Some forerunners of sociology of education in Britain: an account of the literature and influences c. 1900–1950', *Westminster Studies in Education*, vol. 7, pp.13–43

TAYLOR, G. and AYRES, N. (1969) *Born and Bred Unequal*, London, Longman

TAYLOR, H. F. (1980) *The IQ Game: A Methodological Inquiry into the Heredity – Environment Controversy*, Brighton, Harvester

TAYLOR, J. H. (1976) *The Half-Way Generation*, Slough, NFER

TAYLOR, W. (1981) 'Contraction in context', in SIMON, B. and TAYLOR, W. (eds) *Education in the Eighties: the central issues*, London, Batsford, pp.17–37

THOMPSON, E. P. (1970) (ed) *Warwick University Ltd.*, Harmondsworth, Penguin

TIERNEY, J. (1983) *Race, Migration and Schooling*, New York, Holt, Rinehart and Winston

TOMLINSON, S. (1981) *Educational Subnormality – A Study in Decision-Making*, London, Routledge and Kegan Paul

TOMLINSON, S. (1982) *The Sociology of Special Education*, London, Routledge and Kegan Paul

TOMLINSON, S. (1983) *Ethnic Minorities in British Schools*, London, Heinemann/ Policy Studies Institute

TOMLINSON, S. (1984) *Home and School in Multicultural Britain*, London, Batsford

TOWNSEND, P. (1979) *Poverty in the United Kingdom: A Survey of Household Resources and Standards of Living*, Harmondsworth, Penguin

TROPP, A. (1957) *The School Teachers: The Growth of the Teaching Profession in England and Wales*, London, Heinemann

TROYNA, B. (1984) 'Fact of artefact? The "educational underachievement" of Black pupils', *British Journal of Sociology of Education*, vol. 5, no. 2, pp.153–166

TROYNA, B. (1986) 'Swann's song: the origins, ideology and implications of *Education for All*', *Journal of Education Policy*, vol. 1, no. 2

TROYNA, B. and SMITH, D. I. (1983) (eds) *Racism, School and the Labour Market*, Leicester, National Youth Bureau

TURNER, C. H. (1969) 'An organisational analysis of a secondary modern school', *Sociological Review*, vol. 17, no. 1, pp.67–85

TURNER, G. (1983) 'The hidden curriculum of examinations' in HAMMERSLEY, M. and HARGREAVES, A. (eds) *Curriculum Practice: Some Sociological Case Studies*, Lewes, Falmer Press, pp.195–206

TURNER, R. H. (1961) 'Modes of social ascent through education: sponsored and contest mobility', in HALSEY, A. H., FLOUD, J. and ANDERSON, C. A. (eds) *Education, Economy and Society*, New York, Free Press, pp.121–139

TURNER, R. H. (1964) *The Social Context of Ambition*, San Francisco, Chandler

TYACK, D. B. (1976) 'Ways of seeing: an essay on the history of compulsory schooling', *Harvard Educational Review*, vol. 46, no. 3, pp.355–389

TYLER, W. (1977) *The Sociology of Educational Inequality*, London, Methuen

TYLER, W. (1982) *The Sociology of the School: A Review*, London, Social Science Research Council

UNIVERSITIES CENTRAL COUNCIL ON ADMISSIONS (1973) *Statistical Supplement to the 10th Report 1971/72*, Cheltenham, UCCA

UNIVERSITIES CENTRAL COUNCIL ON ADMISSIONS (1979) *Statistical Supplement 1978–9*, Cheltenham, UCCA

UNIVERSITY GRANTS COMMITTEE (1984) *University Statistics 1983–84; Volume 1: Students and Staff*, Cheltenham, Universities' Statistical Record

VAUGHAN, M. and ARCHER, M. S. (1971) *Social Conflict and Educational Change in England and France 1789–1848*, Cambridge, Cambridge University Press

WAINWRIGHT, H. (1984) 'Women and the division of labour' in ABRAMS, P. and BROWN, R. K. (eds) *U.K. Society: Work, Urbanism and Inequality*, 2nd edn., London, Weidenfeld and Nicolson, pp.198–245

WAKEFORD, J. (1969) *The Cloistered Elite*, London, Macmillan

WALBY, S. (1986) 'Social inequality: sociology's central problem', in BURGESS, R. G. (ed) *Exploring Society*, London, Longman

WALDEN, R. and WALKERDINE, V. (1982) *Girls and Mathematics, Bedford Way Papers* No. 8, London, University of London Institute of Education

WALFORD, G. (1982) 'Girls in boys' public schools: a prelude to further research', *British Journal of Sociology of Education*, vol. 4, no. 1, pp.39–54

WALFORD, G. (1984) (ed) *British Public Schools: Policy and Practice*, Lewes, Falmer Press

WALKER, R. (1972) 'The sociology of education and life in school classrooms', *International Review of Education*, vol. 18, no. 1, pp.32–43

WALKER, R. and ADELMAN, C. (1975) *A Guide to Classroom Observation*, London, Methuen

WALKER, R. and ADELMAN, C. (1976) 'Strawberries', in STUBBS, M. AND DELAMONT, S. (eds) *Explorations in Classroom Observation*, Chichester, Wiley, pp.133–150

WALKERDINE, V. (1981) 'Sex, power and pedagogy', *Screen Education*, no. 38, Spring, pp.14–25

WALLER, W. (1932) *The Sociology of Teaching*, New York, Wiley (reprinted in 1967)

WALSH, K., DUNNE, R., STOTEN, B. and STEWART, J. D. (1984) *Falling School Rolls and the Management of the Teaching Profession*, Windsor, NFER–Nelson

WARING, M. (1979) *Social Process and Curriculum Innovation*, London, Methuen

WATTS, A. (1981) (ed) School, Youth and Work, special issue of *Educational Analysis*, vol. 3, no. 2, pp.1–106

WATTS, A. (1983) *Education, Unemployment and the Future of Work*, Milton Keynes, Open University Press

WATTS, J. (1977) (ed) *The Countesthorpe Experience*, London, Allen and Unwin

WAX, M. L. and WAX, R. (1971) 'Great tradition, little tradition and formal education', in WAX, M. L., DIAMOND, S. and GEARING, F. O. (eds) *Anthropological Perspectives on Education*, New York, Basic Books, pp.3–18

WEINBERG, A. (1969) 'Education', in STACEY, M. (ed) *Comparability in Social Research*, London, Heinemann, pp.1–31

WESTERGAARD, J. and LITTLE, A. (1967) 'Educational opportunity and social selection in England and Wales', in OECD, *Social Objectives in Educational Planning*, Paris, OECD

WESTERGAARD, J. and RESLER, H. (1975) *Class in a Capitalist Society*, Harmondsworth, Penguin

WESTWOOD, L. J. (1967) 'The role of the teacher', *Educational Research*, vol. 9, no. 2, pp.122–134 and vol. 10, no. 1, pp.21–37

WHEATLEY, A. (1976) 'Implementing a resource based project', in BODEN, P. (ed) *Developments in Geography Teaching*, London, Open Books, pp.70–79

WHITBURN, J., MEALING, M. and COX, C. (1976) *People in Polytechnics*, Guildford, Society for Research in Higher Education

WHITE, D. with BROCKINGTON, R. (1983) *Tales Out of School*, London, Routledge and Kegan Paul

WILCOX, K. (1982) 'Ethnography as a methodology and its application to the study of schooling: a review' in SPINDLER, G. (ed) *Doing the Ethnography of Schooling: Educational Anthropology in Action*, New York, Holt, Rinehart and Winston, pp.456–488

WILKIN, M. (1982) 'Educational opportunity and achievement', in REID, I. and WORMALD, E. (eds) *Sex Differences in Britain*, London, Grant McIntyre, pp.85–113

WILLIAMS, R. (1961) *The Long Revolution*, Harmondsworth, Penguin

WILLIAMS, G. and GORDON, A. (1975) '16 and 18 year olds: attitudes to education', *Higher Education Bulletin*, vol. 4, no. 1, pp.26–37

WILLIAMSON, B. (1979) *Education, Social Structure and Development*, London, Macmillan

WILLIAMSON, B. (1981) 'Class bias', in WARREN-PIPER, D. (ed) *Is Higher Education Fair?* Guildford, Society for Research into Higher Education, pp.17–39

WILLIAMSON, H. (1982) 'Client response to the youth opportunities programme' in REES, T. L. and ATKINSON, P. (eds) *Youth Unemployment and State Intervention*, London, Routledge and Kegan Paul, pp.99–114

WILLIS, P. (1977) *Learning to Labour*, Farnborough, Saxon House

WILSON, B. R. (1962) 'The teacher's role – a sociological analysis', *British Journal of Sociology*, vol. 13, no. 1, pp.137–158

WOBER, M. (1971) *English Girls' Boarding Schools*, London, Allen Lane

WOLCOTT, H. F. (1982) 'Mirrors, models and monitors: educator adaptations of the ethnographic innovation', in SPSINDLER, G. (ed) *Doing the Ethnography of Schooling: Educational Anthropology in Action*, New York, Holt, Rinehart and Winston, pp.68–95

WOLPE, A. M. (1974) 'The official ideology of education for girls', in FLUDE, M. and AHIER, J. (eds) *Educability, Schools and Ideology*, London, Croom Helm, pp.138–159

WOLPE, A.M . (1978) 'Girls and economic survival', *British Journal of Educational Studies*, vol. 26, no. 2, pp.150–162

WOODS, P. (1976) 'Having a laugh: an antidote to schooling', in HAMMERSLEY, M.

and WOODS, P. (eds) *The Process of Schooling*, London, Routledge and Kegan Paul, pp.178–187

WOODS, P. (1979) *The Divided School*, London, Routledge and Kegan Paul

WOODS, P. (1981) 'Strategies, commitment and identity; making and breaking the teacher role', in BARTON, L. and WALKER, S. (eds) *Schools, Teachers and Teaching*, Lewes, Falmer Press, pp.283–302

WOODS, P. (1983) *Sociology of the School: An Interactionist Viewpoint*, London, Routledge and Kegan Paul

WOODS, P. and HAMMERSLEY, M. (1977) (eds) *School Experience: Explorations in the Sociology of Education*, London, Croom Helm

YATES, A. and PIDGEON, D. (1957) *Admission to Grammar School*, London, Newnes

YOUNG, M. (1958) *The Rise of the Meritocracy*, Harmondsworth, Penguin

YOUNG, M. F. D. (1971a) (ed) *Knowledge and Control: New Directions for the Sociology of Education*, London, Collier–Macmillan

YOUNG, M. F. D. (1971b) 'An approach to the study of curricula as socially organized knowledge', in YOUNG, M. F. D. (ed) *Knowledge and Control: New Directions for the Sociology of Education*, London, Collier–Macmillan, pp.19–46

Index